To my father, Bruce W. Osterman, Sr., a patriot.

For my wife Karyn, my son Daniel and daughter Tori, my brothers and sisters Bruce, Brian, Wendy and Kerry, and my granddaughter Katherine, who's love, support and editing made writing this book an enjoyable and rewarding experience.

TABLE OF CONTENTS

BECOMING KEVIN

FROM WARRIOR TO PEACEMAKER

KEVIN OSTERMAN

PREFACE

I'm not sure exactly when I started rebelling. I'm not even sure exactly when it all began to turn around. I was born and I became. That's all I know for sure.

I'm not preaching.

I've only known one preacher in my life I enjoyed listening to. She was knowledgeable and balanced in her treatment of differing religions. She was confident with an amazing demeanor, vitality, and beauty—all characteristics which I do not possess.

I've always been an observer of human nature. And maybe that's why it all went wrong. I observed things I didn't like. More to the point, I observed things I didn't understand. But this is also the reason it eventually all went right.

Perhaps most teens are rebellious. It probably goes with the territory. Some manage to stay on the straight and narrow. I wasn't one of those kids. But things happened that I didn't realize at the time would change my life forever. Some were subtle, some obvious and intentional.

Each of our paths leads us to our purpose, though we don't realize it as it's happening. If we live long enough to put it into context, we can see how everyone, and everything had its function in preparing us for that purpose.

There are places, people, and incidents I remember vividly. They influenced me greatly, and I began to see that our lives are a product of everything we experience and how we react to those experiences. We take the pound of clay we're given and either make it into a useful vessel or let it dry out until it's useless.

We all have value—something to bring to the world. Sometimes it takes the gift of time, and sometimes it takes others to bring it out of us.

This book is a biography of sorts, a memoir, the history of me and to some extent my ancestors. It is a story about becoming, about everything and everyone that had some influence and value to me.

In a way, it's me putting everything into perspective and something I can hand down to my future generations so they can perhaps better understand their own becoming.

Why should you read the story of my life?

We are all bound together in some way in the vastness of the universe with all of its complexities. There are similarities that go beyond our understanding.

I only ask that you think twice before you write off that young miscreant you're dealing with. He or she may pull their head out of their ass one day without warning, and when that good and beautiful person inside begins to shine outwardly, they may quite surprisingly become a productive member of society who edifies others and contributes to the welfare of the world.

"There are more things in Heaven and Earth… than are dreamt of in your philosophy." (Wm. Shakespeare, *Hamlet*)

"The rule that every general knows by heart: It's smarter to be lucky, than lucky to be smart." (King Charles in *Pippin*)

1

MEDIATION WITH A VIEW

I sat at the conference room table on the 22nd floor and looked across into the pretty, petite, young, and obviously sleep-deprived face of the Respondent's attorney who was there alone representing her client. We had been in mediation all morning. She had flown in from Dallas that morning and had a reservation to fly back home that evening. It had already been a very long day for her.

We had the conference room with the best view. It was a clear, bright Spring day. From our perch, we looked out over the Phoenix mid-town, with the Osborn and Central light-rail platform directly below us and a crystal-clear view of the Papago Buttes, Camelback Mountain, Piestewa Peak, and a hazy view of the McDowell Mountains far in the distance to the east. I could also see the Sky Harbor control tower.

This was a tough mediation. Charging Party alleged that she'd been sexually harassed by the company president, and he denied it vehemently. My sense was that it might have been a brief relationship that had gone awry quickly. Charging Party was unable to produce any meaningful evidence other than a few seemingly innocuous texts containing no intimate language.

The parties had reached an impasse almost an hour ago and all negotiation had come to a screaming halt—literally. Respondent's attorney made a counteroffer of three thousand dollars to Charging Party's opening demand of one-hundred thousand dollars.

I caught my breath when the Charging Party's attorney unexpectedly made their demand early in the open session, even though I'd already asked him to hold off until he had a chance to listen to the Respondent's version of the facts—and again when the Respondent's attorney blurted out her counter-offer before I could suggest a caucus.

I liked talking with the parties separately first before the demands and counteroffers began flying back and forth. For good reason.

The Charging Party lost it. She started weeping loudly, leaned across the table and began yelling at the young attorney across from her. Respondent's attorney was visibly caught by surprise, hardened, and became combative in return.

She leaned forward across the table and glared into the Charging Party's eyes, "This is why you were terminated—for barging into the president's office during an executive meeting and letting loose on him in front of a room full of senior corporate officers. You were justifiably fired on the spot, and I'm confident that a jury will agree, if you're able to get in front of one—which I seriously doubt."

As the stone-faced Charging Party's attorney was silently packing his briefcase and getting ready to walk out with his client, I called for a caucus to meet with both of them in another private room I had already reserved and set up with bottled water and snacks. I moved the Charging Party and her now flummoxed attorney to the small conference room with no windows or other distractions, so we could be alone and talk.

I pacified the Charging Party; she calmed down and cleaned up her running mascara. After several minutes of light talk and pointing out that they had my services all day and should really take advantage of this one-time opportunity, I managed to help them get started again in attempting to find a resolution. I quickly went next door to let the Respondent's attorney know we were back on track.

Ten minutes into the caucus I had the visibly distraught Charging Party and her attorney talking about her issues, interests, and concerns. She had run out of money, including cleaning out her 401K, and her boyfriend had dumped her the week before. She was on the verge of being evicted from her apartment and losing her car. Her life was in complete shambles. Her attorney was no doubt acutely aware that any future payments from his client could be an exceedingly long time in coming—and a long shot at that. Not surprisingly they both agreed that finding a workable resolution and putting this matter behind them would be a good thing.

I was then able to get them right down to business, and through my facilitation they formulated a demand to be conveyed to the Respondent's attorney who sat quite forlornly in the room with a view, staring intently at her cell phone.

When I returned after about a half-hour, she was still slumped in her chair. I asked her to come stand with me at the big picture window, and showed her the various landmarks, including the airport to which she would soon return. Then I explained their counteroffer to her.

The demand was about ten-grand on the high-side and included a written agreement to not challenge her unemployment insurance (which she had initially been denied) and a neutral reference letter. It might require the president to take a few deep breaths but was probably doable. Respondent's attorney made the phone call, and we knew it would be a while.

At my suggestion, Charging Party and her attorney took a long lunch break.

I asked Respondent's attorney if she wanted something from the deli downstairs. She looked up at me and noticeably brightened.

As we sat munching on our sandwiches, she looked more relaxed than she had been all morning, and casually said, "So how'd you get into this line of work in the first place?"

I smiled at her and said, "It all started when I lost my job driving a cab right here in Phoenix." She giggled and gave me a puzzled look.

I explained that my awakening and expanding self-awareness seemed to have gradually been triggered back in 1976, aided by a hard knock on my head in 1980...

2

THE AWAKENING

It was a cool, slightly overcast Wednesday, December 15th, 1976; the meeting seemed hastily called. There was some big news coming—the drivers were milling and talking in a quiet buzz as they packed into the crowded room filled with tables and chairs, waiting to meet the new owner, Walter Arnett.

My world was about to get turned upside-down, and the trajectory of my life would be significantly altered forever.

Walt owned and operated our competitor, Checker Cab of Mesa. About a week before we had heard that he was buying our company, Yellow Cab of Phoenix.

I had been driving a cab for about 2 ½ years. It was a comfortable job, paying me 50% of the meter, plus tips. I enjoyed excellent medical coverage, and it was a decent job, in fact, without question, the best I had ever had.

I was enrolled full time at Phoenix College, attending classes in the evenings, majoring in Business, and receiving G.I. Bill benefits.

As a driver, my usual hours were 4:00 a.m. to 2:30 p.m. One afternoon I came into the office to turn in my keys, cash, and paperwork after my shift was over. The office manager approached me and said, "You sound rather good on the radio. Would you like to try dispatching?"

I accepted his offer. We determined the time he wanted me to report for training, and I left for the day. The following morning instead of taking my cab out, I spent the day in training, and dispatching calls to cabs on the radio. So, for the past 6 months, in addition to driving, I had been working a couple of days every week as a dispatcher.

My training as an Air Control/Anti-Aircraft Warfare Electronics Operator in the Marine Corps, and experience as a Direct Air Support Controller in Vietnam (Marble Mountain, about seven kilometers south of the Da Nang airfield) before volunteering and transferring to the infantry, made me confident that I would be comfortable and effective on the radio.

Every job has a list of knowledge, skills and abilities that goes along with it.

As a driver, I had learned that the entire Phoenix Metropolitan Area had been converted into sectors and numbered cab stands for brevity, efficiency, and effectiveness.

For example, Park Central, in front of the Walgreens (no longer there, and where I'd been a grill cook previously) was 650. Heading east, the stands increased to 700s, and the furthest east stands were designated in the 900s. The stand number increased the further north it was (far South Phoenix was 601, North Sunnyslope, 678).

Going west stands were numbered in the 500s, and farthest west, 300s.

When I needed a cab in the vicinity of the downtown Valley Ho, I would call, "Cab at 630 (Valley Ho), cab at 628 (San Luis Hotel), cab around."

If there was a cab sitting on the stand I called first or second, they would answer with their cab number, and I would tell them where their fare was waiting, plus any additional information I had.

In the event there were no cabs on stand, when I called "Cab around," a free-for-all could ensue on the radio. Multiple cabs might answer, and I would discern the first cab number I could understand and dispatch the call to that cab.

This sometimes resulted in disputes as to who had been first in on the radio. In one instance, an old timer alleged that I "fed" a good call to a friend of mine (Charity) and filed a grievance through the union.

The tape was listened to by management and the union steward, and they heard my friend barely (and faintly) yell her number first.

My former controller experience helped me to quickly master the dispatching job. I continued to dispatch and drive cabs.

Ten months earlier, my son Daniel had been born at Good Samaritan Hospital in Phoenix, and thanks to the Blue Cross Blue Shield coverage I had through the cab company, medical expenses had been paid for.

I spent the entire morning and early afternoon driving and sitting on cab stands all around the Phoenix area and had a chance to see many interesting things: such as one of our local television personalities, Pat McMahon, standing on the driver's seat of a funky looking converted VW with one of those fiber-glass molded bodies that made it look like a sports car, appearing to argue with a "meter maid" about what looked like a parking ticket he had just received and was waving in his hand.

On a hot late-morning Wednesday, June 2, 1976, I sat on stand at "654" in front of what was then the Del Webb Townhouse on Clarendon Avenue, just west of Central Avenue.

I had been distracted while looking for my fare but felt the jolt and heard a muffled boom even with the windows rolled up and the air conditioner turned up high. Suddenly the radio started to light up with chatter about a "car fire," and "possible explosion" at the Clarendon Hotel.

I noted a plume of dark smoke a couple blocks to the west while loading my fare and his luggage. In addition, I heard sirens as I pulled away.

I later learned that a bomb had been set off under *Arizona Republic* reporter Don Bowles' white Datsun while parked at the Clarendon Hotel, mangling him severely and, after eleven agonizing days, killing him.

Most days were much more mundane. I often waited for my next fare while at the airport. The airport was quite a bit smaller than it is now, still with only two runways. There were four terminals, designated as "East" and "West," "Executive" and "International" terminal (last two very small).

I would sit in a line of about 12 cabs at the East Terminal, casually working on school assignments, listening to the dispatcher, sometimes chatting with other drivers, and gradually moving up until I was first in line and my fare walked out of the terminal to my cab.

Many of us knew each other's cab numbers, and sometimes I'd decide whether or not I wanted to sit in line at the airport when I spotted the number of an acquaintance.

A common prank was to creep up behind an acquaintance's cab and tap them lightly on the bumper (almost always catching them by surprise).

There were downsides to driving a cab, and one negative aspect of being a cab driver was that both police officers and fire fighters made clear their obvious disdain for me as I drove the streets picking up fares.

I would sometimes get what we referred to as a "police call," where I would go to an assigned location to pick up someone who wasn't ready to go to the hospital and hadn't committed an offense worthy of arrest.

They would often be very ill, intoxicated, or both, and were usually in pretty rough shape, not having bathed in quite some time, soiled by their own vomit, excrement, and other serious hygiene issues.

They would have already proven to the police that they had cab fare. I would expect payment in advance, and it was sometimes a moldy five or ten-dollar bill that had been hidden in the sole of their shoe.

I once picked up an extremely intoxicated woman who appeared to be in her mid-thirties, slender, wearing a stained skirt and blouse, and her medium-length black hair in disarray.

As soon as we had pulled away from the police, she leaned over the seat, leered at me, and said, "Let's fuck." Her breath was hot spoiled wine and something decaying. Unfazed, I made an unnecessary call to the dispatcher confirming I had my fare and took her to the address she had provided to the police and I had provided in my unnecessary call.

She was very insistent, tugging on my shirt and ruffling my hair, but finally figured out that I had no interest. She stumbled out of the cab muttering obscenities and slammed the door.

As she staggered toward the front door of the small house, perhaps the slammed cab door alerted a man inside the house who rushed outside bare-footed, wearing a "wife-beater" t-shirt and pants, grabbed her, and dragged her into the house by her hair.

Another time I went to a police call, and they had just peeled a vagrant off of the sidewalk in downtown Phoenix; he was in especially rough condition and smelled terrible! As a cop and fireman loaded him into my cab, they both laughed.

I asked them what they were laughing about. The fireman looked at me with a smirk and said, "He just crapped his pants." I protested and asked them why they hadn't warned me in advance, so I could put some newspaper down on the back seat.

They both just shrugged and walked away after closing the cab door.

As a result, after dropping my fare at the 7th Avenue Hotel, I had to drive back to the shop and sanitize my back seat before taking another fare.

I had initially learned about my G.I. Bill school benefits from another driver while sitting on stand at the airport. We were talking about the G.I. Bill home loan, which I'd taken advantage of, and he reminded me that I had a school benefit that would pay me to attend college.

Based on my negative bias concerning college students, I had never imagined myself attending college. After that conversation with my fellow driver, I researched my school benefits and determined that I could be paid a decent amount to learn. Money was becoming more and more important to me as time passed and my life became more complex.

I went through the entire enrollment process at the college, and when I arrived at the last table that night, I was asked to show my diploma or G.E.D. Certificate.

I explained I had taken the tests for my G.E.D. while stationed at Twenty-Nine Palms, California and passed, but was never issued the certificate. I was 17 years old at the time and out of school for less than six months; the Marine Corps informed me that I could apply for my G.E.D. when I turned 18 or had been out of school for six-months. I did not bother.

Without any preparation, I had taken the battery of tests because it was announced that morning while standing in formation that anyone who successfully passed the complete round of testing would get a ninety-six-hour pass.

That was the only reason I had completed the testing. I enjoyed the four days off in Phoenix with a girl I had recently met named Elaine. She was a tall, slender, beautiful, brunette with straight hair running down the middle of her back and an equally beautiful smile.

The helpful college registrar provided me with information on where I should go at the Department of Education and who I should ask for, and also let me know there was a deadline for getting everything back to the college and completing registration.

I did as she recommended, and amazingly, after I explained my predicament to a pleasant, middle-age woman in a small basement office crowded with filing cabinets, she was able to locate my test scores on one of hundreds of microfiches.

The State of Arizona awarded me a G.E.D. within days, which I promptly showed at the college to complete the registration process. I was now officially enrolled to start college.

I signed up for a single class with my friend Andy, and my then wife, Patricia. The class was Conversational Spanish. Patricia didn't enjoy it and dropped the class after the first week.

I enjoyed the class and received a C, and even though I still couldn't speak Spanish fluently, I was convinced that I could attend college without a problem. The following semester I enrolled full time and began drawing my G.I. Bill educational benefits.

Driving a cab was an ideal job for a college student. Between calls, I read assignments, wrote papers, and completed course work. It wasn't unusual for me to have class materials scattered across the front seat of my cab.

Back at the cab company on that cool, overcast Wednesday morning, the word was that Walt Arnett was going to treat all the drivers as new employees and start all of us at 40% of the meter, significantly reducing our income until we proved ourselves worthy of a pay increase.

This meeting would provide clarification to the nervous drivers, many of whom had been driving a cab since the end of World War II and depended heavily on their job to stay afloat. Few of them had done much of anything else for a livelihood in a long time, and were feeling very anxious.

When I first heard the rumors, I stopped by the unemployment office to ascertain my options. It was explained to me that I would be eligible for unemployment insurance if my "new" job offer meant a significant reduction in wages.

Walt walked to the front of the room and took a seat, accompanied by our manager, Bill. The room became quiet.

Bill stood up and got right down to business, explaining the job offer in detail. Mr. Arnett was in fact going to reduce our take of the meter to 40%, treating everyone as a new employee.

Our manager then explained that there would be no break in pay, or other benefits, such as health insurance. We would gradually work our way back up to 50% of the meter.

I then spoke up and shared the information I had received at the unemployment office. Walt shot up, abruptly telling me that I was misinformed, advising the other drivers to disregard me, and demanded that I leave the meeting ("Obviously, this meeting is of no benefit to you.")

As I was escorted out of the room by the front office supervisor, I could hear a great commotion behind me, including Bill letting everyone know that this was a non-negotiable job offer.

While the tumult behind me subsided, I walked to my motorcycle, feeling numb, and in a state of shock.

This had been a decent opportunity for me, and I felt like I had just tossed it away. I would not be driving a cab anymore.

It was ten days before Christmas. I had a ten-month old son I would soon be paying child support for, and a court date to dissolve my marriage set for January 3rd, 1977.

I also had little savings, a mortgage on a house that I'd bought less than six months ago—and faced a worsening economy.

I sat on my Suzuki GT-380 for a few minutes contemplating my next move. My soon-to-be former spouse Patty had already moved out, and she had opted to take the pickup truck rather than keep the house; which she didn't seem to care for at all.

We had completed less than half of the work we needed to do on the house. It was very lightly furnished, and the heat pump had just quit.

I decided to head for the unemployment office and get the ball rolling.

3

STATE JOB SERVICE

My marriage ended quietly, with a brief visit before a court commissioner named James McDougall, who asked a few questions, filled in the agreed upon amount of child support, and signed our decree.

Years later, while I was mediating for the Attorney General's Office, another mediator named James McDougall joined our team. He and I co-mediated and resolved a dispute—and spoke after the mediation. He was the same Commissioner who had signed the decree dissolving my marriage to Patty.

For the following month or so I visited the State Job Service faithfully, at least 3 days a week.

I carried a little tri-folding card the interviewer would annotate with a date and initials at each visit. I was required to visit the unemployment folks upstairs monthly to show them my initialed card and prove I was trying to find gainful employment.

Since I was a veteran, I met with a Veteran's representative named Mel Price nearly every time I went into the Job Service.

After about a month of unproductive visits, Mel said, "You know, I'm not going to find you a job that pays as well as your last one and has the same benefits. I can offer you a position here part time on V.A. Work Study until something comes along. You want to give it a try?"

I accepted his offer, and soon found myself interviewing veterans, helping them find work, and helping them to learn more about their benefits.

The Unemployment Office notified me that they had a concern about me being a fulltime student on work study while drawing unemployment benefits and attempted to stop my benefits.

I requested a hearing where I was able to demonstrate that all my classes were at night, and I had successfully worked and gone to school nights prior to losing my job. I also pointed out that as a work-study student I was well-positioned to find gainful employment.

The administrative judge agreed with me.

Soon, I was working full time on Work Study, and my unemployment benefits were gradually reduced and eventually stopped all together.

Working for Mel was a highly valuable experience. He was a great all-around gentleman who had served in the Army in Korea. He demonstrated a high degree of patience as he mentored me.

I learned all about veteran benefits and interviewed more than twenty veterans or qualified family members nearly every day. It was my first exposure to this kind of work, and the environment was simply electric!

The doors would open in the morning, and a tide of unemployed men and women would fill the lobby. For the first time in my life I had my own desk, cubical, microfiche viewer, phone, and office perks.

I really liked the people I worked with. They were diverse, fun, and professional. I was happily settling into single life, involved with several interesting women, and my house on 10th Street was within walking distance of the office.

I was making my child support payments monthly and barely scraping by financially, but I felt like a new man.

As time went on, my skills as an interviewer improved significantly, and soon, my placement statistics became impressive. I was happy and felt good about what I was doing.

Since I was just barely making it financially, I was also in a position where I could refer myself out to weekend temporary jobs as soon as they were listed. That combined with trips to Park 'n Swap, where I sold possessions, I felt I could do without, kept my nose barely above water.

The other interviewers knew about my availability for weekend gigs and would often walk over and ask me if I wanted to fill a job order. I nearly always cruised and perused the open job orders on Friday afternoon just before leaving for the weekend, just in case.

Not all my weekend gigs were okay though. I took a temporary job removing old overhead light fixtures from a factory ceiling. It required using a drill and some other tools, and working all day standing on a ladder while holding the drill overhead.

I managed to get a steel splinter in my right eye. I went to a doctor (after completing the job), got the splinter plucked out, and had a gauze patch taped over my right eye with strict instructions to keep it over my eye for at least a couple of days.

The following morning, I had another gig lined up to assist an electrician working at an ore-crushing plant in Pinto Valley, Arizona.

I rode out there on my motorcycle with a patch over my right eye and found the plant. When I reported for work, the electrician, an older guy in bib overalls, regarded me nervously, and asked me if I was sure I was up to the task. I assured him I was.

The "task" turned out to be daunting. I followed the electrician across beams high above the loud ore-crushers, feeding him lengths of conduit, and assisting him in snapping them into place. The noise was deafening, with small particles of crushed ore clouding the air.

Here I was, high above huge, loud ore crushers, blinking, one-eyed and left-eyed for the first time in my life, with no real depth perception, on my hands and knees crawling on a three-foot-wide beam with conduit in tow all day for $5 an hour. Did I ever earn that paycheck!

The Job Service office manager, Mr. Claude Brashear was a retired Marine Master Sergeant. He was a tough but fair manager who had worked his way up in the system and treated me like one of his young Marines.

Susan Dean, his assistant manager, was attractive, intelligent, and supportive. She taught me how to separate the various office report print outs, crunch the numbers, and prepare a daily report in addition to my regular duties.

Soon, I was coming in a little early and assembling the daily office activity report every morning. This also gave me an opportunity to see how I was doing compared to everyone else!

One morning, Mr. Brashear called me into his office and offered me a position as a state intern under the CETA (Comprehensive Employment and Training Act) program. I happily accepted the offer. Now I was making a decent little paycheck with benefits, had some real stability, and was happily enjoying what I was doing.

In addition to interviewing and referring veterans and family members to paying positions, I was permitted one day per week to visit employers and cultivate new job opportunities for the multitude of unemployed folks pouring into the job service daily.

Employers now called and asked for me specifically to list new positions, which gave me first crack at filling them!

I was also settling into a nice routine with my infant son nearly every weekend. Patty seemed to be enjoying her new single status quite well, and there were no difficulties other than the on-going need for me to occasionally make additional income.

I would skip getting Daniel on weekends when I needed to work, with no objections from Patty.

School was going well, too. I made the Dean's List and continued to routinely meet interesting women. Much to my surprise, in comparison with my high school days, it was the polar opposite. I discovered that very much unlike school when I was a kid, I liked school, and was a capable student. It was like I was a whole new person in a whole new world.

I was in a position to help out my friends who had accepted Arnett's offer and who had discovered how unworkable it was for them. They were now looking for better employment.

I helped my friend Andy secure a job as a Chemist for the Carling Brewery in Phoenix.

One day, much to everyone's surprise, he marched into the office, walked directly back to my cubicle, and dropped a case of Tuborg beer on my desk.

This created a great stir. I ended up doling out about half of it to my co-workers as they visited my cubicle and inspected the case of beer I'd set in the corner.

It also caused a visit into my boss' office so he could scold me briefly and advise me on the rules about beer being brought into the office.

One of the classes I signed up for was Typing 101. Of about 30 students, it appeared that only one other was a male.

He seemed gay, as did the instructor. They spent a fair amount of time together as the instructor showed him how to position his fingers on the keyboard, and other important instruction.

I liked being surrounded by so many women, and I don't believe I've ever benefited more from any class I have taken. And I've never enjoyed a class so much in my life!

I learned to type 40 words per minute on an IBM Selectric, and I have benefited from this skill perpetually throughout the years. Since then I've been able to prepare all of my own correspondence and other work, significantly enhancing my ability to perform a wide variety of assignments, including schoolwork. I have fond memories of my classmate "Mickie Flickie". A beautiful, fun-loving blonde I palled around with until she eventually met the love of her life.

Everything else seemed to be falling into place as well. I had an interesting roommate named Carol who had left her husband and moved in with me, complete with her piano and a shepherd-mix named Eve.

Carol was pretty, fun, and a little wild, too. We had an Intriguing, tumultuous, and brief relationship.

We met while taking Applied Psychology. Our instructor was a trained hypnotist and asked if there were any volunteers in the class for a little experiment. Carol raised her hand eagerly. She sat before the instructor, smirking, and giggling as he worked on placing her in a trance.

She soon became quiet and sat placidly, eyes closed as he gave her a post-hypnotic suggestion that when he clapped his hands, she would get up and draw the shade on the window.

He then snapped his fingers and she seemed to spontaneously awaken.

She returned to her seat and whispered in my ear with a little giggle that he hadn't hypnotized her.

The instructor clapped his hands, and it was like she'd heard a shot! She leaned over and nervously asked me if I'd mind getting up and pulling the shade on the window for her.

She seemed embarrassed and confused, and when I wouldn't get up and pull the shade, she did; much to the delight of the class!

When Carol moved out, "Evie" stayed. She was a well-behaved dog, and surprisingly, an excellent quail dog. Sadly, she was hit by a car and killed while a friend was watching her for me in the late summer of 1980.

As I continued my work at the Job Service, complete with occasional temporary jobs here and there, women drifted in and out of my life.

I also had the opportunity to hunt quail frequently during the season, shot and ate numerous rabbits, and enjoyed some productive bass and crappie fishing on Roosevelt Lake during the Springs of 1978, 1979, 1980 and 1981.

Life hadn't ever seemed more complete or interesting; I had developed a comfortable rhythm and flow that was quite pleasing. I just needed to solve the problem of a slightly inadequate cash flow.

I would eventually resolve this issue.

4

MY EARLY YEARS

My mother and father both served in the Marine Corps during World War II. Mom was a Sergeant and Dad was a Corporal. Mom was born and raised in the Pittsburgh area, and Dad grew up in Buffalo, New York.

During the Depression years, Mom's father, Brian McDonald, was a successful entertainer with an extremely popular radio show, and at the height of the Depression was earning as much as $10,000 a week. Mom sometimes appeared with her father, singing, or doing a Vaudeville routine.

Dad's father, Samuel, was former U.S. Army, serving as a scout in the Philippines, and learning to speak Tagalog.

They lived an austere life during the Depression years, aided somewhat by my father discovering a crashed delivery truck filled with canned food and other merchandise while out hunting early one morning.

The driver had run off the road and walked away from the accident to no doubt seek assistance. Dad quickly ran home and recruited assistance to re-position the contents of the truck. His family was well-provisioned for quite some time.

Mom served primarily as a recruiter in the Syracuse Armed Forces Recruiting Station. One of her routine duties was to arrange and schedule bond tours for returning combat veterans who would speak to groups and encourage them to purchase war bonds to fund the ongoing war in the Pacific.

She would meet with the veterans and help them develop a talk based on their service experience.

Typically, these heroes had no public speaking experience. Mom would be expected to get them up to speed as speakers, and often escort them to their speaking engagements and try to keep them out of trouble.

At the start of the war, Dad went to work at the Curtiss Wright aircraft plant in Buffalo, New York, quickly being promoted to foreman. He enlisted in the Marines in October 1942 and volunteered as a scout-sniper.

Dad honed his skills as a scout-sniper as he wandered the hills outside of Wellington, New Zealand, shooting deer for the dining hall as the 2nd Marine Division prepared for their first major fight—they didn't know it until they were well-under-sail, but they were organizing and preparing to capture the island of Tarawa.

Dad fell in love with New Zealand. And the New Zealanders fell in love with the 2nd Marine Division. While in New Zealand with Karyn, my son Daniel, and his wife Angela, we spent most of our time on the South Island, then rode the train into Wellington and visited The Museum of New Zealand, Te Papa Tongatewa, located in the center of Wellington. I was both surprised and delighted to find an exhibit dedicated to the 2nd Marine Division during World War II when they trained and prepared for their assault on Tarawa. The exhibit contained photos of the young Marines interacting with the locals, including a number of very attractive local ladies, and wedding photos as well. There was also an article about a Marine lieutenant married to a New Zealand girl, who would never return to her or hold their child for the first time.

The exhibit emanated a certain reverence for these heroic young men the New Zealanders had grown to know so well.

Dad served as a scout-sniper during the battle for the island atoll of Tarawa, a part of the Gilbert Island chain. He was assigned to Lieutenant William Hawkins' platoon. Hawkins, known as "The Hawk," was a highly respected leader, with an important assignment—to capture and secure the island's dock in the first invasion wave.

Nearly all the actual fighting in Operation Galvanic occurred on the island of Betio (pronounced bay-she-oh). This fight was so spectacularly bloody, that the details were initially withheld from the American public. When the awful details began to reach the public based on some pretty graphic film footage and eye-witness accounts by war correspondents such as Robert Sherrod in his 1944 book, *Tarawa: The Story of a Battle*, there was considerable public outcry.

There was a belief that the heavily defended atoll could have been isolated instead and left to whither as Japan became more cut off and surrounded. The War Department thought otherwise. The airfield on Tarawa put the U.S. within striking distance of Japanese defenses close to the homeland and gave the U.S. another significant strategic advantage.

The fight to take Betio—an island strip roughly 2 miles long and only 800 yards at its widest point—had a nearly unparalleled fierceness. It was heavily defended by Japanese Special Naval Landing Forces. These weren't typical soldiers. They were the equivalent of U.S. Marines, many already combat-hardened in China.

The assault force was comprised mostly from the 2nd Marine Division. This was the same Marine Division that I was briefly assigned to before separating from active duty and transferring to the Reserve in April, 1970.

Of the 12,000 Marines involved roughly half actually served in a direct combat role during the assault: 894 were killed outright, 84 more died later from their wounds, and an additional 2,188 Marines were wounded.

Of the 4,690 Japanese military defenders, a total of one officer (Warrant Officer Kiyoshi Ota), and 16 enlisted men survived the battle. Of the 1,200 Korean civilian laborers, 129 were taken prisoner.

The Japanese commander, Rear Admiral Keiji Shibazaki had boasted that "A million men cannot take Tarawa in a hundred years." The Marines did it in just 76 hours at great cost.

The Navy bombarded the island heavily, and it appeared the Japanese had been decimated. Unfortunately, they had not been.

Their defensive positions were still quite intact, only their lines of communication had been seriously damaged, significantly hampering their ability to coordinate an effective defense.

As a scout-sniper, Dad landed with the first wave after an exceedingly difficult ride to the beach on an Amtrak. The Roebling ALLIGATOR was the first in a series of assault amphibians that transported Marines and cargo to and from hostile territory and was referred to as an "Amtrak" pretty much from its inception. This evolved into the AAV7A1—armored assault amphibious full-tracked landing vehicle. Initially, there was some shelling from the smoke-shrouded island as they rode the choppy surf after getting past the coral reef.

The Marines in Dad's craft had initially joked and spoke of their desire to collect some souvenirs. Dad mentioned that as they neared the island, a shell passed just over their craft and splashed with a huge geyser in the water behind them. One of the Marines said, "There's your souvenir, go get it," to much laughter.

As they neared the beach, they were pelted with .50 caliber rounds, followed by 20-millimeter shells, including one that cut the driver of the amphibious tractor in half and spattered Dad with shrapnel in his left hand and arm. Only six of the fourteen Marines in his Amtrak made it to shore alive, four of the six were already wounded before they hit the beach, and only three survived the battle, one unwounded.

Upon stalling at the seawall on the beach, they were confronted with an impressive array of interlocking, mutually supporting Japanese bunkers, machine gun nests, and other fighting positions that had to be fought through.

Dad fought hand-to-hand using his bayonet and jungle hatchet after getting his rifle blown in two by a grenade. This resulted in more shrapnel wounds, including losing part of his right thumb when his rifle was destroyed.

He retrieved a dead Marine's Garand rifle, was placed in charge of a squad, and ordered to flank an enemy bunker. The enemy gunner spotted them and opened up with a burst of machine gun fire as he and another Marine got within fifteen yards of their objective.

The other Marine was killed, and Dad was hit three times in the right arm and shoulder.

Severely wounded, Dad passed out on the beach. At that point he had been shot several times, bayonetted, and hit numerous times with all forms of shrapnel.

When he woke up, he continued to fight on and then began searching for an aid station to get his wounds dressed.

As he crept along the beach, a mortar round landed next to him, hitting him in the face, right eye, and lungs and blew him into the water, where he lay with his head propped up on the leg of a dead Japanese soldier for 27 hours until he was eventually dragged out of the water by a Navy Corpsman named "Doc" Warwick.

"Doc" Warwick loaded him on an Amtrak for evacuation back to the transport.

The airfield located on Tarawa was named after Dad's platoon commander, Lt William "Bill" Hawkins, who received the Medal of Honor posthumously.

Ultimately, Dad lost his right eye, half of his right lung, partial use of his right arm, and required significant reconstructive surgery. After being transported back to Pearl Harbor, then San Diego, he was eventually transported to the base hospital at Samson Naval Training Center in Upstate New York where he spent approximately one year being treated.

According to the March 1, 1945 Samson Naval Base "All Hands" base bulletin, Dad refused a Silver Star and Legion of Merit. His official reason for declining the awards was because, "I was just carrying out orders. Those decorations are for conduct beyond the call of duty." According to Mom, he privately stated, "It's the Medal of Honor, or nothing."

Many years ago, my brother Bruce received a phone call from an elderly gentleman named Tom who was living in Florida. Tom was looking for Dad.

Tom hoped to contact Dad and was extremely disappointed to hear that he had recently drowned. He had been on Dad's Amtrak and had begun wondering about Dad after he learned that he was still alive. He was amazed that Dad had lived.

Tom related that as they had approached the beach on Tarawa, within 50 yards or so they began getting constantly pelted on all sides by 20-millimeter cannon, machine gun, rifle fire, and shrapnel. Nearly everyone aboard was already dead or wounded except him.

He survived the battle without a scratch. He said that when their craft hit the beach and came to a halt, the driver already dead, Dad winked at him, hopped out with rifle and hatchet in hand, and dashed to the beach. He knew that Dad was the bravest man he had ever known.

Bruce related this conversation to Brian who followed up on something Dad had told him over a beer many years before Tom's phone call.

Dad had told Brian about a near miss that occurred while he was on the transport headed for Tarawa. There were frequent and encouraged boxing matches on board ship. Some for sport and, I can imagine, some to resolve grudges. Dad was a talented amateur boxer and got himself onto the card. He was matched up with a guy named "Mo" Sposato. He managed to get a look at Mo prior to the fight and was a bit alarmed. Mo looked like a gorilla! Dad described him as the "hairiest guy I'd ever seen." And he looked like one really mean-motherfucker.

Fortunately, they never fought. As they drew close to their destination, attention turned to last minute preparations.

Brian did some research, checking online to search for Tarawa casualties, and learned that "Mo" was Maurice Sposato and was still alive.

Brian contacted him at his gym in Utica, NY. Mo owned a boxing gym and had been a championship-caliber boxer prior to joining the Marines. He hadn't boxed professionally after Tarawa due to being shot in both legs during the assault.

While being treated for his wounds, Dad volunteered to sell War Bonds, and that's how he met Mom. He cut a dashing figure and had a great story for his audiences that the "Japs aren't 10-feet tall, and we can take them," and Mom was a tall, good-looking brunette with a show-business background and a great singing voice. They hit it off and got married.

Dad was initially retired as 100% disabled. They immediately took an apartment in Syracuse and started a family, with my older sister Wendy being born in early 1946. Dad sought employment as quickly as he could and began selling insurance.

I was born in April of 1950, and my brother Bruce was born in June 1951. My brother Brian was born the day they started moving into a 3-bedroom house Mom and Dad had just purchased on Male Avenue in the suburb of Fairmount, just outside of Syracuse, New York. Before that, we lived in an apartment on Rockland Avenue in Syracuse.

My Grandfather McDonald purchased the adjoining lot as a wedding present. That lot was the future scene of many neighborhood baseball and football games. Mom continued on to have my brother Brian and my sister Kerry, for a total of five of us.

Mom told me that one time she took me for a walk around the neighborhood shortly after we moved into our house on Male Avenue. She stopped and asked me, "Kevin, do you know where you are?" I replied that I did. She asked me where I was. I looked at her and said, "I are here!"

As a young kid growing up, I remember my Mom and Dad being engaged in near-constant community service.

They led the effort to start the first public library in Fairmount, named after the Petit family for their generous contributions of time and money. They also launched the first teen club, initially in our basement. Later it was moved to an abandoned fire house on West Genesee Street that was refurbished by community volunteers.

Dad developed some public-speaking expertise while selling War Bonds and had further developed those skills working at the Syracuse Chamber of Commerce. He decided to run for Town Councilman in Camillus, New York, was elected, and re-elected once.

While on Town Council, he successfully led a move to build a new firehouse to better serve and protect Fairmount. He was also a key negotiator and decision-maker during the launch of Fairmount Fair, one of the earliest shopping malls in Upstate New York.

I remember going to a park in Camillus to hear Dad give a speech on Veterans Day. He spoke eloquently of the valiant men he served with on Tarawa and described Lieutenant Bill Hawkins fighting and leading his men on the island until Hawkins fell for the last time, bleeding heavily, mortally wounded, and died.

He also spoke highly of another Lieutenant (I best recall his name being Mike Hoffman), describing him as one of the bravest men he had ever known. There did not seem to be a dry eye in the park. I looked around and felt amazed as I witnessed the impact of Dad's story on the crowd around me.

Dad tried his hand at selling insurance, distributing quality frozen foods (we sampled many for dinner, and one of my favorites was frog legs), and operating a line of ice-cream vending machines in Upstate New York.

He was hired as Membership Secretary for the Syracuse Chamber of Commerce, where he worked for many years, until shortly before he and Mom divorced.

Mom and Dad ran a tight household while they were still working as a team. We all had assigned chores that we were expected to do, the most important of which was keeping our respective bedrooms clean.

My two brothers and I shared a single bedroom, and we were expected to keep it inspection ready. Any slacking by any one of the three of us had consequences. If Dad conducted an inspection and discovered a mess there could be hell to pay!

We had some tense moments, including corporal (physical) punishment when an inspection went awry. This prepared me quite well for Marine training at Parris Island years later.

When we weren't cleaning, in school, or sitting for a meal, we all pretty much ran wild in the neighborhood. That's what kids did in those days. On our street and the adjoining streets, there were at least twenty boys within a year or two of the same age.

This meant that we almost always had plenty of team members for any of the many games we played, which included war, of course. During the summer, it was nearly non-stop baseball, football, boxing, races, and pretend war games.

Our street provided a long downhill stretch where you could get some real speed with our many rickety wheeled contraptions, and over the course of several years, we planned, organized, and conducted some daring races, with our favorite race involving just about every make-shift wheeled coaster you can imagine.

We would line up maybe five of the odd-looking vehicles at the starting line complete with a flag man. The command, "Ready, set, go!" would launch this perilous competition.

There was a considerable number of pileups, resulting in road-rash, scrapes, cuts, bruises, gashes, and other assorted injuries, but rarely anything that required a visit to the doctor or hospitalization. How we ever managed to avoid any serious injuries, I will never know.

Perhaps most remarkably, the adults either never caught wind of exactly what we were doing, or they turned a blind eye. No police ever showed up to stop us, issue a "blue ticket", which was something they handed out for a juvenile offense (I received one later), or in any way ever interfered. Amazing!

Throughout the summer we played games of baseball, football, and tom-tom tackle (one runner carrying a football, trying to get past two or more defenders) using almost no protective equipment. Team membership constantly shifted and changed.

There were occasional minor injuries, but once again, nothing major. I broke my collar bone once playing tom-tom tackle.

There were no big fights, just a once-in-a-while shoving match and angry words, or someone getting wrestled to the ground. It was the same with boxing.

Most of us shared a couple pairs of boxing gloves, with few injuries other than a bloody lip or nose, or someone getting the wind knocked out of him (I did).

My brother Bruce got his wrist broken once when a neighborhood kid attempted a judo flip on him.

Teams for the war games were almost always formed by streets, and usually sparked by a challenge or agreement. Sometimes the warriors would be armed with wooden swords and protected by "shields," usually holding a garbage can lid.

Some more creative armament included a catapult made from a bicycle inner tube, launching paper bags filled with dirt, as the "enemy" advanced. One team would defend a bunker, and the other team would assault it.

After the assault ended in victory or defeat, there would be laughter and displays of comradery while cuts and bruises were noted.

When I was 14, I got into a fistfight with a 16-year-old kid down the street who was built like a gorilla and dumb as a mud wall. He broke my nose. I broke it again in a motorcycle accident in 1980.

During the last couple of years that I lived in that neighborhood, when many of us were in our early teens, BB gun wars gained popularity.

Once again, there was seemingly no parental or police interference as teenagers hunted each other with BB rifles, accompanied by an occasional shot fired and a yelp!

I shot my brother Bruce in the ass once, from about 50 yards (a long shot with a BB rifle). He was pissed at me until I explained that it wasn't that I wanted to hurt him, it was just that I wanted to see if I could make the shot.

He tended to see my point of view. Bruce is an excellent shot, and if the tables had been turned, I would not have blamed him either!

Being in the suburbs, we had a considerable amount of undeveloped land around us. We had hills where we found an abundance of fossils; swamps (I got chased and bit by a dog in the swamp once), big fields, and even an abandoned munitions storage facility called Split Rock.

Many years before there had been a spectacular accidental detonation of stored military ordnance at Split Rock that could be heard throughout the region, resulting in numerous fatalities—and destruction of the facility.

It provided a great (and highly dangerous) spot for us to explore bunkers concealed by wild vegetation over the many years.

On rare occasion, someone would find an old exploding device. A couple of kids from my neighborhood found what turned out to be a detonator for a mine and threw a rock on it, resulting in several injuries.

When we were not walking, we rode our bicycles here, there, and everywhere. Sometimes we would ride for hours, miles from our neighborhood like explorers, pressing further and further into the countryside.

Toward the end of the day, as the sun inched closer to the western horizon, we would drift back toward home. My mom and dad had a large bell they would go out and ring repeatedly, signaling it was time for us to return.

Even if we didn't hear it, often one of the other neighborhood kids would, and they'd let us know. We would come into the house, get washed up, and head for the dinner table, chattering like magpies.

Our dinner fare often included Sheppard's pie, kidney pie, baked heart, chili con carne, Yorkshire pudding, and any type of fish or game on hand.

Nearly without exception, every night ended with us kids kneeling next to the bed saying our nighttime prayer; as I best recall it went something like: "Now I lay me down to sleep, I pray the Lord my soul to keep. If I should die before I wake, I pray the Lord my soul to take."

We would end our prayer with a special request that Cardinal Mindszenty be freed. The Cardinal had been tried and imprisoned in Hungary by the communist authorities.

Our big collie, Susie, would almost always squat next to us, her paws on the bed, and seem to mutter the words with us, sometimes ending her soliloquy with an enormous dog yawn.

We walked to school every morning and walked home after school as well. It wasn't unusual for Susie to walk with us in the morning, as did several other dogs with their kids. It also was not unusual to find Susie outside the school waiting for us when we headed home.

As she got older, she became incontinent, and had more difficulty getting around. One of her favorite things to do was to lay in the driveway, basking in the sun.

One day a delivery van from one of the local department stores came zipping into our driveway while a couple of kids played in the sandbox next to the driveway. Susie leapt up, chasing and barking at the van, as the young, male driver continued his fast approach. She was run over as she defended what was most important to her.

Paralyzed from the waist down, she attempted to crawl to the house. Dad and Mom picked her up in a blanket, took her to the vet and had her put to sleep. It was a painful experience for all of us, and I remember crying hard when I learned that she was dead.

We often got up and made crepe suzettes (using grape jelly and powdered sugar), pancakes, or whatever was on hand for breakfast as Mom and Dad slept in.

As long as we didn't burn the place down, we were allowed to cook on Saturday mornings. It would often be a collaborative effort.

During smelt or walleye season it wasn't unusual for us to find a bin full of fresh-caught smelt or walleye in the morning when we dove into the fridge to plan breakfast. If there was smelt in the refrigerator, it often resulted in smelt and eggs for breakfast!

I also remember mornings when Dad got up early and led us in cooking breakfast, offering pointers in knowing right when pancakes were ready to be flipped and so on.

Sometimes my Dad would whistle for us to return home. He had a very loud, distinct two-tone, one high note, one low note whistle that could be heard for a great distance. When we heard that whistle, we came running! Susie also came to his whistle, as did both Poika 1 and Poika 2 (golden retrievers) later, long after he and Mom divorced.

During the summer, Dad liked to wear just shorts while he worked in the yard or just laid around. He was quite a sight and a source of fascination for the neighborhood kids. He'd been stitched by a machine gun, had multiple other assorted wounds including a healed bayonet wound, a significant number of shrapnel wound scars, blue freckles on this face from a point-blank explosion, a missing right eye (he normally didn't wear his patch or glass eye, unless he was in public), and tattoos on his arms and chest.

When I was about ten years old, I started to note significant tension developing between Mom and Dad. Dad was working a full-time job at the Syracuse Chamber of Commerce and always seemed to have something else going such as servicing his ice-cream vending machines which were scattered across Upstate New York, distributing frozen food, or selling insurance. He was in constant motion and seemed to be growing more irritable by the day.

As a family, we had talked about a possible road trip to Mexico. Us kids learned what the conversion rate of dollars to pesos was and grew excited about the prospect of travelling there. Dad and Mom finally agreed on a road trip to New Orleans instead.

Dad bought a brand-new light blue 1959 Ford station wagon, with a rear-facing back seat. In the summer of 1959, we took off through the south on our route to the Big Easy.

As we drove further into the south, we started seeing new things. We passed numerous chain-gangs working on the side of the road, and started encountering signs that said, "Whites only."

While staying at a motel in Alabama, we played in the pool, where about ten of us would race up the steps and take a bouncing leap off the high diving board. As I raced up the steps for another plunge, the kid in front of me accidentally kicked me in the mouth, sending me flying from the rear of the board, straight down to the pavement below. This resulted in a quick trip to the emergency room.

Nothing was broken. I just had a sore mouth, and a bruise that extended from my knee to the bottom of my rib cage. Great fun!

We continued to New Orleans uneventfully, and spent a couple of days wandering the French Quarter. Tension only increased between Mom and Dad.

After we returned from our road-trip, I noted a period of loud arguments, punctuated by brief periods of silence. Dad was often head down, glowering and pissed. Mom was frosty.

I became more rebellious, and we had several encounters that did not end well, including once when I decided to go out and wander the neighborhood at 02:00 a.m.

When I finished my fun little reconnaissance and walked into the driveway, I saw Dad leaning against the car, smoking a cigarette.

He said, "Come here." I stepped up to him. "Where have you been?"

I responded, "Out walking around."

He nailed me with a hard right, stood over me, pointed, and said, "Get in the house, now!"

Our father-son relationship was in shambles.

I was aware of the greater world around me, and when there were significant events happening, I learned as much as I could about them.

While I was completing my education at Fairmount Elementary, the Cold War was really heating up, and we students routinely practiced "duck and cover" in preparation for a nuclear strike.

Despite the family turmoil I still very clearly remember the Kennedy assassination, which occurred several months after Dad had moved out. I was in the seventh grade and it was a Friday afternoon. While I was changing classes I heard the announcement from the principal over the P.A. system. President Kennedy had been shot! I remember girls crying in the hallway.

Two days later, as I lay in front of the television in our living room watching live coverage of Lee Harvey Oswald being transferred in the Dallas Police Parking Garage, a local Dallas night club owner named Jack Ruby, ran forward and shot Oswald in the stomach—on camera. Ruby died of cancer while in prison.

While focusing on world events swirling around me, I was caught by surprise when Mom and Dad gathered us together and told us they were getting a divorce. I recall feeling mixed emotions. I knew I wouldn't miss the angry outbursts or Dad's worsening temper and wondered what would happen next.

Mom and Dad, newlywed

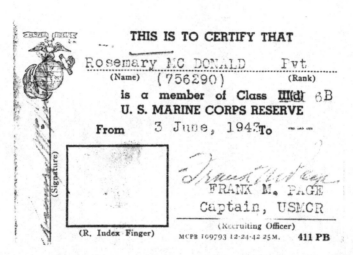

THIS IS TO CERTIFY THAT

Rosemary MC DONALD   Pvt
(Name)   (756290)   (Rank)

is a member of Class **III(d)** 6B
U. S. MARINE CORPS RESERVE

From   3 June, 1943 To   ———

FRANK M. PAGE
Captain, USMCR

(Recruiting Officer)

(Signature)

(R. Index Finger)   MCPB 109793 12-24-42 25M.   **411 PB**

Mom's I.D. card issued when she enlisted

5
—

DELINQUENCY

Dad and Mom divorced. We did not know many of the details. Mom was a Catholic, and we had all been raised in the Catholic religion as was required by the church. Dad appeared to take no interest in Catholicism, and I do not recall him attending church with us, but he agreed to tithe.

I remember we would come out of church and Dad would be leaning against the car smoking a cigarette, waiting for us.

A couple of years before the divorce, I got caught smoking. As punishment, Mom and Dad (who were both smokers) forced me to sit on the front porch and smoke until I nearly turned green.

Rather than eliminating my desire to smoke, after I recovered from an extreme nicotine overdose and thought about it, I decided it was oddly funny, and my inner rebelliousness seemed to be triggered. I became a smoker.

As I grew older, I also became more skeptical of the church. I was required to attend Catechism class and even had one year in a Catholic school, which I strongly disliked. The more I heard, the less I believed.

I frequently calculated the impossibility of Noah's Ark—all the animals of the world in tight quarters for forty days with enough food and fresh water on a massive vessel built by a guy without ship building experience in a time when they weren't even building rafts yet during the greatest storm of all time. Why nobody else seemed to question it puzzled me. I began wondering about all the other stories in the Bible.

I found it unbelievable that every human being and living creature on earth, other than those aboard the Ark had been drowned.

As I grew older, I noted that this story was in complete conflict with all evolutionary theory and scientific research of humans and other creatures.

The Adam and Eve tale also became completely unbelievable to me.

I became very skeptical of many other things as well, such as the "virgin birth." I was unworldly at the time, but understood the concept of being cuckolded, and thought that Joseph's reaction to the news that his "virgin" wife was pregnant seemed puzzling.

The justification for Jesus forcing the authorities to punish him like a common criminal to save us from the "original sin" (thanks to Adam, Eve, and a serpent) seemed totally illogical to me.

All the lecturing in the world could not shake my doubts, and there was no real venue for addressing my doubts with Catholic authorities. Priests seemed isolated and unapproachable and any questioning during catechism could result in a rap on the knuckles by an angry nun.

As I grew older, I learned that the concept of a virgin birth was not new to religion.

The more I thought about it, the surer I was that Jesus was very smart, had learned to become a skilled magician, learning and perfecting the craft and his delivery style as he wandered from village to village, gathering followers and performing such illusions as the miracle of the loaves and fishes, or walking on water. Skepticism in me reigned supreme.

The nuns seemed oddly removed from society. The priests were insular, uninteresting, supposedly celibate, and I could not understand why a man or woman would intentionally choose to not be in a loving, committed relationship with another living person.

The explanations I heard did not ring true with me. I got a strange feeling when I was around the nuns or priests. I found myself rapidly falling away from the church.

Oddly, my Confirmation seemed like the last straw. I came to realize that Catholicism was more than just a religion, it was an institution. It employed thousands upon thousands of people, and involved staggering sums of money internationally, going here, there, and everywhere, but mostly landing in the Vatican, a city unto itself!

It is a business. I thought about everything I heard and experienced during that process and realized that I wanted nothing more to do with the church. That was my last holy communion.

The brewing maelstrom building inside me—the rickety construct of tales, fables, and rituals that had been encoded in Latin over the centuries and built around me over the years—was blown asunder with the force of an Arizona dust devil passing over a pile of debris in the desert.

I lost any faith I had ever felt in a whirling blink of time.

I had devolved into a surly, untethered delinquent with no heroes, role models or religious unction. I felt a complete alienation from society.

Despite my estrangement from religion and society in general, my own personal set of beliefs evolved during my early, formative years:

There is a supreme intelligence in the Universe that is far beyond the reach of our comprehension and miniscule intelligence, and requires no trappings such as churches, shrines, alters, or rituals.

All religions are made up and packed full of falsehoods.

If I leave things better than I find them, I'll be okay.

The time will come when I and everyone else will be completely forgotten, totally erased from all memory and from the face of the Earth; and one day, Earth as we know it will no longer exist either.

After the divorce, Mom soon found a job and bought a brand-new light blue Chevy Malibu convertible, followed by a new wardrobe. I pondered that car and wardrobe. It seemed odd that she would be able to afford it.

It was a nice car, but I had little interest in riding in it. At some point in time I found out with some shock what Dad was paying in child support and wondered how much of that money had gone into the car and clothes.

She worked for WSYR radio/television selling advertising and worked a good number of years for U.S. Air before retiring.

I began to experiment with shop lifting. The store owners and employees would watch us kids like a hawk when we hovered over the candy or merchandise, and I learned to be creative.

I usually would wait until he or she was distracted, then strike. I would purchase some penny candies on my way out of the store, and never got caught stealing.

Boldly, I shoved a quart of beer under my armpit while wearing a leather jacket, one of the clerks spotted me and gave chase. I outran him, laughing, and when I was safely out of any danger, I walked up into some trees, sat down, lit up a cigarette and guzzled beer. I avoided that store for quite some time.

As I became more skilled at shoplifting, I found another store owner, nick-named "Fats", who agreed to pay me 50% of the price tag for selected merchandise from other stores (mostly food products—he especially liked a good steak). He also provided me with alcohol and cigarettes.

One time when I walked into his store, he and a fellow shoplifter named Bobby offered me a small airline-size bottle of "whiskey". I took the bottle and held it up to the light. It had a suspicious yellow cast to it. I unscrewed the lid and took a sniff. It was piss. I held the bottle at arms-length and began tipping it.

As a small dribble of the liquid started spilling, Fats, very nimble for his girth, dashed around the counter to stop me. I tipped the bottle back up and slapped it on his counter. I looked at Bobby and Fats and said, "Don't do that again."

Several of us had discovered that a huge neon dairy billboard on West Genesee Street with two Dutch boys see-sawing and advertising a local dairy was a great source for empty soda and beer bottles that had been thrown from passing cars, or otherwise discarded there, all of which could be returned for two or five cents apiece.

One time when my brother Brian and I were walking past it, I picked up a baseball-sized rock, and gave it a good fling. I must have hit the billboard in just the right spot, as it blew out the sign with a pronounced flash and accompanying sound. We ran like hell, laughing like little maniacs all the way!

This billboard kept me with money in my pocket, and by the time I turned thirteen, I was smoking about a half a pack of cigarettes daily. For some time, that billboard bottle graveyard and shop lifting were staples for my personal economy.

Years later, Brian told me that he had become a prolific shoplifter, and upon sharing experiences, we agreed that we employed many similar techniques.

Mom and Dad had a stocked bar in the basement. Although most of the liquor had been removed after the bar became inactive, there was still a variety of partial bottles of this and that, and over the course of about a year, I polished them all off.

I began to spend increasing amounts of time on the street, and I started skipping school. My grades soon reflected my disregard for the classroom. By the time I was 15, I was making a regular habit of ditching, and I was openly not doing homework or studying for tests.

On several occasions I sat through the test and handed it in blank. I am not sure why, but I recall the teacher's reactions being confused or mystified, and my Mom never seemed to be aware of what was happening with me.

I started combing my hair in a wave, wore pegged pants, and began to make some real money shop lifting. I purchased a pair of black, pointed-toe shoes, followed by a wardrobe more to my liking.

I pegged a pair of pants for Brian. He wore them the next day. One time, he sat too quickly, and the seams ripped out. His teacher would not excuse him, and he spent the rest of the day walking around with his pants flapping, torn all the way to his crotch. Obviously, tailoring was not my forte.

I came home really drunk one night and got nabbed by Mom. She was mightily pissed, and really raised hell with me, torturing me until late into the night. But seeing as how I was quite drunk, I didn't care.

I began routinely getting in fights at school. My most frequent source of conflict were the many school athletes who walked the hallways like little lords, sometimes seeming to dare a confrontation, which I was glad to provide by not giving way, and sometimes resulting in words spoken and punches thrown. Early on, I learned not to get into a wrestling match, instead circling my opponent with an ongoing assault.

Fights were almost always stopped by spectators or fellow athletes. On one occasion a fight that had gone on for more than a few seconds caught the attention of a school employee, and we were both cited and required to meet with the principal. I ended up meeting with the Assistant Principal and received a warning.

I was living a day-to-day existence, with no concept of a future. I had no positive influences, no role models, and I never gave a thought about what I would do if I ever reached adulthood.

In class I would hold the text *du jour* upright in front of me with a more interesting book tucked in, such as *Portnoy's Complaint* or *Black Like Me*, and pay no attention to what was being taught. Sometimes I'd read my history book, enjoying it far more than any of the other textbooks.

I became more and more reckless, and over a three-year period, I managed to fail two grades in school and couldn't have cared less.

I don't remember ever connecting with a single adult, except for an elderly, retired neighbor who lived behind us. He and I drank several beers together and talked about his life. He was severely disabled after many years working for Solvay Process, a chemical processing plant that made sodium carbonate or soda ash, which has now been associated with tumors and premature mortality. But he was a good guy.

I totally disliked and distrusted all my teachers, never connecting with any of them. Any other authority figure also received a high degree of distrust, especially cops.

To my mother's credit, by the summer of 1964 she realized I was coming off the rails and sent me to summer camp at a place called Lourdes, run by the Catholic Church. Although by that time I had begun to eschew all things Catholic, I found something I really enjoyed: swimming.

This rustic camp is located on the shore of Skaneateles Lake, one of the Finger Lakes in Upstate New York. The water felt ice-cold but was clear and clean (one of the purest lakes in the world). Once I got in the water, I adjusted quickly and loved the freedom of that big lake.

I was (and still am) a strong swimmer, learning all the requisite strokes, and easily swam the mandatory 300 yards on test day, achieving my Junior Life Saving certification.

I found the counselors to be tolerable (most of them were on the younger side of adulthood), and for a few weeks got some good sleep, ate well, and stayed out of trouble. One of my cabin mates was also somewhat of a delinquent, and we would slip out into the woods, have a smoke or two and listen to music or a fight on a small transistor radio I'd brought.

As soon as I got back to the neighborhood, I fell right back into my bad ways. After a pretty serious confrontation with my sister Wendy's then boyfriend, who tried to force me to get a haircut (I pulled a knife on him), I hitch-hiked, heading for Canada, tossed the knife, and made it just past Watertown on U.S. 81, about 70 miles north of Syracuse, before being picked up by a State Trooper.

After Christmas break when I was 15, I stopped going to school. I knew that I could legally drop out when I turned 16, but I just couldn't wait. I disliked every day in school and all I could think of as I sat in class was the time when I would not be forced to sit there anymore.

I had two girlfriends, both of whom I cared for, and one I was deeply fond of. She was a foster-child, being cared for by a single woman. We talked on the phone quite a bit, and we would sometimes rendezvous at night (her foster mom worked nights). She became my first lover.

It was miraculous that Darlene did not get pregnant. After I stopped going to school, we saw little of each other, and finally never saw each other or spoke again.

She was beautiful and sweet. She seemed to really care about me, and I cared about her. We called each other "Ma" and "Pa."

Shortly after I turned 16, my mother finally seemed to get wind of the fact that I had stopped going to school. I honestly do not know if the authorities finally contacted her, or if she put 2+2 together. She insisted that if I was not going to attend school, I find a job.

A priest friend of hers referred me to Crouse-Irving Hospital for a position as a hospital porter, and I was hired.

As a porter my job was primarily to clean things up. If a patient made a mess, I would be there with cleaning implements to tidy up and make things as sterile as possible. I cleaned rooms, mopped, and waxed floors.

I kept moving all day long cleaning, mopping, picking up after extremely sick people, and any other duties I was assigned. My work hours were 6:00 a.m. to 2:30 p.m. with a half hour for lunch, which I rarely took. I would usually read instead.

I typically would begin hitch-hiking to work at about 4:30 in the morning, and perhaps take the bus back to Fairmount in the afternoon. I quickly grew tired of this commute and found the job to be completely distasteful.

Previously, when I was running away to Canada, Dad spotted me at the Northern Lights traffic circle. He pulled over and called to me. I was still extremely pissed and gave him the finger. He waved me off, jumped back in his car, and drove away.

We hadn't spoken again since that day, until I went to work at the hospital. He called and asked me to meet him after work one day, and he made a proposition. He would set me up with a full camp on a river for the summer.

He would expect me to be willing to watch my brothers (including my step-brother) responsibly as they rotated through, and the camp would be mine for the rest of the summer.

He would provide a 14-foot aluminum boat with a 3 ½ horsepower Mercury outboard motor, two oars, an extra fuel tank, and fishing gear.

He would resupply me weekly with food and any other necessities and give me a weekly stipend of $15. He would also check in on me periodically.

In return, I agreed that at the end of the summer I would stay with his girl-friend and her three children, behave myself, go back to school, and achieve passing grades in all subjects.

He would employ me at his Syracuse Howard Johnson's Motor Lodge located on Carrier Circle, Friday, and Saturday nights, working as the Night Auditor/Desk Clerk. I agreed.

It was one of the smartest deals I've ever entered into.

Street punk, shoplifter

6

SUMMER OF 1966

Dad and I struck our agreement and proceeded to carry it out. I began working at the motor lodge and learned to run the front desk.

Elly Mae, the daytime clerk, showed me how to check guests in, make entries on the accounting sheets, and how to spot common accounting errors.

She fully explained the guest register to me and taught me how to use the switchboard. In addition, I learned how to track room completion as the maids called in to the front desk, track completed maintenance, and take reservations. She also showed me how to charge credit cards. At that time, the two big credit cards most used and accepted seemed to be American Express and Diners Club.

Elly Mae was an attractive, vivacious, brunette from the hills of Kentucky. She had a beautiful smile, dark shiny hair, a great laugh, and I liked her. She was helpful and determined to make sure that when I took over the desk, I was ready. And I was.

I already knew the motel well. In 1962, the year Dad moved out, he had resigned his position with the Chamber of Commerce, worked briefly for Sysco, a food distribution service, and soon after accepted employment working for a millionaire named Howard Aronson serving as his General Manager for Ho Jo Corporation.

They had met during Dad's duties as Membership Secretary (selling memberships) at the Chamber, and Howard was impressed. Howard was a good guy, and they struck a deal that worked best for both.

Dad became the General Manager for two Howard Johnson Motor Lodges in Syracuse, one located at Northern Lights and the other on Carrier Circle across from the Carrier Plant and went to work making them profitable and building Howard's business.

The deal had Dad living at the lodge while he got his finances sorted out. After about a year, he took an apartment a couple of miles away with a roommate we called Harris.

Harris owned a Porsche and drank scotch. He had a grey-blonde brush cut and somewhat florid complexion and seemed like a good-natured fellow.

Dad and I had an on and off again relationship. When we were "on" I would often do some work at the lodge for minimum wage. It became a nice little source of income.

I would paint curbs, re-set and level the cinder blocks around the pool before we opened it, and a multitude of other jobs, including cleaning rooms and washing linens.

Dad was quite the entrepreneur, and the name of the game in the hotel/motel world was occupancy. Dad set out to attract businessmen.

One of his initiatives that proved quite popular was "Steak and Poker." Every Wednesday, Dad would host this event in the motel conference room 'by invitation only'.

He would buy some good steaks, a bag of potatoes to bake, sour cream, butter, lots of salad fixings, dressing and other condiments, and quart bottles of beer which we'd put in the ice-filled bathtub.

If the attendees wanted another beverage, they were welcome to bring it. The fee to participate was $15 which included $5 in poker chips.

Starting at about 5:00 p.m., attendees would drift into the conference room and Dad would have the grill going, cooking steaks to order. It was a great meal of steak, baked potato, salad, and beer topped with poker, drinks, and laughter.

During his early years as a new bachelor, Dad relied on his poker winnings to remain afloat. After Dad died and we started sorting things out, we found 200 silver dollars under his bed. He had won them playing poker.

No matter what time of the year, nearly every Wednesday the Carrier Circle Howard Johnson's would be at or near 100% occupancy.

Based on lots of talk during poker, Dad got an idea. We typically opened the pool in May, and it usually required a fair amount of cleaning and other work before it was swimmable for guests.

Prior to the annual cleaning and squaring away of the pool and surrounding area, we went down to Onondaga Lake and caught some big carp. At that time, Onondaga Lake was horribly polluted with a real stench that was detectable for miles, but the carp seem to thrive. They were easy to catch, and carp are a hardy fish.

We put them in big buckets and drove them back to the motor lodge, as many as eight or nine at a time. After a couple of days of fishing, we had at least thirty big carp swimming around in the motor lodge pool, tossing them pieces of bread daily.

While we fished, we had also cut approximately ten-foot lengths of cane growing along the banks of Onondaga Lake, and we fashioned fishing poles with roughly ten feet of line and tackle.

Dad advertised amongst his poker night attendees the "Annual Huck Finn Fishing Contest." First prize was a bottle of Cutty Sark Scotch for the largest fish.

Second prize, also a bottle of Cutty Sark, was for the winner of the fish race. Dad ran it much like a Steak and Poker night without the poker (although after the competition was over many adjourned to the conference room for poker anyhow, bottles in hand).

The entry fee was $20. That got each participant a pole, dough bait, and a colored balloon with a number written on it. Besides the chance to win a bottle of scotch, it also included a good steak dinner, plenty of beer, and excitement.

The event started out orderly. Businessmen in casual attire began trickling in for all the beer they could drink with a good steak dinner. The other motor lodge guests gathered on their balconies to watch as the fishing contest began. The desk clerk had mentioned the upcoming fishing event as guests checked in—probably to avoid noise complaints.

The guys started fishing and the hungry carp were caught and tagged with numbered balloons. The fishing event got rather chaotic, but that was nothing compared to the race that would follow!

Meanwhile, motel guests were sipping their beverages and enjoying the show tremendously.

After a while, all participants had caught a fish, which was netted, weighed, tagged with a balloon, and returned to the pool. There were many fish-attached balloons circulating around in the water.

All the fish were herded to the shallow end of the pool using cane poles to nudge them into a tight, milling mass. All the participants clustered at the shallow end of the pool, and Dad started the race.

It's not as easy as you might think to get a fish pulling a balloon to cross the finish line. All participants could use their poles to nudge the fish. Talk about chaos! A few partially or totally inebriated guys waded into the shallow end of the pool, trying to move their fish or untangle balloons, with other participants yelling, "Foul!"

The guests were almost delirious from laughter. Ultimately, the first fish crossed the finish line, and the bottle of scotch was claimed and consumed at poolside or during the subsequent poker game back in the conference room.

All the carp were returned to the pool and later netted for the employees who wanted them or returned to the lake.

Along the way, playing poker on many Wednesday nights, Dad had managed to win and hold onto a couple hundred silver dollars, which us kids divided, much later, as part of his estate. When it was time for Dad to set up camp for me for the summer, he and I chose a spot on the Oswego River/Canal, at an abandoned commercial dock less than a mile north of Three Rivers, right off of County Route 57.

It was a beautiful spot. We had a contentious dialogue at the time, and I could be surly, but when we drove to that spot on the river, I had to try to contain my excitement.

It was secluded, and breath-takingly beautiful. There was a big open area that included a nice clear spot for a tent, and plenty of rocks to build a good fire-pit.

The dock had been built to secure and load a barge. It appeared that it had not been in use for quite some time. It seemed ancient, but had been built sturdily, and

I could fish right from it. There was vegetation on either side, with a nice clear spot to secure the boat.

Less than a mile downriver was Three Rivers which at that time included a dock, gas pumps, a restaurant and a hotel. Going the other way for about a mile there was a market in Phoenix, within easy walking distance from the shore after you pulled the boat up out of the water.

There was a nice spot that river travelers often used, and you could see the back of the market and a trail leading to it. I visited this market the entire time I was camped on the river.

We pitched the tent, set up camp, and brought the boat down to the water. After we finished unloading all the gear and supplies and Dad provided some instruction regarding the boat, we surveyed the camp, sat, and talked for a while. Dad gave me 15 dollars and told me that he would be back in a couple of days.

He also reminded me that my brothers and stepbrother would probably be spending time out there and I would be responsible for them. We shook hands and he left.

I sat down and lit a cigarette. I looked around. It was a great spot and I liked everything about it. For the first time, I felt an unfamiliar sense of freedom. I walked onto the dock and admired the great, wide river. I made sure my bedding was all in place and thought about dinner.

I built what I considered to be an adequate fire-pit—which I would add to later—and gathered wood. I pulled out a bottle of pre-mixed screwdriver that I had brought and took a good slug.

Over the next couple of days, I caught fish, cleaned them, cooked them, and fried up potatoes, which I smothered in ketchup. I took the boat out and rode up the river to the spot where I could beach it and walk up to a market.

I loved the freedom. Every night I built a great, roaring fire, drank, smoked, ate fish and potato chips, and howled at the moon!

I was out on the river in the fourteen-footer when I saw Dad pull up to the camp site. I guided the boat to the landing spot next to the dock, cut the engine, and nudged the shoreline with the prow of the boat. I got out, pulled the boat up, and walked over to him.

He seemed quite cheerful. He asked me how I was doing. I told him about the fishing and showed him the fire-pit. I also told him about the easy hop to the market.

We unloaded a few supplies including more gas for the boat, and he looked around for a few minutes. We sat and talked. He told me he planned to swing by periodically and reminded me that one of my brothers would be joining me soon.

Over the course of the summer he came by frequently, and often spent many hours talking and fishing with me and my brothers. We got along better than we ever had.

While on the river, my lack of discipline was reflected in my care for my brothers.

One time, Brian came out to spend the weekend. We rode the boat to the landing for the market in Phoenix. Long story made short—we came out of the market and discovered that the boat had drifted out about 30 feet into the river and I demanded that Brian swim out to retrieve it while I stood on shore yelling instructions!

We did get the boat back, but in retrospect, I was older and a strong swimmer. I should have been the one to swim out to get the boat, particularly since I was the one who did not verify that the boat was secure.

Dad helped me to devise some jugs for jug fishing. Jug fishing probably isn't legal anymore (maybe never was). You take an empty plastic bleach bottle, tie and wrap a generous amount of fish line around where the cap screws on, and screw on the cap, leaving enough line to tie your tackle.

When I would get out on the river, I'd bait them, lower the line down until the bait touched bottom and then reel about 2-3 feet back on the threads of the bottle and screw the cap back on.

I'd throw five or six of them in the river, cast the line on my pole, and lay back. If one of the bottles started bobbing up and down, that meant there was a fish on.

I'd reel in my fishing pole, start the motor, or row over to the jug, and begin reeling the line in on the jug. It got exciting when a couple of my jugs started bobbing at the same time! I had great fun over the next couple of days, fishing and exploring the river.

One day I decided to try entering a lock on the canal system and it proved to be quite an adventure. Each lock was large, over 300 feet long and about 50 feet wide. On my first trip through, I was in the lock with a good-sized commercial ship, which added to the excitement.

After I left the lock, I rode upriver a fair distance before turning around and going back through the lock and to my camp site.

Over the next month-and-a-half, I rode the lock system extensively, passing through all seven locks on the Oswego canal in my 14-foot fishing boat.

I was out on the river when I saw a car pulling up to the campsite, and it wasn't Dad's. I reeled in the jugs and my pole, started the motor, and rode back to the shoreline.

I pulled the boat up and walked over to see Elly Mae standing next to the fire-pit. Dad had asked her if she would mind dropping off some supplies to me, and she had agreed.

She asked me if I would take her for a ride in the boat. We rode out on the river and I cut the engine. We lightly rocked in the boat, laid back on the seats and talked.

We admitted to a mutual attraction and kissed. She came out the following day and spent the night. We continued frequent visits throughout the summer.

Dad came out randomly, and whenever one of my brothers was coming or going, he would bring them out or pick them up and spend time with us at the camp and on the river. Dad had just purchased a more powerful boat that could pull skis, and my brothers and I had a great time!

My brother Bruce and I took turns trying to ski. Bruce demonstrated an athletic prowess. Once, I was driving the boat and I didn't make the turn tight enough. Bruce skied through some reeds close to shore with ease.

I spent the entire summer exploring, learning, experiencing, and enjoying. I greatly enjoyed the solitude and will always remember the many nights I sat next to the crackling fire, watching an occasional insect dance around the flames. I would lay on my back and study the night sky, and sometimes listen to a gentle breeze rustle through trees and surrounding vegetation. As I listened, I would imagine that the breeze was thousands of spirits moving and gliding over the surface of the earth. Sometimes I'd fall asleep and wake up hours later.

Finally, one day Dad drove down to the campsite and we pulled the tent down, loaded the boat, packed everything else up, cleaned the site, and left.

Just before school started, I began clerking and auditing at the motor lodge Friday and Saturday nights. It was a great job. I would hitch-hike to work on Friday, starting out early evening, grabbing a meatball sandwich at Cavallero's on Thompson Road, and easily arriving in time to start my shift.

The morning person would relieve me, and I'd update him or her on any issues or concerns before heading to whichever room was available for a snooze.

I had the run of a 90-unit motel all weekend. I typically would take a room if one was available, or just stay in the conference room if there were no rooms, and remain all weekend, hitch-hiking back on Sunday to the Danforth Street apartment where I was staying with Dad's girlfriend, and later his wife, Gladys.

Guests would call down to the desk and leave wake-up call times. We had an alarm that made sort of a grumbling sound and would alert us. We would call the guests from the roster laying on the switchboard. Sometimes I'd have to be persistent.

One morning, I made a wake-up call and the guest didn't answer. I tried again every five minutes for fifteen minutes and assumed that he was already up and out.

About fifteen minutes later, his friends started collecting in the office. They were all supposed to meet at the restaurant for breakfast, and when their friend hadn't shown, they grew worried. I tried calling his room again. No answer.

I grabbed the master key, locked the office, and set off for his room with a small mob following me. I knocked on the door. No answer. I pounded on the door, no answer. I tried the master key. The chain was on.

I had a small screwdriver in my pocket. I reached around the gap in the door, and un-screwed the deadbolt. It dropped and the door swung open.

According to his friends, they'd had a wild night, and our guest had gotten quite intoxicated. He lay on his back in the middle of the bed, blanket and sheet neatly pulled to his chin, and his hands clasped on his chest. All he needed was to be clutching a daisy to complete the picture of absolute repose. His bare feet stuck out from the blanket and sheet.

His friends grew silent. I bent down and studied him closely. He was absolutely silent and motionless. I said, "Sir" as I looked down at him. No response or reaction. I said it again louder. Still no response.

I walked to the foot of the bed, reached out, and grabbed his big toe. He sat up, glared angrily at me, and yelled, "Who the hell are you, and what are you doing in my room?" His friends were overjoyed, and he cooled off quickly.

In the fall, I brought my 16-gauge Lefever side-by-side shotgun to the office and left it in the back room throughout the pheasant season. All fall and winter I frequently hunted pheasant on many Saturday mornings after I left work.

There was a nearly unlimited stretch of hedgerows, tree lines, and fields, directly behind the motor lodge. All I needed to do was walk out back. After I hunted, I'd clean everything up and get some sleep.

Gladys was good to me and treated me gently. Her son, Robert, was a James Bond fan; a big, mild-mannered, good fellow. Her daughter Marilyn was a gorgeous and gracious brunette, and her younger daughter Sheila was equally trim and cheerleader pretty, an attractive blonde with a beautiful smile.

They were all exceptionally good natured and forgiving. I was feral, but I was determined to keep my agreement with Dad.

When I initially started back in school, I was placed in 9th grade at Grant Junior High. As a 16-year old, I was a mature 9th grader! They quickly tested me and promoted me to 10th grade, sending me to Henninger High School in Eastwood.

I was absolutely determined to keep my end of the deal with my Dad. I maintained good grades and had an easy school year. I did my homework as required, never missing an assignment, or playing hooky. I studied and passed my tests. I made a few friends.

The only fight I got into during that entire school year happened away from school. I was hitch-hiking to work one Friday just past twilight. As I walked past a convent on Court Street between rides, three young guys who were leaning against the wall near an unlighted portion of the sidewalk stepped out in front of me.

I had never been in a fight with three guys at the same time. I'd had a couple of fights where my opponent's pal jumped in, but never three all at once.

There was one time when I was hitchhiking to Fairmount Fair—a car with three guys whipped past me and just barely missed me, and I flipped them the bird. They slammed on the brakes, jumped out and came barreling toward me, appearing to be mightily pissed. When they got close, I pulled a knife on them. We exchanged insults and I made it clear I was not kidding. They jumped back in their car and took off.

Hitchhiking to work that night, I was wearing dress pants, a nice long-sleeve shirt, and a tie, and probably looked like an easy mark.

The tall guy in the middle said, "Get on your knees." I punched him square in the nose.

The other two guys piled on and started throwing punches and kicks at me; trying to wrestle me to the ground, and I threw punches and kicks back with enough accuracy to break away from them, stagger one of my attackers backwards, and make the other one completely let go of me.

I recognized him from Grant Junior High, and yelled, "I know you," as I pounced on him and started throwing as many punches as I could at his face. Meanwhile, the other guy was standing over me pounding on my head and kicking me in the ribs!

He had a ring on his right hand. I was trying like hell to avoid his punches as best I could and continued to work on the guy I was kneeling on.

I finally could not stand the guy behind me pounding on me anymore and jumped up to face him, throwing a few punches and kicks that connected. He was caught by surprise and backed away. I felt my left wrist and realized I was missing my watch! I was furious.

I began looking around in the growing darkness. I kicked the guy on the ground and told him to find my watch! I continued to look around and noticed that the first guy I'd hit and the guy with the ring seemed to be conferring in the growing darkness.

I decided it was time to move on. I stepped out on Court Street and almost immediately caught a ride by a very surprised motorist after I climbed in his car and he got a look at me.

I told him what happened, and he drove me all the way to work.

Later, Dad bought me a new watch, which unfortunately got ruined in Vietnam during the monsoon of 1969.

When I walked into the office at the motor lodge, the guy I was relieving, Pete Vascillio, took one look at me, laughed, and said, "What the hell happened to you?" I told him about the fight, and he laughed hard. He was a tough, street-smart guy. I was a real mess.

With his advice, I went into our lost-and-found in the back of the office and selected a reasonably good-fitting wardrobe that was a significant improvement over my current attire.

I then went into our office bathroom and cleaned up. I had a few golf ball-sized lumps on my head from some good shots the guy with the ring had gotten, and my face didn't look so good either.

I also had a couple of good-sized bruises starting on my right ribcage too.

I dressed in my new wardrobe and went to work.

While I was desk clerking, I learned that one of our guests was unable to pay his bill and bartered his black 1960 Chevy Bel Aire for three extra weeks at the motel.

The keys were in the cash drawer, and in the early-morning hours I would often take it for a spin.

It was a 3-speed on the column (H pattern), and I learned how to drive much as I did with my first motorcycle. I got in, started it, and learned to clutch and shift.

I began with ponderous explorations around the motel, and ultimately drove out onto the circle. I would occasionally refuel it by getting a can of gas from the Shell station on the corner, operated by a guy we called "Chopper."

I continued to drive it secretly until my father gave it to Gladys. Dad gave me a few driving lessons in his station wagon, which had an automatic transmission (please keep in mind that I flunked my driving test in his car), but I'm completely self-taught with manual transmissions.

The same holds true with motorcycles. When I purchased my first motorcycle, I paid for it, climbed on, asked the owner how to shift it and what the shift pattern was, started it, and then drove off.

While attending school at Henninger, quite often I was able to get a ride to school with a friend of mine, David Sansone, and his two brothers. David's older brother was doing some sort of internship with the school. All three of them were rock-solid dudes.

David and I crafted a paper mâché tiger in art class, using flashbulbs for its eyes, and painted it orange with black stripes. The tiger was the school mascot, and it was cool enough that it was put on display for a while in the school.

Every morning as we drove to school, we would listen to the news. In early June, we listened to reports of significant tension rising between Israel and its Arab neighbors.

Suddenly, the Israelis launched a brazen air attack, followed by Israeli sweeping victories on the ground. My head was spinning!

Here all these things were going on in the world, and I was sitting in high school. I needed to join the Marines and be part of what was going on. I told my carpool mates what I planned to do.

At first, they dismissed my declarations. As time progressed, they began to take me more seriously after I visited a Marine recruiter and got all the paperwork I needed for my mom and dad to sign.

Mom was fully on board and immediately signed the paperwork. Dad was quite a bit more reluctant and spoke with the recruiter at length first. He finally relented, tearfully wiping his left eye as he signed the consent form.

I returned the paperwork and received my reporting instructions from my recruiter. I understood that I would report back to swear in and board the bus for Parris Island, South Carolina early on the morning of Thursday, June 29, 1967.

I had traded in a paper mâché tiger for some real ones.

My last day of high school was June 23rd. I was advised to travel very lightly, as everything I needed would be issued to me at the recruit depot. I brought only a toothbrush and the clothes I wore. I wasn't shaving yet.

Before I left, I met Elly Mae for drinks at the Holiday Inn across from the Howard Johnson's on Carrier Circle. She was beautiful and wished me well. She said she looked forward to me returning safe and sound.

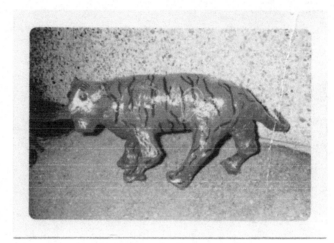

Paper Mache tiger made by

David Sansone and Me

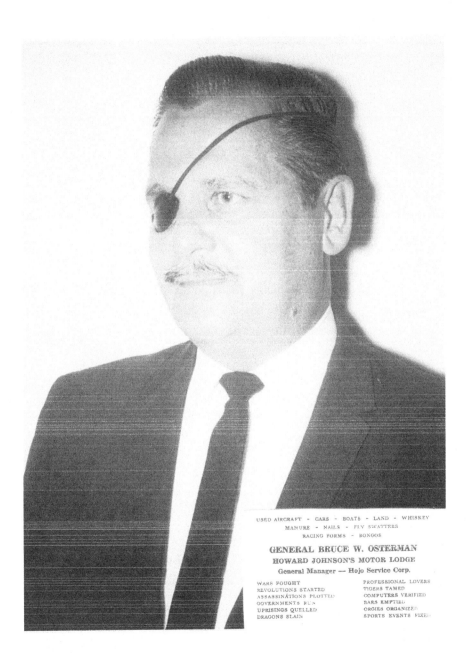

USED AIRCRAFT - CARS - BOATS - LAND - WHISKEY
MANURE - NAILS - FLY SWATTERS
RACING FORMS - BONGOS

GENERAL BRUCE W. OSTERMAN
HOWARD JOHNSON'S MOTOR LODGE
General Manager — Hojo Service Corp.

WARS FOUGHT	PROFESSIONAL LOVERS
REVOLUTIONS STARTED	TIGERS TAMED
ASSASSINATIONS PLOTTED	COMPUTERS VERIFIED
GOVERNMENTS RUN	BARS EMPTIED
UPRISINGS QUELLED	ORGIES ORGANIZED
DRAGONS SLAIN	SPORTS EVENTS FIXED

7

—

SUMMER OF 1967

I reported as directed to the recruiting station in the Chimes Building, downtown Syracuse early on the morning of June 29, 1967. There were a number of other recruits and inductees for all the branches nervously milling around and awaiting instructions.

The first thing we did was complete a physical. After checking our blood pressure and other vital signs, they stood us in ranks and began the physical examination. We all took turns, pulling our undershorts down, coughing, bending over, and raising each foot off the ground as we were inspected by the doctors.

I noted a few guys being culled from the group, but I had no difficulty with the inspection. We all signed our enlistment contracts, raised our right hands and were sworn in, then sat in the hallway and waited for orders to load up on the bus.

The ride to South Carolina was occasionally interrupted as we stopped at other recruiting stations until nearly every seat was filled. There was a perpetual murmur of quiet discussion as we proceeded south. I did not feel chatty.

We finally drove through the brightly lit gate at Parris Island in South Carolina and continued to the reception area. The bus came to a halt. I could see a group of Marine Drill Instructors standing at the right side of the bus, staring intently at us.

The door of the bus swung open and one of the Drill Instructors climbed into the bus and began to speak in a booming voice. Essentially, not mincing any words, he told us he wanted us off the bus ASAP and standing on the painted footprints at attention.

The last one off was all his! We scrambled to get off as quickly as possible.

As we jostled down the aisle, off the bus, and onto the parking lot, Drill Instructors yelled and snarled as they stalked around us; we all stood on the painted footprints at attention, eyes forward as instructed.

The Drill Instructors paced up and down the ranks, stopping occasionally to single someone out for more personalized attention.

The night was a seemingly endless blur of standing in line for a haircut, mattress cover, linens, towels, washcloths, uniforms, boots, and a "chrome dome" (a helmet liner spray-painted silver).

What a shock when I saw myself almost bald for the first time! Of course, the night was also filled with a great deal of yelling and a variety of threats.

Ultimately, all members of Platoon 199 scrambled across the drill field, arms full, and ended up in our "barn," located in the First Battalion area of Parris Island.

This was the oldest part of the recruit depot, sitting right on the edge of the swamp, and the only battalion that still had wooden barracks. We all dropped onto our assigned racks exhausted, in our new skivvies, laying silently in anticipation. I could hear someone sobbing and someone else yell, "Shut up." I fell right into a deep sleep.

After what seemed only a few hours we were all shocked awake by a Drill Instructor banging two garbage can lids together and rapidly yelling, "Get up, get up, get up!"

When the clanging trash can lids banged together, I had already been lightly awakened to a small commotion coming from the direction of the Drill Instructor's office, so I was poised for whatever came next. The fun and games had begun.

For the next 9 ½ weeks we were whipped into great physical condition. We learned how to drill proficiently, gained a rudimentary knowledge of hand-to-hand combat, and learned how to fight with a bayonet. Most of us qualified with the M-14 rifle as well.

Throughout boot camp I never doubted that I would complete the training and graduate.

Also, throughout the training I remained the platoon smart-ass. I was very probably the youngest kid in the platoon, just barely 17.

Thanks to Mom and Dad, I felt like I had grown up in boot camp, and always understood that the Drill Instructors were not going to make me do anything (intentionally) that resulted in permanent injury or death.

At about the fourth week of training, due no doubt to my obvious attitude, I was selected for one day of what was affectionately labeled "Motivation." With relish, the Drill Instructors made it clear that I was in for a really bad experience.

As directed, I stood in front of the barn early the next morning as a formation marched about the Platoons 196-199 Series Area collecting participants one at a time.

I watched them march around the Company area until they reached me; as previously instructed, I stepped immediately into the ranks and we marched on.

The plan was to put us through the wringer for the day and then deliver whatever was left of us back to the barn at the end of the day. Off we went.

At the time, Parris Island had a flag system in use to identify the level of physical activity that could not be exceeded. As I recall it was: white flag (no restrictions), yellow flag (some minor restrictions), red flag (significant restrictions) and black flag (no strenuous physical activities permitted).

I learned later that the flag system had been developed due to some catastrophic miscalculations that had resulted in significant injuries and death.

There was also a serious effort being made to curb any potential abuses such as the Ribbon Creek incident involving 74 recruits in Platoon 71 who, in 1956, were marched into a swampy tidal creek at night by a junior drill instructor named Staff Sergeant McKean, and six recruits drowned.

For that reason, rules preventing these types of incidents were strictly enforced, with potentially severe sanctions for anyone who violated them.

This was late-July at Parris Island, and we had experienced a few yellow and red flag days which the Drill Instructors took advantage of to have us work on academics, clean our areas or the barracks, clean our rifles, spit-shine our shoes, and other non-strenuous activities.

My day at Motivation rapidly devolved into the one black flag day I can recall on the Island.

We spent most of the day sitting in a barracks that was nicer than the one my platoon occupied back in the First Battalion, watching film footage of Guadalcanal, Iwo Jima, Okinawa, Tarawa, and Vietnam.

It was a fun day, and when we were marched back to the First Battalion area, I was in good spirits and motivated to be the same smart-ass I had always been, with greater restraint.

We all took IQ tests. The score from the test was called our GCT score, with a score of 100 being average, and it was my understanding that a score of 120 or above was considered a qualifying score for consideration of appointment to the officer academy.

We were treated gently for the day preceding the testing. I was already benefitting from many nights of uninterrupted sleep, a good diet, plenty of exercise, and I've always been a good test taker when I wanted to be.

Our Drill Instructors ordered us to "get on line" (stand with the toes of our boots touching a painted line on both sides of the long barracks, at attention).

We were informed that we were coming up on a week when we would be assigned either mess duty, or "weeds and seeds" (picking up debris from the roadsides and surrounding areas).

One lucky private in the platoon would be assigned to supply, and that assignment would be based on the highest GCT score.

The following day, the scores were received and read aloud. I got a 137.

I was directed to walk to the Depot Supply building and report to a corporal who turned out to be a really good guy. He was just back from Vietnam and had come to strongly dislike being a Marine. He was getting out soon and was a self-described "shit bird." That was the first time I'd ever heard that term.

I spent a really good week inventorying the warehouse, one shelf at a time, spending the entire day walking around with pencil and clipboard checking off items and counting.

We always spent a little time talking about the Marine Corps. He was very unpretentious and down-to-earth.

On the second to last day I worked in the warehouse, he told me to ask my Drill Instructors if there was anything they could use.

Upon returning to the barracks I did just that.

It seemed fairly unusual for a private to voluntarily go to the Drill Instructors' office to address them without being called in first, and they seemed a bit caught by surprise when I approached them with the corporal's offer.

They pondered for a minute or two and had a brief discussion as I stood at attention, eyes forward; one of the drill instructors turned to me and told me to stand at ease.

The following week we would be entering Drill Competition, where each platoon in the Series (four platoons) would compete to see who drilled best.

The Drill Instructors all agreed that brand-new, polished belt buckles would give us some real pizzazz. I returned the following day with enough new buckles for the entire platoon, and we immediately set to work stripping off the vanguard (protective clear coat) and polishing them. Man, did we look sharp!

We won the drill competition.

For most, the greatest challenge in boot camp is the rifle range. Every Marine is considered a Rifleman first, and being a good shot is important.

The rifle range was divided into several days of "snapping in," where you learned the art of shooting, to include good sight picture and adjustment, and the various positions: prone, sitting, kneeling, and off-hand. The second part was actual shooting.

I grew up shooting and felt confident that I would have no trouble once I sighted my rifle in. On the first day and every day thereafter, I shot a qualifying score, feeling little pressure.

Not all were so fortunate, and for the poor Marine recruits who didn't shoot a qualifying score, there was hell to pay!

On Day One, I and several other Marines fired above 190. When we got back to the barracks, we were permitted to sit in the head and read and write letters, or study. We also snuck in a little bit of conversation.

The rest of the platoon was subjected to some serious harassment. On Day Two, there were more Marines sitting in the head listening to the carnage in the barracks. On the final day, I missed Expert by 3 points and fired Sharpshooter with a score of 217.

A black Marine named Jackson fired the highest score, and as the platoon honor graduate received his PFC stripes and a set of dress blues, which he graduated in. He looked sharp. His handsome, chiseled face and well-pressed dress blues made him look like a model for a poster.

The unfortunates who didn't fire a qualifying score on the last day were forced to walk in a separate small formation, heads down, rifles slung upside down, behind the platoon, chanting "unk, unk, unk" (un-qualified) all the way back to the First Battalion.

A couple of days before graduation, we were called on line, and one of the Drill Instructors read us our MOS (Military Occupation Specialty) assignments.

I was profoundly disappointed to hear that I was to be assigned as an Air Warning and Control Operator. I had hoped to be assigned to the infantry. From that day on, I made a determined effort to be re-assigned as an infantryman, ultimately succeeding.

I reported to Camp Lejeune, North Carolina for my abbreviated infantry training, which was minimal due to my assigned MOS. We learned basic squad maneuvers, threw a grenade, fired an ancient 3.5-inch anti-tank weapon, and fired the M-1 Garand.

One day we went into the woods for a compass march. We received training on map reading and orienteering. We were formed into groups of four, and we were expected to follow our map to specific points and return to the encampment. Off our team went.

We found the first few points easily and could hear other teams nearby. Then we missed a point, and the woods grew silent. We walked for a very long time in the dark of night, and finally walked up on a highway with a sign that said, "Camp Lejeune 7."

We made our best guess on a direct vector to Camp Geiger and headed in that direction. We stumbled into camp right at first light.

Just as we walked in, a group of bleary-eyed fellow trainees converged on us. They were just being released from a miserable night of POW training, and breakfast was being set out.

As each team had arrived back from the compass march, they had been taken "prisoner," and herded into the mock POW compound for a night of harassment.

Apparently, we hadn't been missed.

I still felt profoundly disappointed that I hadn't been selected for the infantry.

I took some leave that included a fun pheasant hunt with my Dad and a Marine Sergeant Major on land controlled by the Syracuse Marine Reserve detachment; Dad and I both shot our limits and "gifted" our birds to the Sergeant Major.

I was then off to 29 Palms, California, to be trained in my MOS.

The only ground transportation to 29 Palms at the time originated in Banning, California. We packed into an old van, our sea bags strapped to the roof, and raced east toward 29 Palms with the van swaying back and forth.

We jokingly referred to this van service as the "Banning Bullet."

Never one to consider the rules to be terribly important, I purchased a red 1963 Renault Caravelle for $200 on base from a guy being transferred overseas within a month of my arrival, and proceeded to drive on desert roads to destinations all over the place, never bothering to get a driver's license or properly register or insure the vehicle.

I drove fast across the desert with one or two guys stuffed into the car as we headed toward Phoenix, Las Vegas, or Bakersfield.

One night while I was staying with my then-girlfriend Elaine in Bakersfield, before heading to Vietnam, I borrowed her girlfriend's 1957 Chevy for a quick spin. As I cruised down Columbus Avenue, a police cruiser pulled up behind me and the lights were flipped on.

I calmly continued driving for another block until I reached the entrance for the JLJ Apartments (where Elaine lived); and formulated my plan. I turned into the parking lot, parked, jumped out, and ran like a jack rabbit.

The two cops leaped out and realized I had disappeared into the thick vegetation of the field behind the complex in the blink of an eye.

After I was certain I'd lost them, I circled back to observe them. They eventually contacted Elaine's friend, who walked down to the car, and I watched her reclaim it.

The following month, I was pulled over on the Black Canyon Freeway in Phoenix, detained by the Highway Patrol, and handed over to a couple of Navy Shore Patrol guys who transported me back to 29 Palms in a brig van for a conversation with my commander.

I never saw my car again and received a counselling for my infraction. I managed to get an Article 15 later for a drunken rampage, but I did complete my training. I didn't bother to get my driver's license until December 1970.

In early May 1968 I received orders for Vietnam.

My Parris Island graduation photo dated September 2, 1967

Me at Camp Lejuene, September 1967

Dad and me holding our bag limit in pheasants shot on the USMC base just before we gifted them to the Sergeant Major

8

VIETNAM

I landed at the Da Nang, Vietnam Air Base mid-morning of June 24, 1968, on a United DC-8.

As we entered Vietnam airspace there was a hushed wonder as we all peered out the windows with great expectation. I had my set of orders and a packed sea-bag. We clambered down the stairs, picked up our bags, and headed into the terminal building.

I was informed that a "deuce and a half" (2 ½ ton truck) would be transporting me to my unit in Chu Lai and I set out to find it. I located the driver, loaded my sea-bag, and climbed in the back with other Marines.

We roared down a mixture of paved and unpaved roads, through villages, past rice paddies, and over at least one small bridge.

There was a constant flow of three-wheeled vehicles and small motorcycles, often ridden by Vietnamese soldiers with rifles slung—we nicknamed them "cowboys"—sometimes with a woman or another soldier on the back of the seat, and people walking, including women wearing the traditional Ao dai.

After a long ride and several stops letting other personnel off, we pulled into the compound for Battery B, 2nd LAAM Battalion. I walked up to the Command hooch with my sea-bag to check in.

I was told to have a seat on the bench out front and the Commander would meet with me as soon as he was available.

I sat down and looked around. A few guys passed by me and didn't say a word or seem to even notice me. Pretty soon a guy wearing sunglasses sat down next to me and introduced himself. He asked me if I had checked in yet, and I told him I was waiting on the CO.

He asked me if I smoked. I tapped the pack of cigarettes in my pocket and said, "Sure I do."

He pointed to a dirt road off to my right meandering up a hillside and informed me that he and some others would be in a fighting position up there having a smoke just before nightfall, and I was welcome to join them.

I told him I'd be there. He got up and wandered off. I reflected on my good fortune to meet someone friendly in this strange new place so quickly! The clerk came out and told me the CO was ready for me.

My Commanding Officer seemed pre-occupied as I sat in front of his desk. He conducted a cursory review of my Service Record Book, asked a few questions, and told me where I was to be billeted and who to report to. I got up, did an "Aye, aye, sir" and headed to my new hooch. I found my NCOIC (non-commissioned officer in charge).

He seemed helpful, providing me with some instructions on reporting in the morning, made sure I knew where the chow hall was, directed me to supply where I picked up bedding, jungle fatigues, and boots, and was issued an M-14 with a synthetic stock, magazines, and some ammunition.

I wandered back to my hooch, unpacked a few things out of my sea bag and set up my new living area. I hefted my newly issued M-14, took time to inspect it, and loaded my magazines.

I had fired the M-16 at Staging in Camp Pendleton, and did not think much of it, so I was glad to have an M-14 that looked new.

I found the dining hall and got a quick meal. The food was decent, and I ate quickly. I stepped out of the dining hall and looked around.

I could see the radar antennae, not turning, and spotted a Hawk missile launcher, no missiles loaded, and covered with a tarp. I noted that we were on a hill, with the sea on one side. I would learn later that this place was called "Hawk Hill."

Then I wandered back toward the CO's hooch, oriented myself, and walked up the dirt road looking for the fighting position.

After curving around the side of the hill, I spotted my new friend with a couple of other guys sitting in a depression surrounded by sandbags off to the right of the road.

Much to my surprise, he asked me if I'd brought a beer with me. I hadn't, so he handed me a can of Rheingold. They talked, I listened. They asked me various questions including where I'd taken my training and where I was from.

Just as it was starting to grow dark, one of them asked, "Ready?" They all looked around, assented, and my new friend lit something that didn't quite resemble a cigarette, and definitely didn't smell like one!

I had never smelled marijuana before, and it caught me totally by surprise. They passed it around, each taking a deep hit and holding it before exhaling; then it came to me.

I gave it a puff and almost in unison they said, "Hold it in!" I did. The joint came around again, I did the same, and then again.

Pretty soon I started to feel the effects. It wasn't unpleasant, but I was feeling a little vulnerable, as it grew dark. I sipped my beer and asked them about Chu Lai.

They explained that our next-door neighbor directly down the hillside was the Americal Division (renamed the 23rd Infantry Division after WWII).

About that time, I saw a bright flash in the distance where they had pointed. At the count of three I heard the explosion, followed by several more similar flashes, and more distant blasts.

The guys in the fighting position started saying, "Ooh, those poor bastards are getting hit again!"

Pretty soon I saw what appeared to be greenish-white tracers streaming one way, followed by distant crackling reports of automatic rifle fire. In response, pinkish-red streams of fluorescent tracers beamed outbound with the same delayed reports.

My fighting position mates were making all kinds of comments and carrying on about "Poor America!" It was surreal. At least one more joint had been passed around, and at that point I felt the full effects of the marijuana—I was totally stoned!

I finished my beer, hefted my M-14, and excused myself. They were all quite congenial and offered bits of unremembered advice and comments.

I wandered back down the hill and found my way back to my new hooch in an anxious daze. I lay down on my cot and thought about my strange, new world. I'd been in the Marines just a few days short of a year and had three more to go. My head was spinning.

One of my hooch mates came in and we talked briefly. I told him where I'd been, and he seemed to respond knowingly.

Thus, began my first tour in Vietnam.

I soon learned that the North Vietnamese had long ago stopped crossing the DMZ with their MIG fighters. Too many had been lost north of the demarcation line to risk operating south of the DMZ, and there was no advantage to taking that risk with their finite number of operational aircraft.

Instead they focused on the B-52s, strike aircraft, and escorting fighters that came north in significant numbers. We were never going to shoot down a MIG with a Hawk Missile.

My duties became quite routine. I spent most of my time on perimeter duty and performing any other odd jobs my NCOIC assigned me to do.

One of the routine duties assigned to me was burning the shitters. I would open the back door of the latrine and using a long metal handle, pull the partially full receptacles from the back, and shove an empty replacement back in.

The receptacles were former 55-gallon barrels that had been cut down to about ⅓ of their original volume, with a handle welded on one side.

I'd douse the contents liberally with diesel fuel and throw big wads of toilet paper in before igniting the slow-burning diesel.

They would burn until there was barely a trace of anything left in the barrel— and you could smell them burning from far off.

One night when I was on perimeter duty in a position overlooking the sea, my fighting position mate and I smoked a joint, and soon he started talking about being hungry.

He slipped out of the position, down to the dining hall, got inside and grabbed the first number ten can of whatever he could get his hands on, then returned to our fighting position. It was a can of stewed tomatoes!

We opened it with a p-38, a small, folding can opener we referred to as a "John Wayne," gulped handfuls of tomatoes and laughed hard.

Almost every night I wasn't assigned to guard the perimeter was spent in the club. Only beer was available to the junior enlisted, with wine and hard liquor reserved for senior enlisted and officers, who rarely made an appearance in the club hooch.

We had a reel-to-reel tape player, containing all the newer music of the 60's. The club shut down fairly early in the evening. So, for some of us that meant drifting off with an extra can of beer or to go smoke some pot.

Every great once in a while there would be an altercation, and once, a pretty good fight ensued between a big red-haired Irish guy and the guy I'd gobbled down the stewed tomatoes with.

Another night when I was on duty with the stewed tomato guy, we got quite stoned, slipped down to the club, got in, opened a beer each, and played some Mamas and Pappas on the reel-to-reel. He told me about his dream to start a motorcycle club called the Marauding Huns when he got out of the Marines.

As the Mommas and the Papas sang, "California Dreamin," and "Monday, Monday" I felt dread gnawing at me, certain we were going to get caught, but we did not.

One morning the First Sergeant called me in. He had become aware of my deteriorating attitude after I got into it with my NCOIC and he gave me a less-than stellar proficiency and conduct rating.

I explained to the "Top" that I had not joined the Marines to party. I told him that I had a strong desire to serve in the infantry.

He told me that as a young Marine he too had wanted to serve in the infantry. Unfortunately, he told me that once the Marine Corps invests time and money to train and qualify you, you're usually stuck.

He then agreed to help me try to get transferred to the infantry. He assisted me in writing a letter to the Commandant of the Marine Corps, requesting a transfer. In my letter, I stated that I had a "burning desire" to serve as an infantryman.

At the time, this was referred to as a "Letter to the CMC." We finished the letter together, I signed it, he endorsed it, and we sent it off.

About one month later, we received notice that the battery was being pulled out and returned to the states. For some of us, that meant being transferred to another unit in Vietnam.

I received orders to MASS-3 (Marine Air Support Squadron), MACG-18 (Marine Air Control Group), 1st MAW (Marine Air Wing) on Marble Mountain, just south of Da Nang. I reported in on September 21st, 1968 and was quickly qualified as a Direct Air Support Controller.

I normally sat at a radar scope waiting for fighter and attack aircraft to check in with their location and altitude. Depending on where they were coming from or going to, if they passed over the coast in-bound, they would call "Feet dry," and if they flew back out over the water, outbound, "Feet wet."

After they came up on my frequency, I would identify them on the scope and provide them with naval gunfire and artillery information to help them avoid getting shot down by a really big bullet while in route to or from their mission.

I would also provide them with vectors and hand them off to the forward air controller (FAC) they'd be working with.

My former First Sergeant had been transferred to the same unit. Every once in a while, I'd run into him and we'd exchange greetings.

One morning I was sitting in the dining hall eating breakfast when he came up from behind me, slapped me on the shoulder, and said, "Congratulations, boy. Your request has been granted!"

I had received orders to report to Company A, 5th Recon Battalion for re-training and assignment. I was soon on a military transport headed for Okinawa.

Alpha Company was located on Camp Schwab, Okinawa, which had been named after Private First-Class Albert E. Schwab, a posthumous Medal of Honor recipient. The village of Henoko was just outside the gate. Alpha Company was currently on Okinawa in a training cycle, and I immediately started learning the craft of being a reconnaissance Marine.

Almost every morning began with a seven-mile run. Doing the "recon shuffle" out of the front gate and through the streets of Henoko, then back to base.

As we ran through the village, some of the early rising bar girls would be standing on their little balconies. They would yell to us, "Hey, recon, see you tonight?"

Many nights indeed included a trip to Henoko.

The training was rigorous, with breakfast following a run at first light, and then training all day—and sometimes all night, too. When able, I would dash back to the billet, shower, change into civilian clothes, and head downtown for one of the bars with girls. The bars with "that" kind of action had a red torch-like flame painted on the side of the bar. This was universal throughout Okinawa.

Drinks were cheap. The girls were young, pretty Japanese women. The cost was $3.00 for a "short-time," and $5.00 for a "long-time" (all night). The girl often requested a drink first, which would be a very weak drink, or perhaps a little cup of hot sake. The deal would be struck, and off we'd go. They were courteous and clean. Each girl received a periodical medical exam to ensure they were disease-free.

I arrived on Okinawa with some money and left flat broke!

While assigned to Alpha Company we did some interesting things, including training on a submarine to do "wet deck" landings and departures in a rubber raft called an RB-7. It held seven of us—six paddlers and a coxswain.

We went out on the sub, launched from a big tank on the back of the boat after it surfaced, and as the sub re-submerged, we paddled like hell to get away from the undertow and head toward our destination on shore.

We later rendezvoused with the sub at a pre-ordained time and location. As we spotted the boat below us, we once again paddled like hell to position ourselves over the deck, and up it came, streaming sea water.

It was great fun! Being on board the sub was quite interesting. Meals were served family-style as we sat around a table laughing and talking.

I always liked the Navy guys, and the submariners were no exception. The two submarines made available for training were the USS Tunny, and the USS Cusk.

On occasion, we trained with Navy Seals and Green Berets, and during my time in the Marines, I noted that some of the black Marines I served with had exceptional night vision.

One night, led by a black Marine named Terry Jones (a veteran of Hue City during Tet 1968 while assigned to Delta Company, First Battalion, Fifth Marine Regiment) we crawled into the base-camp of our exercise opponents, Green Berets up in the Northern Training Area. We decided to catch them by surprise in the middle of the night. They were all asleep! We grabbed one of them and crawled back out, leaving him tied up on the side of the road.

The Green Beret guys were mightily pissed and got their revenge the following day when they caught us in an ambush while we were screwing with a farmer pulling a trailer loaded full of pineapples.

I learned all manner of hand-to-hand combat techniques, including fighting with a knife. I learned to rappel. I practiced with a variety of weaponry, too. The entire experience was a good one.

The end of February 1969 I received orders to go to the Twenty Sixth Marines, First Marine Division, part of the massive III Marine Amphibious Force.

Major General Ormund R. Simpson had taken command of the 24,000-man 1st Marine Division in December 1968 and he had been the Commanding Officer of the Parris Island Recruit Depot when I completed my training there.

The 1st Marine Division was trained, equipped and deployed for mobile offensive and pacification operations. The Division was constantly operating to protect Da Nang, the second largest city in Vietnam and the surrounding population centers.

The 26th Marines became part of the 9th Marine Amphibious Brigade (MAB).

I was assigned to Charlie Company, 1st Battalion, 26th Marine Regiment, commanded by Lieutenant Colonel Clyde W. Hunter while we were still up in the Hai Van Pass, an area of strategic importance between Hue City and Danang. That's where I got shot at for the first time.

The Pass was beautiful. I was told that it had been featured once, years back in National Geographic Magazine.

A rail line, a good portion of it long since destroyed, had run the length of its 21-kilometer span through a great mountain range, and there was a winding road that ran down through the pass, heading back south to Da Nang with Hue City to the north. Further south at the edge of the Pass was the Lieu Chieu Esso Depot.

The Pass also sat at the Northern-most boundary of the 1st Marine Division's Area of Operations and Responsibility. Further north was the 3rd Marine Division. Their northern-most boundary was the DMZ.

Colonel Robert H. Borrow, Commanding Officer of the 9th Marine Regiment, part of the 3rd Marine Division, commented on the difference between the type of combat environment faced by units in the 3rd Marine Division and the 1st Marine Division.

He stated:

"… (in the 3rd Marine Division) anything that moved you could shoot at because he was the enemy; you did not have to separate the armed threat from the civilian population… which was a daily occurrence in the Da Nang area. Those Marines went out day after day conducting combat patrols, always knowing that somewhere along their route of movement, they were going to have some sort of surprise visited on them, either an ambush or an explosive device. I think that is the worst kind of warfare, not being able to see the enemy. You can't shoot back at him. You're kind of helpless. It is easy to become fatalistic, as indeed a lot of our young men did."

We ran patrols and ambushes daily and had frequent contact with the Vietnamese as we patrolled through the many villages and hamlets.

ARVN (Army of the Republic of Vietnam) and PF (Paramilitary Forces, kind of like a national guard or reserve) personnel walked and zipped up and down the road constantly on scooters, small motorcycles, or little 3-wheeled vehicles, and we would sometimes meet with the ARVN, PFs or the PRU (Provisional Reconnaissance Unit) while on patrol.

I began to learn a little Vietnamese. I was assigned as First Fire Team Leader.

One night while on listening post with my fire team, I was quite surprised to hear a round whizz over my head, followed almost immediately by the crack of the shot, and then several more shots fired.

After reporting the contact, we were directed to beat a retreat and headed back to the Company area. Pretty soon, contact became routine. The NVA was up to something.

We then moved down to Nam O Bridge. Nam O (we pronounced it "name-oh") had been severely damaged in April 1967 and re-built. The Marine Corps was determined to not let the enemy destroy it.

The village of Nam O was less than a click from the bridge. There was a large restricted movement area around the bridge, and it was a busy little place.

We guarded the bridge in shifts and we would throw small fused blocks of TNT or grenades in the surrounding water all day and night randomly in 5 to 10-minute intervals.

We also shot at anything floating or visibly submerged, as that was how the sappers had approached the bridge to set explosives the first time.

This gave us an opportunity to sight our rifles in and get better at snap shooting. A variety of motor vehicles and pedestrian traffic zipped across the bridge all day long. The bridge was closed to all traffic at night.

The Marines on the night shift, including me, often purchased bottles of a diet concoction called Obetrol on the black market, which was a formulation of amphetamine mixed with salts that included methamphetamine, and a half-bottle worked very well to keep us wide awake all night!

One night, one of the black guys on my shift spotted movement in the dark about 100 meters away and was sure it was someone who was armed.

He aimed and fired one shot and soon we heard wailing in the distance. We investigated in a sweep which included the guy who had fired the shot and found a young Vietnamese girl kneeling over a man lying face down with a rifle slung over his back.

He'd been hit in the back of the head and his brains were laying directly in front of where he fell. Talk about a great shot in the dark! Apparently, based on the uniform, the dead man was a PF from the village—perhaps having a little rendezvous in an off-limits area.

A small delegation of ARVN and Paramilitary Forces leadership soon arrived at the scene, and as we set up a perimeter around the body, they carefully examined the dead soldier, interviewed the young girl, and carted the dead man away.

The black Marine was awarded an Achievement Medal based on truly excellent marksmanship.

That was one of the problems with the PFs. They wore odd uniform combinations, carried a variety of weaponry, and played by a different set of rules than the ARVN. They were sometimes mistaken for Viet Cong or NVA.

On April 1st 1969, Lieutenant Colonel George C. Kliefoth took command of 1/26, we were merged into the now huge 9th Marine Amphibious Brigade, and soon were boarding an LPH-3, the U.S.S. Okinawa, the second Iwo Jima class amphibious assault ship of the U.S. Navy. (LPH stands for landing platform, helicopter).

Just about the time we were getting comfortable on board, we were launched on our first operation, "Daring Rebel."

This operation was on Barrier Island, a strip of island about 30 clicks (kilometers) south of Da Nang, a known staging area for the 2nd NVA (North Vietnamese Army) Division close to Chu Lai, and unfortunately a place we would return to again later.

I learned later that much like the U.S. had divided Vietnam into four Corps, the North Vietnamese had divided South Vietnam into five headquarters. The I Corps Tactical Zone was home to the 4th Front. The major unit we dealt with was the 2nd NVA Division (North Vietnamese Army Division).

The 2nd NVA's subordinate units included the 1st Viet Cong, 21st NVA Regiment, 31st Independent, 36th NVA, what was left of the 38th NVA, 141st NVA, and the most onerous in many ways: the 68B NVA Artillery (122- and 140-mm rockets) and the 368B NVA Artillery (122 and 140 mm rockets).

In 1969 the Quang Nam Province was infested with 21 enemy battalions constantly on the move, and looking to strike at us here, there and everywhere. The NVA could quickly and easily launch rockets. The launch pad typically consisted of two bamboo stakes, and although aiming them was a crude affair, they almost always could hit something because the military installations and civilian populations were relatively dense.

Daring Rebel was a big operation involving us, the ARVNs, Korean Marines (part of the 7,800-man 2nd Republic of Korea Marine Brigade which I served with several times), and Americal (23rd Infantry) Division.

We were helio-lifted for the first time on board a Sikorsky UH-34D Choctaw helicopters. What a wild ride that was!

First, we were awakened at "oh-dark-thirty," threw water on our faces, and got ready for a long stint in the bush.

We had the traditional breakfast and lined up at the many tables in the hangar below deck where we were issued our weapons, ammo, grenades, claymores, LAAWs, pop flares, C-rations, and whatever else our squad leader wanted us to carry.

We were fully assembled with gear arranged, and after a quick inspection by our squad leader, lined up to climb a stairwell to the deck and board our helicopter (one of 24 on board the ship).

We climbed in, shoulder-to-shoulder on the bench seats, the door gunner swinging a machine gun into the doorway, and off we went!

When the formation of helicopters arrived at its destination, they arced around and came in close to the trees, before dropping precipitously into our designated landing zone, where we jumped out and formed a perimeter.

This was what I call my "booby trap 101" course. The NVA had modern armament and somewhat sophisticated mines and booby traps that were deployed everywhere.

Later, when I became a scout, I learned that they also sometimes posted well-concealed markers—some of which I learned to spot—for the benefit of their troops, and the "friendly" civilian population.

In addition to pushing the NVA into the waiting maw of the other forces, we carefully worked our way through a maze of explosive devices, and sniper fire designed to cause casualties and slow us down.

I witnessed my first horrible injuries and death on that operation, including seeing Marines lose hands, arms, feet, and legs.

Throughout my time in Vietnam, whenever I noted a Marine who was extremely mutilated or was missing one or both legs from a mine or booby trap, as a corpsman or corpsmen struggled to stop the bleeding, I would hope that the wounded Marine hadn't lost anything else.

This operation was a continuation of a concept called "County Fair" where we would cordon off a village, along with a battalion of ARVNs and a battalion of Korean Marines, sweep through it, search it thoroughly, and move on.

We found weapons, ammo, and other armament.

We took several prisoners. The Vietnamese villagers were sullen, and once in a while, an old mama-san would give us a real scolding.

We provided medical treatment and medevac'd a few wounded or injured civilians but did not seem to score any points with the populace.

They had been co-existing with the NVA and Viet Cong for quite a while—there had been marriages and who knows what else, and they did not want to cooperate with us. They hated having their stuff picked through, and generally seemed to find us to be offensive.

Sometimes a handful of women would squat in a circle chewing betel (which stained their teeth red and gave them a mild buzz), spitting red saliva, warily eyeing us, and chattering amongst themselves. We would walk around them and leave them alone.

This operation had several desired outcomes. In large part, it provided training for the ARVNs on how to work with the Marines. It seemed like there were ARVN soldiers everywhere!

I even encountered an ARVN having sex with a woman behind a hooch on one occasion. I didn't know if it was consensual, but nobody seemed to be forcing anything or struggling. They both glanced at me, neither of them seemed disturbed, and I just kept walking.

I also observed ARVN scouts waterboarding prisoners when they refused to divulge demanded information. It was a crude affair, often involving a couple of guys holding the hog-tied prisoner (who had a handkerchief or rag tied over his face), and the interrogator would begin steadily pouring water from a tea-pot, pail or other utensil, and yelling questions as the prisoner gagged and struggled.

We spent a couple of miserable weeks out there and took casualties. One day after patrolling, we gobbled down C-rations and a quick cup of coffee, filled in our fighting positions, and the helicopters returned (as they had several times already to pick up casualties and drop supplies).

They loaded us up and carried us back to the U.S.S. Okinawa. We were dirty, bone-tired, and ready to be done with Barrier Island.

Once back onboard ship, we fell back into the routine of laying around, writing letters, eating well (food aboard ship was hearty, tasty, and plentiful), smoking on the fan tail, and roaming around the ship.

One morning my friend Dale Thompson ran up to me while I lay in my bunk and said, "Come on, you got to hear this!" I jumped up and followed him as he quickly walked to another compartment filled with Marines on bunks. He approached a lounging Marine and said, "Hey, play that again!" It was a bootleg tape with songs that included Arlo Guthrie singing "Alice's Restaurant," and Country Joe and the Fish singing "The Vietnam Song."

I thought both were awful, but Dale howled with laughter.

One morning while I was down below sitting on my cot, I heard someone yell my name a couple of times, then a big tough looking blonde-haired sergeant walked up to me and said, "You Osterman?"

I affirmed that I was, and that began my time as an S-2 (Intelligence) Scout. He took me on a quick tour of the little S-2 office and introduced me to the S-2 Officer in charge.

After answering a few questions, they offered me an assignment as a scout with the understanding that it was purely voluntary on my part. I looked around. After living down below deck as a grunt, this all looked good to me. I said yes.

That was the last time I ever saw that nice little office.

I was re-assigned as a scout, and initially attached to the same company I had worked with as a grunt. I kept the same bunk and locker on board ship even when I changed companies.

Nothing changed except my duties. I would now be expected to routinely be part of the point element when there was a movement, and often walked point for patrols and ambushes, too.

As part of my S-2 duties I had a whole laundry list of things that I did.

I carried a neat little publication I used to identify weapons and where they had been manufactured based on the markings on the receiver and barrel or tube (mostly AK-47s, RPGs, light machine guns, 62mm mortars, and SKSs).

It also had depictions of various signage and nearly every weapon (including mines and Chicom grenades) that might be encountered. I was to identify and report them to the S-2.

The areas we worked were commonly infiltrated with NVA and Viet Cong. For years they had made use of Dodge City and Go Noi Island as haven sites and staging for their incursions into various low-land areas between Da Nang and Hoi An.

Intelligence estimates always placed between 7-9 enemy battalions consisting of approximately 2,500 NVA and between 200-500 Viet Cong infantry and sappers (enemy troops specially trained to penetrate our defenses).

Another scout named Chris, a Khe Sanh veteran, (as was our First Sergeant, a Silver Star recipient) showed me how to mark booby-trap trip wires using C-ration toilet paper, and I got in the habit of carrying multiple packets of it in my fatigue pockets along with a number of grenades.

I would often leave a trail of scraps of toilet paper wrapped around trip wires as I picked through approaches to bunker complexes, or whatever we were in the process of sweeping. To the best of my knowledge I never got anyone hurt or killed who followed me and I never tripped a device.

One time when I was out with Chris, we decided to occupy a position that had been gouged out of the earth by something big, like a bomb or an artillery round. The force of the explosion had thrown a great pile of loose dirt behind us. The hole was a perfect size for both of us, with room to spread out and a good view in front of us.

Shortly after dark, we found ourselves engaged in a firefight with an unseen enemy about 100 yards from us. It was more of an annoyance than anything else. Every once in a while, Chris or I would fire back laying side-by-side peering into the darkness and talking.

Suddenly, we heard something good-sized whiz between us and hit the embankment behind us. We decided to stop attracting so much attention and spent the rest of the night one up and one down, no more shooting at the invisible enemy.

In the early morning light, we looked behind us, and saw the tail of an unexploded RPG stuck in the loose dirt behind us!

I would often have a Kit Carson Scout attached to me. These scouts were former Viet Cong/NVA who had left the enemy ranks under the Chieu Hoi program and became "Hoi Chuan." I understood *chieu hoi* to translate as "open arms" (aka: rally to the government). I assumed the open arms were often held above their heads, not in an embrace.

They were tough fuckers with a rock-solid knowledge of enemy tactics and more. I never forgot that at one time they'd been trying to kill us.

When we swept through a village, they could spot an infiltrator immediately.

They knew where to look for stuff, and of course interpreted for me as needed. They were mostly decent shots and an asset, but not to be trusted as far as I was concerned, except for one Kit Carson I worked with and trusted.

I never felt completely safe alone with a Kit Carson, except for Tran, when we wandered far from the unit. I finally ended up quitting scouts because I reached a point where I could not stand working with one particular Kit Carson anymore who was assigned to me.

One of our assigned duties as scouts was for three of us to take a convoy down to Chu Lai to pick up and transport new Kit Carson Scouts to the battalion in Da Nang. I found our new "allies" to be quite interesting.

They came from many different Viet Cong and NVA units, but still seemed to have a bond of fellowship and a common language that few of us understood. By the end of 1969 they numbered a total of 597.

They were wild gamblers. I often watched them play card games. They would squat in a circle with a small pile of piasters in front of them, and take turns throwing piasters and cards into the center.

There would be considerable yelling, heckling, and gesturing as they won, lost, shuffled, and continued to play. I had no idea what the game was.

When Tom, Ken and I arrived at the American Division Combat Center in Chu Lai that afternoon, we checked in to pick up a new batch of Kit Carson Scouts, found three cots in transient billeting, and settled in.

We managed to get our hands on a bottle of Jack Daniels from the officer's club, and between several beers apiece and the whiskey we got quite drunk! We picked up our charges in the morning, caught a north-bound convoy and headed back to the battalion.

As previously mentioned, I worked with one Kit Carson—Tran (who I would see again later)—who was fearless, and I grew to trust.

Life as a Viet Cong was quite miserable, and he had felt generally looked down on by the North Vietnamese he served with, even though he had at one time served with the Viet Minh guerilla army. He was probably in his late-30s, and told me he had been forced to Chieu Hoi after he caught an NVA lieutenant screwing his wife and killed him.

At the time he decided to surrender, he was the equivalent of a Master Sergeant assigned to a combined unit (such as Q-80, Q-81 or Q-82, mostly NVA). Through the years beginning when he was fairly young, he had opposed the Japanese, French, and Americans.

He was a mercenary. He was lean, angular, and as tough as a hickory stick.

I worked with Tran during Operation Mighty Play, back on Barrier Island. He was invaluable. Once again, we were sweeping the Island, and again the toll from mines, booby traps, sniper fire, mortars, and combat was grisly.

As he and I were walking the perimeter one afternoon I heard the familiar buzz and crack, crack, crack, crack of automatic fire from an AK-47 as several rounds whizzed and snapped past me. I dropped, immediately peering over my sights, looking to return fire.

He crouched placidly over me peering out in the direction of the shots and said, "He shoot like Viet Cong. No can shoot!" I stood up, feeling a little embarrassed and dusted myself off. I really liked working with Tran.

I think the Texans would say, "Once he signed on, he rode for the brand."

Often when the company or battalion was on the move, as the S-2 scout I'd be on point or prowling around, sometimes well-ahead of the troops. I would often have a Kit Carson Scout with me. At times, there would be ARVN forces or Korean Marines moving around and fighting, too, and I'd be watching for them.

Our Kit Carson and I might sit and watch a village or hamlet for a while. When we were convinced that there were no enemy soldiers lurking around, we'd wander in.

Sometimes when a mama-san spotted us, she'd raise an alarm, and on occasion, multiple mama-sans would be doing the same. It was like walking into a covey of quail and hearing them make their little bitching noises before they run, flush, or tuck into the foliage. There would be very few adult males in the village or hamlet, just women, kids and old men.

That's when our Kit Carson's language skills came in handy. We'd find a mama-san willing to prepare a meal for us. I never knew quite what I was eating, but the food was generally pretty good.

I'd ask the mama-san if she had any beer and she would often produce a lukewarm bottle of 33 beer. The name on the label was Ba Muoi Ba, with a number 33. This was a big national brand, sold universally throughout the I-Corps.

Both my Kit Carson and I would hold our bottles to the light and make sure there weren't any other foreign objects in the beer, then open them and happily sip beer while village life continued around us. Then I'd pay the mama-san in piasters and we'd move on.

Operation Pipestone Canyon on Go Noi Island was the most difficult operation I served on. The "island" was a large piece of real estate (roughly 55 square kilometers) located about 28 clicks south of Da Nang.

It was actually a piece of land surrounded by channels of the Hoi An River and was situated just south of a place called Dodge City, the scene of many fights between the Marine Corps and the NVA.

On May 26, 1969 we were dropped at the base of Hill 37 and began moving toward Dodge City. We eventually set up blocking positions on the western edge of our area of responsibility, aligned with a long-abandoned rail berm as the "anvil" for a hammer and anvil, with one force pinning down the enemy and the other smashing them with an encirclement maneuver.

At the time, my brother Bruce was coming up on draft age. I felt like I was seasoned at that point, and if I could delay or prevent him from coming overseas, it might be worth it (unless he wanted to).

I also had a pal, Dale Thompson who had six months to go on his tour, so I knew I would have someone I trusted around. Dale and I had been grunts together, and I had seen him fight. He could be trusted.

I dreaded the prospect of two more years in the "crotch" (our unkind term for the Marine Corps), being well-pressed, starched, spit-shined, and routinely inspected, and harassed by chicken-shit, stateside Marine NCOs and officers. Although I had served under one lieutenant I admired, I found most officers and NCOs to be quite indifferent when it came to my welfare.

I had no interest in rank progression or a leadership role—and certainly no interest in making the Marine Corps a career.

I had thought about it and decided six more months in Vietnam would be fine to at least delay the inevitable, so I signed the paperwork for a six-month extension in Vietnam just prior to Operation Pipestone Canyon.

After I became a scout, Dale was made squad radioman, an extremely dangerous job. The radio man would carry a PRC-25 radio (we called it the "prick 25"), with a big-assed-antennae constantly marking his position and role as squad communicator.

The radiomen developed techniques for concealing the antennae, but it was always somewhat visible.

I started the operation scouting for Bravo Company, then Charlie Company started making contact with the enemy and I was directed to join them immediately.

This was early June, and it was getting hot. As I recall, daytime temperatures ranged somewhere around mid-90 degrees Fahrenheit with high humidity, and the nights were fairly pleasant. I recall at least one day when I believe the temperature broke 100 degrees.

I knew it would stay like that until the monsoon season kicked in and it started raining in September. We moved all day, interspersed with sporadic combat and waiting for medivac helicopters. I carried up to eight canteens of water.

It was a tough slog through everything the enemy had to offer. On the early morning of June 7th, the NVA attempted to overrun our perimeter, grabbing a machine gun and killing several Marines before getting beat back into the waiting arms of the Korean Marines and ARVN.

My close friend, Lance Corporal Dale Thompson was killed during the early morning incursion by an RPG round.

When his squad leader, Corporal Ken Chase-the-Bear and I pulled Dale from his fighting position, he still clutched his radio in one hand, and his rifle in the other, both eyes wide open. Obviously killed instantly. He was a wonderful young man, and a great loss to the world.

I have never felt more depressed than I did that morning as I noted the dead rolled in ponchos in the middle of the perimeter waiting to be lifted out by helicopter—including my friend, Dale.

As I walked around the perimeter in the early morning, I found a boot with the foot and part of the calf still laced up in it. I walked down to where the rolled-up ponchos were, and with the assistance of a corpsman, re-united the associated remains.

I jumped in one of the helicopters and escorted the "dead gear" back to the battalion rear area.

I discovered while I was in the shower that I had been hit by a small piece of shrapnel, which I squeezed out of my hip. A corpsman swabbed the small wound for me with some anti-septic and put a bandage on it. I had no interest in pursuing a purple heart, and apparently, the corpsman didn't report it, which was fine by me. The still bright-red scar on my right hip was noted in my fitness for sea duty exam before I separated from active duty.

It was also a brutal operation for the North Vietnamese Army, with 852 confirmed killed, 58 prisoners, 410 weapons captured and who knows how many wounded.

The Marines lost 71 men killed, 498 seriously wounded and 108 with minor wounds documented.

Straight out of Pipestone Canyon I took my "special leave" that I had acquired by extending my tour for six months. It was thirty days of leave not charged. A freebie.

While waiting for my flight out of the Da Nang air terminal I was able to send a message to Dad using the MARS System (a HAM radio network developed by Barry Goldwater), letting him know I was on my way back to the States.

I flew back to the States a real hot, wet mess. Literally right out of some bitter combat, and I hadn't been able to process it yet. I was young and very sure of myself, but I had little idea of how to conduct myself in the civilian world as an adult or talk about what I'd experienced.

Dad threw a big dinner for me, with champagne included. The dinner also included the ritual of over-filling the guest's wine glass (mine), accompanied by requisite "oohs and aahs" of all the other family members and guests seated around the table, as I raised the glass to my lips trying not to spill it (I'd seen it done to other guests, numerous times) and calmly sipped off just enough to make it stable.

I was invited to attempt knocking a crystal from the chandelier with an aimed champagne cork, which I succeeded in doing.

When I announced that I had volunteered for a six-month extension, a pall descended over the table. Dead silence. Dad looked at me with his glaring left eye and said, "Kevin, if your brains were as big as your balls, there'd be no stopping you!"

There was a polite titter. Dad raised his champagne glass and said, "Here's to big balls!" Everyone raised their glass (including me) and drank to it. That was it. Dad never mentioned it again.

On July 20, 1969 I heard my Dad yell, "Kev, come here, you'll want to see this!" I walked into my Dad's living room just as Apollo Eleven landed and stood transfixed as Neil Armstrong uttered his historic words.

Dad rented a brand-new dark blue Chevy Biscayne and showed me where the keys hung in the kitchen. I did fine until the 28th day of my leave.

I drove out to a night club called The Scene with my brother Bruce. I drank, danced, and nearly got into a fight. Bruce stepped in and cooled things down—so far, a good night.

I drove my brother back to his place, and he said, "Are you alright?" I said I was, but I was really feeling the alcohol at that point. Off I went, driving too fast and impaired.

I almost made it back. Racing down Shotwell Parkway on a one-way stretch, I hit the left curb and bounced off into two parked cars, one which I hit quite squarely.

My windshield was shattered, and I could see the hood crumpled in front of me with steam rising. I forced the driver's door open and stumbled out, feeling broken glass under foot. I was missing my shoes.

I crawled back in, felt around, and pulled them out from under the brake pedal. I saw a light turn on, and heard someone yell something that sounded like, "Hey, you!"

As I crouched next to the car, I looked up and saw a guy still tying his robe, standing in the doorway one house down peering in my direction.

I slipped into the darkness, took off and ran all the way back to my Dad's house, where I was staying, still holding my shoes.

I ran through the dark median, dodging trees, and sobering quickly. I ran to the wrong house and started pounding on the door. Fortunately, Dad's house was next door, and my younger brother Brian was asleep on the enclosed front porch.

He woke up, called to me through a screen window, ran out and got me, and brought me into the house. I told him what had happened. He looked at me and said, "Where's Bruce?" I told him I had already dropped Bruce back at Mom's apartment before the wreck.

Very fortunately, I apparently had not awakened the next-door neighbors when I banged on their door. I went upstairs to my father's room, and said, "Hey Dad, wake up. I just wrecked the car." He immediately sat up and said, "Are you okay?" I told him I was.

He got up, pulled me into the light, and looked me over. He told me to strip out of those clothes, take a shower, and go to bed. He predicted that the police would be there soon, and he planned to report the car as stolen when they arrived.

I did as I was directed, and as Dad had predicted, not too long later, two city cops were on his doorstep.

He went downstairs in his robe, hair rumpled, appearing to be just awakened, and opened the door to the officers, inviting them in.

I had fallen into a deep sleep but became wide-awake and listening as best I could after I heard the knock on the door and subsequent commotion downstairs. I listened as they confirmed that he indeed had rented that vehicle, and Dad seemed shocked that it wasn't still parked out front where he had last seen it!

I heard one of the officers ask if Dad had any kids living at home. Dad told him that Brian was asleep on the front porch (right about that time, Brian stuck his head out of the door and peered into the living room) and that I was upstairs, staying with him, home from Vietnam.

They asked if he would call me. He did, and I appeared at the top of the staircase appropriately rumpled and sleepy looking, and said, "Yes, Dad?"

Then I turned to the officers and casually acknowledged them before turning back attentively to Dad. One of the seated officers said, "So you're on leave from Vietnam?" I replied, "Yes sir, I'm getting ready to return tomorrow."

Dad looked to the two police officers who said something along the lines of no further questions. Dad told me he did not need anything, go back to sleep.

And that was it. The car had been stolen and was insured. I limped back to Vietnam a day early. Nobody other than me got hurt, and Dad never mentioned it again.

Back in Vietnam, while hitching a ride with two other scouts from LZ Baldy (Hill 63) we were passing through the nearby village and I spotted my only trusted Kit Carson Scout, Tran. I called to him and he yelled back, "Hey, Recon!"

I banged on the roof of the truck. The driver stopped and I told him we were getting off. My two companions were caught by surprise but joined me without question.

We ended up spending the night. Tran's wife was very pretty, and we met some ladies from the village who spent the night with us, too. We were treated graciously, had a little feast, and a great time!

In the morning, we stepped back out onto the road and flagged down the next convoy coming through. Our S-2 Officer seemed to not notice that it had taken us an extra day to get back to the battalion.

Mid-way through the time we were a BLT, we transferred to the U.S.S. Iwo Jima. The other ships in our little convoy included the U.S.S. Whetstone (LPD) and the U.S.S. Deluth (LPD). The LPD had a big interior harbor, where smaller landing craft floated.

We conducted most of our activities on or around two islands, Go Noi and Barrier, and spent time in a place we referred to as the "Arizona Territory," which included the western portion of Go Noi Island.

I assume it was given that name because it was mostly level rolling terrain, had some trees and vegetation similar to the high desert, and was filled with lots of people who were hostile toward us, much like lightly-inhabited Arizona must have seemed to the U.S. Cavalry.

When we would sweep into a bunker complex, we were sometimes greeted by sniper fire and a concentration of booby-traps and mines. When we spotted a bunker entrance we'd go to work, methodically approaching it.

I pitched many grenades and other explosives into bunkers and down spider holes, including fused blocks of C-4.

Sometimes we would take fire as we worked toward a bunker. We would call for the occupants to "Chieu Hoi," maybe pitch a canister of CS into the entrance and at times the occupant(s) would come out sputtering, all teared up, dripping snot and yelling rapidly, with both hands quite visible.

Surrenders often occurred when a Kit Carson Scout sweet talked them or scared the crap out of them, after they briefly yelled back and forth to each other.

The trapped V.C. or NVA soldier might defiantly greet our invitation to surrender with a few shots or a pitched Chicom grenade, and we would respond by blowing them up.

One time, I crawled into a bunker and found a badly wounded NVA with a large splint on his leg and dirty bandages. I could smell what was probably gangrene. I stuck my .45 and a flashlight in his face and he waved both hands, making it clear he was done fighting.

The squad I was working with had a hell of a time getting him out of the cramped bunker. His big, bulky splint kept getting caught and he would yell in pain! His leg was a putrid mess, and I'm sure he lost it, if he survived.

Once, as I stood at the entrance of a bunker with a member of the squad I had temporarily attached myself to, after the usual approach to the bunker under cover fire, the occupant tossed a grenade out, which I immediately kicked back in.

It exploded immediately.

We looked at each other with a quick startled laugh, then took turns pitching grenades into the bunker entrance, followed by a satchel charge of C-4 brought up by the engineers that blew the top off of the bunker straight up in the air with a tremendous roar.

Then I moved on.

We would typically spend days fighting like this, and it became a blur of shots fired, lots of booby traps, casualties, attempts to coax a surrender, and the liberal use of explosives.

One time a new replacement was flown out to the field, and for lack of anything else, they stuck him with me until they figured out where he was going to go in the Company. As usual, I was attached to a company as we advanced as the "hammer" for a hammer and anvil maneuver. He hadn't been with me for more than ten minutes when we came under fire from the next tree line over.

We'd been putting up with this harassment designed mostly to slow us down and inflict a few casualties all morning. Several of us returned fire, including a tank.

I saw a guy running from tree-to-tree, firing as he ran, so I lined up midway between the next two trees and when I glimpsed movement I snapped off three quick shots and saw him tumble (I wasn't the only one firing, and don't claim to have hit him). I turned to this poor kid and said, "Okay, let's go!"

I ran toward the tree line until I could clearly see the wounded NVA soldier doing a low crawl to some cover. I turned to this now wide-eyed replacement and said, "Go ahead, put a couple of rounds into him!"

He just looked at me, so I pointed my rifle from my waist and snapped off a shot, which hit a Chicom grenade on the NVA's web-belt, resulting in one hell of a big bang, and a dinner plate-sized smoking crater in the hapless NVA's back.

I turned to the replacement and said, "Are you okay?" He nodded with a look that told me he was in near shock. I walked over and did a quick frisk of the now quite dead NVA soldier and took his rifle before we strolled back. I tossed the AK-47 up to a tanker.

A few minutes later someone claimed the newly vetted Marine for assignment to a squad. Welcome to Vietnam!

After we came off of the "float," we relocated back to the battalion base camp, within walking distance of a large cluster of shacks and oddly assembled buildings known as "Dogpatch."

This was where you went if you were looking for some marijuana, other illegal substances, or a girl. It was a nasty little stretch filled with camp followers and petty criminals of all types. In other words, just perfect!

By the end of October, I'd had enough. I was totally disgusted with the Kit Carson Scout attached to me, and I was extremely disappointed with my S-2's response when I aired my concerns about this young Kit Carson's penchant to go AWOL continuously.

When I brought my concerns to my lieutenant, he lectured me on good leadership, suggesting that I needed to use some skills that obviously required development. I fumed.

My delinquent Kit Carson wandered back into camp, claiming he had just married and couldn't stay away from his new wife. I was furious and, lacking any other options short of homicide, I marched into the S-2 lieutenant's office and quit.

I was transferred to Bravo Company as an infantry rifleman, and that's where I spent the rest of my six-month voluntary extension.

Back in the battalion area, some of the black Marines had started to complain about their treatment. They voluntarily segregated themselves into a hooch where only black Marines were welcomed.

At the time, black Marines were often referred to as "splibs," or "brothers." Neither term was considered pejorative. Black Marines often referred to white Marines as "chucks," and it was common to hear blacks and whites using these terms in daily conversation.

But now, relations had grown tense.

A black Marine I had frequently palled around with stopped talking to me and moved into the segregated hooch.

The battalion flagpole was located right in front of their segregated hooch, and one night, I was awakened by a very loud bang that I initially thought was incoming, until I noticed it wasn't followed by any others. I already had my .45 in hand and ran toward the blast.

Someone had blown down the flagpole. A small delegation of officers and NCOs gathered and surveyed the scene.

When I looked at it, I immediately thought it looked like someone had used det cord, because the pole was so neatly lopped off right at the base and lay nearby like a fallen tree.

That brought things to a head quickly, and the command element apparently had to deal with the pissed off black Marines.

I never learned what their issues were or what the outcome was, other than that the segregated living arrangement seemed to be resolved. Jeff and I never resumed our friendship.

One day I was summoned to the see the battalion clerk. He informed me that I was number one on the R&R (rest and relaxation) roster for the entire battalion, and I needed to take it. I had not signed up for an R&R, and the pogue was insistent that I needed to take one. I opted to go to Sydney, Australia, where I had a wonderful time.

When we landed in Sydney, our first stop was the R&R Center, where we were able to purchase some suitable civilian clothes, get cleaned up, receive a briefing on the rules, and get some assistance in finding a hotel.

During the briefing, we were cautioned that there were some places we should stay away from due to the prevalence of drugs, other criminal activities, and numerous unsavory characters.

One of the forbidden locations was identified as the Down Under Club. I changed into civilian clothes, went to the Crown, and checked in, then two other guys and I stepped out to the street, talked briefly, and hailed a cab. One pulled up and we jumped in.

The cabbie looked back at us and said, "Where to mates?" In unison we yelled, "The Down Under Club!" I met a tall, beautiful Australian woman named Roz, and we ended up spending my R&R together.

After five days in Australia, I was totally rested and relaxed (and broke) when I reported back to the R&R Center to return to Vietnam.

Back in Vietnam I became nearly despondent. By my calculations, it appeared that we were employing a losing strategy, and I was vocal when we sat on hilltops and let the ARVNs or PFs duke it out with the NVA or Viet Cong and no American ground combat arms assistance.

I was very concerned and skeptical about the "Vietnamization" that was taking place, and significantly doubted that the Vietnamese were up to taking on the NVA without us, based on what I had observed.

The South Vietnamese were plenty brave and well-equipped, they just didn't seem to have very good leadership, and the NVA could really fight hard and well. Plus, with the Ho Chi Minh trail still intact the government of Vietnam was already at a significant disadvantage.

I spent the next three months patrolling the rocket belt around Da Nang, occasionally making contact with the enemy. Often, contact would consist of a burst of automatic fire in front of us, followed by the sound of dropping Marines and equipment as we all got down and awaited what was to come next. Sometimes someone would trip an explosive device and there would be the usual awaited helicopter, ground transport, or order to continue moving. Usually, we would eventually get word to start moving again with no further contact.

The monsoon had arrived in mid-September, and many nights were wet with cold rain that leaked through my poncho or rain gear, soaked my jungle fatigues, and chilled me to the bone.

One time our squad was going out on an ambush when we stumbled into some NVA or Viet Cong. It was pitch-black dark, with an overcast sky, and they were probably on their way to do the same thing.

There was about five seconds of intense automatic fire and grenades going in both directions. I held my rifle over me and snapped off about 3 rounds in the direction I believed the shots had come from—then silence.

As per usual, they melted away.

Our squad leader did a quick inventory—nobody was hit! We called for illumination and did a quick sweep. No dead enemy soldiers or visible blood trails were spotted.

When somebody's hit squarely with a round, whether it's the M-16's 5.56 mm (.223 cal.), which tended to begin tumbling on impact, or the AK-47's 7.62 Soviet round with a medium velocity but a bigger heavier round that seemed to just punch right through, they bled profusely, and it was relatively easy to see blood trails when I would poke around.

That is the thing about fighting in the pitch-black dark; you don't actually have much to aim at anything other than pinpricks of light.

I participated in a Stack Arms, where we all had a couple days filled with beer, good steak, unlimited hot showers, lots of rest, clean uniforms and no duty at the 3rd Amphibious Tractor Battalion cantonment just south of Marble Mountain. Throughout my time in Vietnam, leeches were a minor annoyance that I quickly adjusted to. After we walked through a rice paddy, a moist, heavily vegetated area, or crossed a stream, I would inspect myself at first opportunity.

Sometimes I would discover one or more nice, big, fat leeches hanging just above my boot line, waistline, or higher up depending on what I'd just waded through.

Removing them became quite routine. I would stand them straight up, tugging very lightly, and touch my cigarette to their ass-end.

They would immediately detach. I'd then place them in a small C-ration can sitting on top of my "stove" (another small can that had previously held crackers or bread, with vent holes notched in its top and bottom), light a heat tab or some C-4, and roast them.

C-4 was my preferred cooking fuel. It burned bright hot and intense once you got it lit. I almost always had at least one 2 ½ pound stick of it in my backpack with little nibbles taken out of it.

Sometimes a few of us would sit around removing leeches and sharing the same can for disposal.

After nearly twenty months overseas, on February 13th, 1970, I hastily threw my meager possessions together, picked up my orders and my Service Record Book, headed for the air terminal in Da Nang, and prepared to leave Vietnam forever.

I gave away my prized .45 to a total stranger, a surprised young corporal just coming in-country, who I passed in the air terminal.

I quietly rotated back to the "world."

Initially, until I was able to place things in perspective years later, I was enormously pissed at God, whoever, whatever…

The two publications I can recommend for detailed, accurate accounts of the operations 1/26 and other Marine units were involved in during 1969 are: *An*

Illustrated History of the United States Marine Corps by Chester G. Hearn, and *U.S. Marines In Vietnam High Mobility and Standdown 1969* by Charles R. Smith.

Another helpful publication is: *Where We Were In Vietnam* by Michael P. Kelley.

I confess to using the term, "gook" many times. Once, an Asian-American friend of mine named Nancy was listening to me and became upset, remarking that whenever she heard me use that term, she felt like I was talking about her. I have not used it since.

Based on my experience, the North Vietnamese Army was unprepared for Marine squad tactics. We were often able to get into their flank(s) quickly during a fight, and nearly always defeat them or send them in retreat in a knock-down-drag-out fight. We seemed more fluid and nimbler when the fighting got really hot.

To the best of my knowledge, they never won a battle involving the Marine Corps.

I always disliked handling dead men. A fair number of men lose control of their bowels when they die violently, and they reek of urine and shit. Hideous injuries, burst intestines and other internal organs, lots of blood, rigor mortis, and decomposition add to the unpleasantness of handling dead men.

Overall, the Vietnamese are beautiful and interesting people. I liked them when they weren't trying to kill me.

Of the total U.S. casualties in Vietnam, 303,644 were wounded, and 58,220 killed. The Marines lost 88,633 wounded, and 14,899 killed.

I do not even remember the flight back to Okinawa, or the one to the States.

I felt like a dead man walking.

Me wearing Korean Marine tiger stripes. Handwritten note on the back: "January 6th, 1970 Stack Arms Center Danang. Happy New Year!!"

THE ROLL OF THE DEAD	

OPERATION DARING REBEL	
CPL James D. Johnson, USMC	Charlie Company

OPERATION PIPESTONE CANYON	
HM3 Richard L. Cox, USN	Alpha Company
HN Joseph C. Wiltsie, USN	"CHARLIE" Co. ~~Alpha Company~~
PFC Isaac Sapp, USMC	H&S Company
S/SGT Ernest Munoz, USMC	Charlie Company
CPL Thomas L. Blevins, Jr., USMC	Charlie Company
CPL Max Lisenby, USMC	Charlie Company
L/CPL Larry C. Davidson, USMC	Charlie Company
L/CPL Henry C. Ettel, USMC	Charlie Company
L/CPL Leslie T. McMacken, USMC	Charlie Company

L/CPL John T. Pavlin, USMC	Charlie Company
L/CPL Dale E. Thompson, USMC	Charlie Company
PFC William C. Costa, USMC	Charlie Company
PFC Clarence Jones, Jr., USMC	Charlie Company
PFC David A. Patton, USMC	Charlie Company
PFC Ronald H. Porter, USMC	Charlie Company
PFC Kenneth L. Small, USMC	Charlie Company
PFC Harry N. Thompson, USMC	Charlie Company
PVT Gregory Welch, USMC	Charlie Company
PFC Scott W. Thornburg, USMC	Delta Company
CPL Albert J. Cartledge, USMC	Alpha Battery 1-13
PFC James P. Hickey, USMC	Alpha Battery 1-13
PVT Gail G. Sanderson, USMC	Alpha Battery 1-13
Cpl. Oats - USMC	"CHARLIE" Co.

9

TWENTY AND ALIVE!

I reported for duty with Company E, 2nd Battalion, 8th Marine Regiment, 2nd Marine Division, Camp Lejeune, North Carolina on March 25th, 1970.

When I reported in, I met with the unit clerk (aka: "pogue"). The first thing he said to me was, "Don't get too unpacked, we're headed for Guantanamo."

I was shocked. I pointed out that I'd already been overseas for about the last twenty months and asked him if there were any alternatives. He pondered over my Service Record Book, and said, "It looks like you're eligible for an early out, if you want one."

I still had approximately one year and three months to go on my four-year enlistment. Because of the amount of time I had overseas as an 0311 (Infantry Rifleman) I qualified to get an early separation from active duty if I so desired. I did.

I was leery of stateside duty but was quite prepared to finish my hitch in the Marines; I simply had heard nothing good about Guantanamo.

I had no idea what being a civilian would be like, but I was more than happy to give it a try versus the alternative of being trapped on an island with a reputation for being unpleasant with a bunch of stateside NCOs and officers and very few civilians.

I had disposed of most of my uniforms other than one complete set of khakis and my shoes. My dress greens were long gone, as well as my stateside utilities. My attitude was poor. I was essentially unfit for garrison duty.

The pogue informed me that I would need to wear a full set of greens for my separation, so with mild irritation I went to supply and picked up a uniform, including a long-sleeved shirt, tie, and service blouse. I sewed my stripes on and picked up some ribbons. I was ready.

On the morning of April 3, 1970, I stood on the 2nd Battalion "grinder" in formation. I looked down my rank and spotted a friend I knew as "Tennessee." We had been in the same squad of First Platoon, Charlie Company, 1/26 and had seen a fair amount of action together.

At one time, we'd had a second big guy from Tennessee join our platoon, so one of them became "Little Tennessee," and the other "Big Tennessee." Big Tennessee was about 6'3", probably weighed about 190, and was a tough guy. He spoke with a low, slow drawl that almost sounded like a growl.

A mortar round landed on Big Tennessee while we were on Go Noi Island, and Little Tennessee became simply, "Tennessee" again. We rarely spoke of the dead, and I worked hard to erase the memory of their demise with some success. These were men who often died with gruesome wounds and in great pain. I always tried to remember them alive, even if I'd seen them get killed.

One day Charlie Company walked into a big ambush on Go Noi Island. Tennessee had been on point and walked square into an awaiting NVA machine gun. The gun opened up on him, and down he went.

He lay there, hit, and at the first opportunity got a bead on the busy gunner and shot him dead. Amazingly, despite the great number of rounds fired at him, and the proximity of the machine gunner, Tennessee had only been hit twice in the ass.

He was sent to Japan for treatment and awarded a Bronze Star and a Purple Heart. When he returned to us on board ship, we were surprised to see him again. He wasn't quite healed, had to sleep laying on his stomach, and stayed on board ship for the next operation.

Now, standing in the ranks, we looked silently at each other with big grins. I held my hand like a pistol and mimed a couple of shots, and he grabbed his ass with a pained look. Just about that time we were called to attention.

A major walked down the ranks handing each one of us a large manila envelope containing our DD 214 (with a reenlistment or "RE" code; mine was RE-1), Service Record Book, and some assorted other paperwork, said, "Thank you for your service," and followed with a salute.

We were then dismissed and went in different directions.

Tennessee was the last guy I ever saw whom I had served with in combat. Before I walked off the grinder, I stood there for a moment and thought to myself, "I'm going to be twenty in nine days, and I'm still alive!"

I was assigned to a reserve tank battalion in Syracuse, New York. It was in fact the same reserve base where the Sergeant Major had so graciously allowed my father and me to hunt pheasant, and the same Sergeant Major I'd "gifted" my two birds to after the hunt.

He'd known me right out of boot camp, and no doubt had kept track of my antics since then.

The assignment to a tank unit didn't particularly appeal to me. I had developed a dislike for tanks in Vietnam. They were big, noisy, impractical for much of the terrain I'd worked in, and the enemy took pot-shots at them at every opportunity, making them hazardous to be around.

I took a bus back to Syracuse and headed directly for my Dad's house. I stepped into the kitchen, stripped out of my uniform, and changed into civilian clothes.

I called the Sergeant Major and asked him what the procedure would be for reporting in. He asked me if I had any interest in continuing my service in the Marine Corps. I unhesitatingly responded with a firm, "No, Sergeant Major."

He said that wasn't a problem, told me to mail him my Service Record Book, and he'd place me in an inactive reserve status. I did.

I picked my greens up off Dad's kitchen floor and stuffed them in the trash, ending my active service in the Marines on a quiet note.

After I was long gone from Syracuse, in 1973, my Honorable Discharge was mailed to my Dad's address, and he slipped it into his drawer.

While helping get Dad's estate in order years later, I found my cast-off greens hanging in the basement. He had pinned a note to them that said, "Maybe someday you'll want these." I still have them. Thanks, Dad.

I also found my Honorable Discharge, along with a folded flag that Dad had flown the entire time I was overseas, with a note from Dad to me enclosed; there was also a bundle of letters from me to him while I was in Vietnam.

One of the letters contained a small set of denominations of MPC (Military Payment Certificates), the currency legally used in Vietnam by military personnel (and not meant for use by the Vietnamese). Another contained photographs that I had forgotten all about.

I hadn't brought back a single souvenir from Vietnam.

I got right down to business. I registered my DD 214 with the County Recorder. I visited the V.A. for counselling. The guy I met with almost immediately referred me to a job at a local restaurant called "Scotch and Sirloin" as a bus boy. They hired me and I went to work.

It was an awful job and I immediately cast my net for a new opportunity. I ended up working as an instructor/salesman at Holiday Health Spa in Geddes Plaza.

At the time, I could easily do one-arm chin-ups, pushups, and more. I had just come from a job where I had routinely humped ten clicks carrying up to sixty pounds of stuff, plus a rifle, and fought on occasion. I was in great shape.

I entered into a relationship with the receptionist that was uncomplicated and fun. After we closed the club at night, the two of us would make love and skinny-dip in the pool and spa.

While instructing and trying to sell memberships, I had befriended a fellow instructor named Dave. Dave was a little crazy, which worked fine for me. We got to talking about going to Yellowstone National Park on motorcycle. My job dissatisfaction grew quickly and one day Dave and I agreed to launch.

I took off on a 650 Triumph. Dave was a blast to travel with. We made good time getting to Yellowstone, with no issues.

I had never seen any of this countryside and seeing it from a motorcycle was superb! There is a certain freedom you feel riding on a motorcycle that you cannot get anywhere else.

We first stopped at the Grand Tetons. The Tetons were breathtaking. I rented a horse and took a ride partially around the Tetons. It was beautiful. Then, we were off to Yellowstone.

In 1970, Yellowstone was well-visited, but there was some room for privacy. I struck up a relationship with a park worker I called "Murphy." She had dark brown hair cut in a bob, a beautiful smile and was very serious. She was a student working there over the summer. We had some very fun times, and the park was amazing.

I met a guy named Dennis riding a Suzuki 500. We talked and I learned that he had been a CIA recruit at the Bay of Pigs. He told me what a miserable experience that had been, and about how he narrowly escaped.

His mom and dad owned a little ranch just outside of Riverton, Wyoming. She taught elementary school on the Wind River Indian Reservation. I loved the ranch—and his mom and dad. They regularly provided me with employment, and I had a little travel trailer I could stay in.

For a good part of the late-summer I happily worked on their ranch and attended a pow-pow on the Wind River Indian Reservation, during which a white man who ran the trading post danced around the fire. If you're unfamiliar with Native American pow-wows, this was not a common sight.

The man was somewhat of a hermit, and the natives had nicknamed him "Seldom Seen." He was a tall, lanky, pale guy with an unkempt mop of long dark hair that shined in the fire light, and as he danced, the Shoshone and Arapaho attendees howled with laughter!

I finally bid them adieu, heading for parts unknown. By that time, I had sold my bike to fund my excursion. I headed out riding my thumb and ended up getting picked up by some guy driving a new Thunderbird.

He was a driller for Hi-Tower Drilling Company out of Canada, and he was responsible for putting in an oil rig in Colorado the following week.

He still needed one crew member. Did I want to do it? I said, "Hell yes." Off I went to Naturita, Colorado. The rig we put in was twenty-two miles out from Naturita in a canyon.

Several of us drove to the rig construction site together in the driller's car. The early morning drives to the rig site where quiet and quick. He typically drove at speeds of 85+ miles per hour.

The drives back and forth from Naturita to and from the rig were sometimes punctuated with our driller rolling his window down to take a shot at a crow on the wires. He carried a .22 pistol in his lap, and every time he spotted a crow, the window would come down and he would snap off a shot.

We'd be flying down the road and when he rolled down the window, the riders in the back seat got one hell of a blast of wind, and the car would start going all over the place as he aimed and fired. There would be a great howl from the back seat, and some laughter.

I never saw him hit a bird.

The work of erecting the rig was demanding and hazardous. We worked ten hours a day, six days per week. The first forty hours were straight time, the next ten, time and a half, and anything beyond that, double-time.

The other "hands" were old timers, both my roommate and I were new, and we were referred to as the "worms" on the drilling crew.

We had a dumpy little place in Naturita, but girls from the town spent time there with us anyhow. Because the drinking age in Colorado was 21, I was the one roughneck in town who had to drink 3.2% beer at the only bar. It tasted awful.

One day my driller asked me to swing by his room. He had a question for me. He wanted to know what my plans were. He didn't have any problem with my work, but he didn't feel like I planned to make a career as a roughneck.

Another roughneck had just come into town looking for work. This was a guy the driller had worked with over several years. I looked at my driller and said, "Hire him." I gave my roommate almost all my cash before I left, to cover my portion of the rent.

I told my driller that I planned to hitchhike to Phoenix, and he forwarded my final check to me at the Phoenix Post Office by general delivery.

While I hitchhiked to Phoenix on I-25 South, I was picked up by a truck driver headed to Phoenix. He offered me $10 to help him load some frozen pancreases (used for making insulin) at the stockyards. I accepted the job offer. He also bought me a couple meals.

After finishing that job, I reassessed my situation. I had $16.

While out hitch-hiking previously, I had met a Phoenix native named Robert and his pal Kirk. They both had just graduated from high school and had taken off on a hitch-hiking adventure.

Robert had clear blue eyes, was handsome, with shoulder-length hair, and could play a little guitar, including some riffs from my favorite band, Crosby, Stills, Nash and Young. Girls were clearly attracted to him.

Kirk had a pale, pock-marked complexion, black, shoulder-length, tangled hair, and a somewhat nervous demeanor.

I purchased a loaf of bread, a package of baloney, and a quart of beer, and we feasted.

Robert said, "Hey, if you're ever in Phoenix, here's my address," which he proceeded to write on a scrap of paper, and I stuck it in my wallet.

Later, I found myself in Phoenix and pulled that address out of my wallet. I had minimal knowledge of the Phoenix layout based on my previous time there while in the Marines, but I was able to navigate to his address easily and knocked on the door.

A short, medium built, middle-aged woman with a very direct gaze answered the door. Her name was Peggy. She was Robert's mom. She listened to my story, and then turned, and yelled for her son to come immediately.

She asked me to tell my story again, but Robert recognized me and welcomed me in.

Robert borrowed his mom's Polaroid camera and one night the three of us wandered into the Bob's Big Boy at Central and Thomas, approaching two nice looking young ladies seated in the restaurant.

I explained to them that we were shooting photos to land some advertising work with the restaurant and wondered if they would mind being photographed.

They were happy to pose for us eating, sipping, smiling and looking pretty. I asked them for their phone numbers so I could contact them in the event we were successful. They were happy to comply.

We ended up joining them in their booth and Robert, Kirk and I left with them after they finished their meal. One of the gals, Laura, invited us to come back to her place, and we did. Pretty soon, Laura and I kissed, and were happily tucked in when we heard a commotion coming from the room next door.

Apparently, Kirk had dropped some acid, and had begun freaking out shortly after he and Laura's girlfriend had climbed into bed. He was sitting in the far corner of the bed, naked, ankles together, arms wrapped around his knees, and his head buried behind them, sobbing.

Laura's nearly naked friend was yelling, "What's wrong with you?" and finally dressed and stormed out. Laura and I shrugged it off and picked up where we had left off before the interruption.

I continued to see Laura for about a week until her husband returned from a construction job down in Tucson.

I spent about one more week sleeping on the floor in Robert's room before I met Annie.

Annie was a goddess. She lifted me up and protected me. Plus, she was extremely attractive, and wild as all hell.

She and her previous boyfriend had been nabbed after shooting out some streetlights in Black Canyon City, Arizona, and being in possession of an ounce of marijuana.

Her boyfriend at the time worked for a guy named Ned Warren Sr., and made it clear to Annie that he absolutely could not have any convictions on his record. Annie took the fall for the dope and shooting, and in return her boyfriend hired a good Prescott attorney to represent her and work out a plea deal. Annie and I rode up to Prescott on my newly acquired Triumph 650 when she went to George Ireland's office in Prescott and signed the plea agreement.

Ned Warren ended up being a convicted swindler involved in shaky land deals and became known as the "Godfather of land fraud."

Annie was an automobile insurance claims adjuster. When I got arrested for driving while intoxicated on my Triumph, after running a stop sign, being pulled over by a motorcycle cop—and spending the night in the drunk tank—Annie bailed me out and got a lawyer friend to represent me.

A deal was struck to reduce the offense to running a stop sign, provided I completed an alcohol awareness program, which I did.

In the Spring on 1972 I was helping my friend Stanley sight in his new .270. I would fire a couple of shots, dash the 100 yards to the target, study where my group was, and dash back to correct the sights. After my second lap, I was winded, and a little surprised.

That surprise prompted me to quit smoking cigarettes. Dad had quit the year before and was quite proud of himself. I followed his lead.

I stopped by the drug store and bought an over-the-counter product called Bantron. I read the simple instructions. At noon, the following day I smoked my last cigarette, brushed my teeth, popped a tablet of Bantron chewing gum in my mouth, and never lit another cigarette.

I was a heavy smoker, typically smoking 1-2 packs a day. Annie thought it was interesting and did not believe for a minute I was really going to quit. She'd seen me try before. We'd be sitting somewhere having a drink, and she would smile at me demurely, take a puff of her cigarette, blow some smoke toward me, coo softly, and say, "Come on darling, don't you want just one?" I successfully resisted all efforts to bring me back into the nicotine fold and have never lit another in forty-eight years (since Spring, 1972).

She was a great pistol shot, partier, lover, and a beautiful woman. I will always love her memory. She moved on, as did I.

I went through a series of jobs starting with dishwasher at the IHOP at Central and Thomas. As I moved from job to job, I became a grill cook, assistant manager, construction worker, landscape laborer, warehouse worker, shoe salesmen (which I greatly enjoyed), and bartender.

With the patience of a tough old rancher, Arizona expected me to pull my weight one way or another and gave me room to run a little bit wild. I gradually became a productive member of society.

10

MR. LUCKY'S

After Annie and I split up, I rented a little trailer in Sunnyslope, which was then considered the northern part of Phoenix. The trailer park owner, Vi, took a liking to me. Vi's son, Steve, was just coming off active duty from the Marine Corps, and she introduced us.

Steve was a tall, handsome guy and we agreed to get a larger, two-bedroom trailer together in another park his mom and stepfather owned in central Phoenix. The fact that we were both former Marines helped.

He was a good guy, and a real straight arrow. He'd been an M.P. in the Corps.

At the time I was selling shoes at Christown Mall and decided to try construction. I worked construction and then started driving a truck for a local appliance dealer. Meanwhile, Steve got hired by a local nightclub called Mr. Lucky's as a bar back. He told me they were still looking for another bar back, and I should apply.

I did, and they hired me. I continued driving the truck and delivering appliances during the day for another year, and worked at the club nights, wolfing down a quick meal, and heading to the nightclub until about 2:00 a.m., with Sundays, Mondays, and Tuesday's off.

I had been driving for about four years unlicensed. Annie had suggested that since I was driving her car sometimes, I probably should have a license. I complied. I loved that woman.

I acquired my first driver's license in December of 1970, in Arizona, but by now I had acquired a chauffer's license which was a requisite for driving commercial vehicles in Arizona.

I had originally first tested for my driver's license in New York in 1966. The examiner flunked me for doing five miles per hour over the posted speed limit.

Had I passed that test, it probably would have changed everything. I might have felt some real affinity for New York State. I never have. Ultimately, Arizona was a much better fit. That experience also nudged my lack of respect for authority, which was already dim, and growing dimmer.

So, I started out as a bar back upstairs where they featured country western music and dancing. The main act was Virgil Warner & The Rogues who played many of the nights I worked at the club. They were a particularly good band. Even though I had never been a fan of country western music, I really enjoyed listening to them all night.

They were about more than simply good music. They added real color to the place. They would kibitz back and forth between tunes, tell jokes, and make fun announcements, such as announcing a newly-divorced lady by name, "sitting right over here" (pointing).

You could count on her getting a lot of attention that night.

Mr. Lucky's was advertised as the "King of Clubs," and it was. The Prince of the Club was clearly J. David Sloan. He was an excellent fiddler and entertainer, having toured with Willie Nelson in Nashville.

He exemplified everything you could hope for in an entertainer, including humility. He was a genuinely nice man, a gentleman, and could he ever play that fiddle and sing!

After a while, I was approached by my manager, Steve Matherly, with an offer. They were thinking of starting a bartending class and he wondered if I'd be interested in attending. I was. It would be off the clock for two hours before I started my shift behind the bar. No problem.

The training was great. I learned to manage the liquor in my well, accurately pour one-ounce shots, and do drink strings by setting the glasses in proper order. One of the waitresses volunteered to be the "server," coming up to the bar, rattling off a drink string to us.

I practiced and learned to memorize the string of drinks as she dashed them off. We would then begin filling glasses with ice, setting them in the correct order, pouring the shots, adding the mixer, using the soda gun, and more.

After a couple of weeks of class, Steve declared us as ready to bartend.

My first bar was in a small enclave downstairs nicknamed "Doper's Cove." Downstairs, the music was hard rock. The bands played the music of the day, and some from the past.

The bands were mostly good. The tips were meager, and the customers were often stoned, difficult, and cheap. But it was still a great experience.

Steve Matherly seemed slightly taller than me (I'm six foot), a good-looking guy with a curly perm. He dressed well, had a well-groomed mustache, and had the ability to deal with bouncers, bartenders, food preparers, pretty cocktail waitresses, and a wide variety of customer and employee issues.

He had worked his way up through the ranks, ran a tight business, and he was fair.

After a while (after I'd proven myself downstairs), I was offered a bartending position upstairs, and I took it. It was a whole different world upstairs, featuring the aforementioned excellent county-western music, dancing, and an ambiance you couldn't find anywhere else. And the tips were great.

This was where I had bar backed, and I had a whole new appreciation for it as a bartender, particularly after working downstairs with the rockers.

Every Friday there was a delicious fish-fry, all you could eat at a very reasonable price. I loved Fridays. I would come in early and feast on fish before I started what I knew would be a lucrative evening.

We had some top-quality entertainers come through our doors to perform— Charlie Pride, Glen Campbell, Ray Price, and more. One of my favorites was a Cajun fiddler named Doug Kershaw. He had a Cajun yell that I mastered.

During one of his performances, I gave a yell from the bar. He looked out in my direction and said, "That sounds like me back there!" We called back and forth all through the rest of his set.

We also had a huge dance floor where groups frequently line danced. There was always a whole bunch of navel-rubbing going on too.

Fights were infrequent, but sometimes spectacular. When a couple of cowboys started swinging, the bouncers would swoop in immediately. One of our bouncers, a fellow named Benson, kick-boxed very effectively.

I never saw him break a sweat, and his expression was typically inscrutable. If the fighters saw Benson coming, with his black hair combed back, dark shirt and tie, coal black eyes, and his Fu Manchu mustache, often they just stopped swinging, broke away from each other, and waited for Benson to hustle them out either as gentlemen or rogues.

If they continued fighting, or resisted Benson, they would usually be on the floor or fully restrained in a blink!

The cocktail waitresses were all attractive interesting women. And, they were all business when they came to the station at the bar. Working with them reinforced my enjoyment of working with women.

I was never alone unless I wanted to be. I always had money in my pocket. I had a nice trailer, and later an apartment, a 1950 Willys short-bed pickup with 4-wheel drive (and a spare engine), and my motorcycle of choice, a 650 Triumph Tiger.

From time-to-time one of the owners, Bob Sikora would come through. He had originally opened Mr. Lucky's in 1966, hoping to make it into a casino. He met great resistance from the State and opened it up as an incomparable entertainment venue instead.

Mr. Lucky's was *the* place to go in Phoenix. Whether you were a cowboy or a hippie, it was understood locally that it didn't get any better.

One Friday night an attractive, slender, brunette cowgirl danced up to my bar and batted her eyelashes at me while ordering a drink for herself. I bought the drink. (I never gave drinks away. That would have gotten me fired.) I would only buy a drink for someone if I thought a free drink was in order, and I did.

We chatted for a while between other customers and visits from the busy cocktail waitresses, with the loud music coming from the stage—and I got her phone number.

Her name was Patricia, Patty to her friends. She danced away and I followed her with my eyes for the rest of the night. Before she left, she swung by my bar and reminded me to give her a call.

We started dating and had a lot of fun. She was attractive, had a prettiness about her, and a brand-new Pontiac Ventura with a 350 cubic-inch V-8 that flew!

She also had a high school diploma, I liked her family, and I felt a closeness to her that seemed like love. I was yearning for some stability in my life, so, I asked her to marry me.

In December, 1973 we had a church wedding, and my father flew into Phoenix from Syracuse to be my best man.

At the time, we were renting a little ranch just north of Happy Valley Road, surrounded by 600 acres of State Land, and there were a handful of geodesic dome homes scattered around the area. There was also a juvenile corrections facility about 2 miles south of us.

I had started bartending in a saloon about five miles north of us in Pioneer Village. The saloon was called Whiskey, the Road to Ruin. The sign over the saloon had the letters "Whis" followed by the picture of a key and the words, "the road to ruin."

It was an interesting place to work. One of our waitresses operated a nudist retreat nearby with her husband, and we had a band from Australia play.

I worked behind a solid-wood bar from the 1860s that had been hauled down from Mayer, Arizona. The bar had wells cut to accommodate whiskey and beer kegs. At the time, I made an observation that those wells must be where the term "well drinks" came from.

The owner, Al Pepe, carried a little revolver in his pocket, and felt compelled to show it a couple of times to unruly cowboy customers.

I kept a hat rack behind the bar where I hung gun belts when an armed cowboy entered the establishment to drink, and I also kept my .38 special in the drawer, but fortunately I never had to pull it out. I was a pretty good bartender and I could always reason with a cowboy who started to lose it.

Treating my customers with respect was key to maintaining good order. Bartending is where I started developing my peacemaking skills.

Dad was now General Manager over a little empire on the East Coast. On Carrier Circle in Syracuse, he had two motor lodges and restaurants: Howard Johnson's and the Marco Polo. He still had the Howard Johnson's at Northern Lights in Syracuse.

He also had a Howard Johnson's in Baltimore on the turnpike to Washington, D.C., a Howard Johnson's in Concord, Massachusetts, a Howard Johnson's in Buffalo, New York at Niagara Falls, and an upscale mobile home park in Fort Pierce, Florida.

He offered me an employment opportunity with his growing business, Ho Jo Corporation. Patty and I discussed it and decided to give it a try.

When back in Syracuse, Dad and I discussed the possibility of Patty and I immigrating to New Zealand and ranching 2,000 acres, which we would split when he came over.

He would purchase the land. I could train as a Ferrier (we located and I interviewed at a school just outside of Syracuse), and we would begin the immigration process. Patty was appalled and resisted, fiercely.

While in Syracuse, we lived in a room at the Marco Polo and I bartended. I never progressed beyond that position, and Patty became terribly homesick—she had made it clear that she wasn't moving to New Zealand.

She cried nearly every night, and I soon realized I needed to take her home. Dad was extremely unhappy with my decision, but I felt I needed to support my wife first.

We moved back to Phoenix, and the appliance dealer, Herold's T.V. and Appliances, immediately re-hired me to haul and install appliances.

My friend and truck partner had been hired by Yellow Cab Company and told me it was a great job. I got a haircut, applied for a position, was interviewed, and got hired in July 1974.

11

MARRIAGE

Once back in Phoenix, working and going to school, I found myself fully occupied day and night, usually not able to crawl into bed before 10:00 or even later on a school night.

Patty worked about 20 hours a week in the same office as her mother, a debt counselling firm called Family Debt Counselors.

We rented a nice little 2-bedroom yellow brick house on 10th Street in Phoenix just north of Virginia Avenue. The house was bare and needed a refrigerator. As luck would have it, while delivering a new refrigerator to a residence, they asked me to take the old one out for them. It was clean and appeared to still be working just fine.

When I got back to the store, I asked Jim Herold how much he wanted for it. He told me that it looked too old to sell, so I could have it. We found some serviceable used furniture and soon had a pretty nice place.

Our carport was behind the house, just off from the alley. Often, when I picked up my cab at 4:00 a.m., I would "dead-head" up to my house and sit in the backyard listening to my radio. My pretty little bride would be safely tucked in, and not even aware that I was there.

I carried classes four days a week, and three nights each week I did not get out of class and back home until about 9:30 at night.

I needed to be back up at 3:00 a.m. to get ready for work, get out the door and to the cab company on time. We clocked in, so attendance was monitored closely.

Patty started hanging out again with her single friend Cass, and sometimes came home late. We started having disagreements. I wanted to support her, but it was becoming increasingly difficult.

I was quite surprised when I discovered that Patty was pregnant in July of 1975. Shortly after I found that out, Patty hit the Bayless Store on McDowell and 7th Street with our new Dodge truck.

Our truck was not drivable, and she left it there. I was called on my cab radio and told to "10-19" (place a call to the office). I called and they informed me that the Bayless store wanted me to move the truck immediately. I was caught totally by surprise.

I returned to the office, turned in my cab, and headed for the store to move our truck.

The front fender was smashed into the driver's-side front tire, and I put my back out for the first time ever while successfully prying the fender away from the tire so I could drive it home.

Patty did not come home for a week, staying at her mother's apartment because she was upset. I ultimately had to go over there and coax her into returning home.

The pregnancy really jolted me, and ultimately jolted our marriage as well. I believed that Patty was taking her birth control, and that we were going to wait to begin having children until we were more established.

Patty decided that she could not wait.

She gave birth to our son Daniel in February 1976. We took Lamaze training, and I was present at his birth. I held him and made a commitment to always protect him as best I could.

I was very leery of the idea of causing anyone to be born into what seemed like a lion's den to me. I sold Patty on the idea that anyone who was born into the current world needed the courage or luck that the Biblical Daniel had exhibited when he survived confinement in a lion's den, and she agreed that if we had a son, his name would be Daniel.

The first few months were difficult for me. I was already a little sleep-deprived, and an infant crying in the middle of the night didn't help, but I persevered.

I also knew I could never be confident that Patty would not do the same thing again.

When Dan was still quite young, Patty began leaving him with her mother so she could continue spending time with her single friend, Cassie. They had hung out as young bachelorettes and were close friends. I realized that Patty was missing the night life, and I just couldn't fulfill that need.

By my second semester carrying a full load, I was starting to get the hang of it. It was demanding, but I could manage it. Most importantly, I was enjoying some of my classes.

What I didn't enjoy was coming home to an empty house at 9:30 at night from class. Sometimes there would still be dirty dishes in the sink as well. I wanted to give Patty all the room she needed, but this was new territory for me.

One time I complained about being tired. Patty got a little chafed and pointed out to me that I didn't need to go to school at night. She believed I could find a decent paying job without college. I suspected that she was right, but I wanted a little more out of life.

One night, Patty came home at about 10:00 p.m. I was sitting at the kitchen table doing my homework and stewing a little.

After she walked in and closed the door, I mentioned to her that we did not seem to be doing very well and suggested that we get a divorce.

She simply looked at me and said, "Okay."

"Do what you can, with what you have, where you are." —Theodore Roosevelt

My son Daniel at about 10 months

12

NEW START

One day while working in the State Job Service Office, I was approached by my co-worker Carmen. Carmen had a lush beauty and happiness about her that beamed maternal love and concern, and I greatly enjoyed working with her.

She had some exciting news to share with me. She was deeply involved with the Chicano community and knew all the Hispanic movers and shakers in town. She very excitedly told me that Chicanos Por La Causa, Inc. was looking for a Job Developer, and she thought I would be perfect for the job. She encouraged me to apply and told me that she would put in a good word for me.

I applied and received a call the next day inviting me to interview for the position. I made an appointment for the following day, and let my boss know I would be taking a longer and earlier-than-usual lunch.

That night after class, I sat at my dining room table and thought about the pending interview. I contemplated the questions they would probably ask me, and rehearsed answers to those possible questions.

I then pulled out my Conversational Spanish textbook and practiced some Spanish while I sipped a beer. I laid out some decent clothes for the interview and got a good night's sleep.

My interview was set for 10:00 a.m. in the morning. I told my office manager Claude what I was up to, and he wished me luck.

At about 9:30, I jumped on my motorcycle and headed for the Chicanos Por la Causa, Inc. Westside Manpower Training Center, arriving about fifteen minutes early.

I sat quietly waiting to get called in for my interview, while contemplating my planned responses to possible questions. Rose Horowitz, the assistant director came out and got me.

I entered the room, greeted the panel which consisted of Art Othon (Director), Rose Horowitz (Deputy Director), and Pete Garcia (Vice-President). I sat down expectantly.

The interview went as expected. I had anticipated many of the questions they asked me, and the interview had a conversational tone.

Pete Garcia, looked me squarely in the eye, held up his index finger, and said, I have one more question to ask you, "¿Por qué te interesa este trabajo?" (Why are you interested in this work?). I looked at Pete in real surprise. I couldn't believe it.

This was one of the few questions and answers I had practiced in Spanish the previous night. I responded, "Este es el tipo de trabajo me gusta hacer." (This is the kind of work I like a lot).

There was a brief silence amongst the panel members, then they turned to each other, nudged each other, and laughed.

Art turned to me and thanked me for coming in for an interview. He let me know that I would be hearing from them soon.

I stood up, thanked them for the opportunity to meet, shook hands, and walked out. Had my responses been appropriate? I was by no means fluent in Spanish. I jumped on my motorcycle and headed back to the office.

Claude stopped me as I walked back into the office and asked me how the interview went; I told him I thought it went well.

Next, Carmen spotted me and asked the same question. I told her about the last interview question and my response. She gave a happy laugh and said that my response was probably just fine. Art Othon called me about thirty minutes later and offered me the job.

It was an immediate pay increase of about $3,000 per year (roughly $12,000 in 2020 dollars). This was more money than I'd ever made before. I was assigned to the Green Team as the team job developer.

The team consisted of five members: the team counselor, Margarite; the job developer, me; the team clerk, Pearl; the training and development specialist, "No" (Norvelle); and team coach, Moses.

Moses had just come in 5th in the "Mr. Phoenix" body-building competition. He was massive, tough, handsome, and reliable.

As the job developer, it was my responsibility to cultivate employment opportunities for program participants assigned to our team. The other teams were the Red Team and the White Team.

The White Team conducted Intake interviews and qualified applicants. After the White Team qualified the prospective participant based on their income level, they would be assigned to either the Red or Green Team. The teams were named based on the colors of the Mexican flag.

When the prospective participants were referred to us by the White Team, each Green Team member would interview them individually, and at the end of the day we would compare notes and vote on whether to accept them or not.

My main concern was always whether I would be able to place them in a job, and the team understood that this was especially important to me.

It was rare that any team member would be overridden by the other team members, but sometimes there would be a spirited debate concerning a prospective participant.

We would interview about forty people to select roughly thirty participants in each cycle. After being selected, the participants would first participate in a two-week "orientation to the world of work" program, and sometimes I would develop jobs for the folks we hadn't selected.

I would provide them with interview training, culminating in a video-taped mock interview of each participant, during which I would interview them for the type of work they were seeking.

Based on my work experience, I could ask them the type of questions they could expect in the real interview.

123

The team participants would watch the video-taped interviews as a group, often with great hoots and laughter. As a group, we would critique each interview. I would also have each participant complete an application which I then edited.

They would carry this "draft" application with them when I referred them to a company to be interviewed.

As a result, when they applied for a position I had developed, their application would be polished and get them off to a good start in the selection process. I had an exceptionally good batting average.

The second year I worked for CPLC; my team was evaluated as part of a Department of Labor manpower program assessment. Of all the valley programs funded by the Department of Labor, our team had the highest average starting wage and percentage of placements—and the best retention rate.

I loved working with the folks at CPLC. They were all deeply dedicated to lending a helping hand to the many people coming to us for assistance. The economy was in the tank, and the job market was highly competitive.

Our focus was on many of the community needs, and I found myself involved in activities far outside of job development. One such activity was our community Christmas celebration.

One year we arranged for a local celebrity, Jerry Foster, who flew a news helicopter, to deliver Santa Claus by helicopter onto a large athletic field in South Phoenix for a major Christmas celebration.

At the time, I owned a little green Datsun pickup truck. We mounted an antlered deer's head on the front of the truck (donated by Art), with a bright red partially cut out ping-pong ball taped on its nose.

I dressed as a clown and stuffed my pockets full of candy. We decorated the truck to make it sleigh-like.

Thanks to a joke by one of the staff members (a tall, somewhat sultry, very attractive brunette named Olga, with long brown hair, distinctive features, and a wry sense of humor), I quickly acquired the moniker, "Kinky the Clown."

I drove my truck. In the truck bed were two of our lovely CPLC ladies dressed as elves, one of them (Pearl) holding the reins to the front of the decorated Datsun, riding the "sleigh" onto the athletic field.

There had to be at least a thousand kids there. Before completing the drive out onto the field, I pulled up to the stage, jumped out, climbed up onto the stage, and proceeded to whip the kids into a frenzy as I talked about Santa coming and threw candy into the crowd.

I spotted the inbound helicopter, yelled, "Here comes Santa!" then climbed down off the stage and headed to my truck for part two of the operation.

I was instantaneously mobbed by at least twenty kids who knocked me down. As I lay there clutching my wallet, watch and keys tightly, I could feel many little hands combing my pockets, and picking me clean of every morsel of candy in my possession.

My elves and other CPLC employees rushed to my aid and got me back on my feet and brushed off. I still had my wallet, watch and truck keys. Every bit of candy was gone! We drove out onto the field just in time for Santa to come swooping in on the chopper.

It all went great. Dave, a CPLC Counselor for the White Team with a doctorate, played Santa. He jumped onto the sleigh and took the reins on the way back to the stage. He had numerous large bags of little toys for all the boys and girls; the event went without a hitch and a good time was had by all!

Although I had eschewed team athletics while I was in school, I agreed to coach a basketball team, the Pistons, in the Marcos de Niza league.

I set out to round up a team. I made friends with two kids living down in one of our largest housing projects, the Marcos de Niza Public Housing, also referred to as the Martin Luther King Freedom Center.

With their aid, I went door-to-door and recruited a team. CPLC paid all fees and provided uniforms and equipment. Despite my total inability to play basketball, I concentrated the training on drawing fouls close to the basket and throwing free-throws.

We came in third. I enlisted some of the same kids to be on a baseball team I agreed to coach later, once again, despite my total lack of knowledge in the game of baseball, we came in third again.

I tried to make it fun for the kids. Many of them had parents (usually a single mom) who did not speak English and were isolated. We had practice on Wednesdays in a local high school gym and the parent(s) often attended the Saturday games.

I would start by picking up the team captain, Jerry, and we would begin my circuitous trip through the housing project. The kids would be waiting on the curb and jump in the bed of the truck as I stopped for them.

On occasion a kid would be missing, and one of the other boys would jump out, bang on his door, and bring the delinquent team member along.

Once I had the whole team in the truck, we headed for practice or the game. After each practice or game, we would stop at the Dairy Queen and everyone got a single-scoop cone of their choice (Sam's suggestion).

Then I would drive back into the projects and drop them off one at a time.

Back at the office on one of the days we spent interviewing our next round of participants, we interviewed a prospective participant who seemed awful to me.

She had stabbed her husband in the leg during an alcohol and drug-fueled argument, and surprisingly, he died weeks later from a blood clot. She took a plea for manslaughter.

She was currently in what appeared to be an abusive lesbian relationship. Her partner, a short, heavy-set, rough-looking woman, stood out in the hallway, and constantly peered into our office as our prospective participant was being interviewed by each team member.

She looked awful, expressionless, with dark bags under her eyes and a puffy lip. She answered my questions in a lifeless monotone.

The other four team members voted to take her, and I voted against selecting her based on my perception that she was probably unemployable. The team overrode me. She completed the first phase of training without a hitch.

She ended her unhelpful relationship and every day she looked better. We selected her for bank teller training at the Maricopa County Skill Center and she progressed wonderfully.

One day I went out to the Skill Center to do my usual updates with each team participant, checking to see how the training was going.

I looked at her and realized for the first time that she was an attractive woman.

She was getting ready to complete the training, and I had been cultivating a relationship with one of the local banks. I asked her if she was confident that she was fully prepared to continue her current successful trajectory, and she told me she was.

I did my usual job of preparing the prospective candidate and employer. I started giving the bank HR director updates on her training progress shortly after she entered the Skill Center, and by the time she was ready to graduate, they had already given her a "courtesy interview," and let me know they were ready to interview her for a position at one of the bank branches.

They interviewed and hired her.

After I resigned my position with CPLC and took off on my motorcycle, I stopped in a bank branch to get some money.

I spotted her in a teller window and got in her line. When it was my turn, she asked me to meet her for lunch.

At lunch, she told me that she was getting married and transferring to another branch in northern Arizona. She told me that she was pregnant, and it seemed to be going well.

She was radiant, and I noted how beautiful she was! I have always been glad the team overrode my vote and we selected Linda.

Things were not going very well for me, however. I had become quite despondent as a relationship I'd been in for about a year came to a painful end.

Her name was Sam, and I had been crazy about her, but she had lost interest in me and moved on. It was the deepest hurt I had ever felt.

I woke up one morning and decided that it was time for me to move on, too. My Dad had drowned down in Florida a little less than a year before. I had just turned thirty, and I could hear the clock ticking loudly.

I sold my house, truck, and everything else I could not fit in a 5x10 foot storage locker and resigned my position at CPLC. Pearl walked outside with me when I left the office for the last time.

I embraced her and told her that I loved her. I told her that I had deeply enjoyed being on the same team with her and greatly admired her. She held me and told me that she loved me too, and we kissed. We parted and haven't seen each other since.

I took off on my 550 Honda with some good camping gear, and hit the road, literally.

Marcos de Niza Little League players with me on game day

My basketball team, the Pistons

13

DO YOU TAKE EX-MARINES?

Prior to working at Chicanos Por La Causa, while still with the D.E.S. Job Service, I had developed a workflow that rarely changed from day-to-day.

I came in early to burst the print outs and highlight the daily statistics for all the interviewers, then posted them. Next, I would get a cup of coffee from the back, walk around to see what existing job orders remained unfilled, and chat briefly with the other interviewers as they trickled in. Finally, I would settle down to review the daily microfiche that contained all the open job orders statewide.

Nearly every morning, without fail, I would note a job order posted by the Arizona Air National Guard. I would scan it quickly as I moved on, seeking potential openings I might be able to refer someone to.

Recently, a phrase in the Air Guard job order had started to catch my attention: "Don't let your usable past service go to waste." I would briefly ponder that, wondering how it could possibly apply to me. I hadn't thought of my time in the Marine Corps as translating to "usable past service." On my DD214 it showed my related civilian occupation as being: "Proof Director Small Arms," whatever the hell that was.

I had no plans to re-enter the military. I did have the lingering frustration of just scraping by month-to-month; a problem that I still needed to resolve.

One morning I picked up the phone and called the number on the Air Guard job advertisement. A friendly Technical Sergeant named Bill Gilliam answered the phone. My first question was, "Do you take ex-Marines?"

He answered me by stating that based on my qualifications, I could be a good fit on the Air Guard team, and my prior service would be useful in several ways.

I took the bait, asking what my next step would be. He simply said, "Come on down and let's talk." I did.

I have often said that had the Army National Guard, and not the Air National Guard, had a job posting that caught my attention, and their recruiter had been as engaging as Bill, I might have gone in that direction instead.

I made an appointment and went to meet with Technical Sergeant Bill Gilliam.

He was a collegial fellow, and fun to talk with. Quite interestingly, he always appeared to be looking in two different directions due to an eye that had wandered slightly to the side. I picked the eye that was looking at me to talk to.

He was a military history buff, had a basic knowledge of the Marine Corps order of battle, and had a knowledge of some of our operations. I decided to enlist. On October 11th, 1977, I raised my right hand and was sworn in.

I missed my first drill. My NCOIC, SMSgt Howie Howlett called me and wanted to know why I didn't come to drill. I told him I hadn't received a report date. He provided me with the date of the next drill and told me to be there.

I told him I did not have a uniform. He told me, "No problem, it's just important that you be here." I spent my first three drills in civvies and made up my missed drill.

I was enlisted as an Airman First Class, radar operator in the 107th Tactical Control Squadron (later re-designated as the 107th Air Control Squadron after the Tactical Air Command went bye bye).

The equipment was vaguely familiar to me, and I assisted the Training NCOIC in writing a letter requesting to waive a formal technical school requirement.

It was waived. The radar scope, a UPA-35 was easy to operate, with two "joy sticks" and switches and buttons that enabled various functions and intensities, and I soon gained a complete understanding of how to operate it.

I made friends with a couple of fun, interesting enlisted women, Mary, and Patty. We hung out together and did some very entertaining things, like going to the Rocky Horror Picture Show at the old Cini Capri Theatre on Camelback Road in Phoenix.

It was a riot; especially seeing both singing, acting out the show tunes, and just being crazy! I had no idea this movie had such a huge cult following.

They were both extremely fun ladies in different ways. I discovered that they were also both talented belly dancers. One time when my unit was having something akin to a talent show, they got up and did a dance in veils, zills (finger cymbals), and all, and brought the house down!

I eventually was fully uniformed, fully qualified as a radar operator, checked out on the rifle range, and had been on a couple of deployments.

A Technical Sergeant named George Steigerwald who had come out of the Air Force entered the unit at about the same time I did. Howie retired and George became the fulltime NCOIC. Eventually George was promoted to Chief Master Sergeant and served with distinction.

George had served in Thailand during the Vietnam conflict and had many colorful stories to tell about "habu" snakes (a pit viper), the many characters he'd known and worked with, and much more.

George was the Operations NCOIC during my time serving as the Operations Officer. A tall, slim guy with a fun personality, he was quite the character. Always a heavy smoker while I knew him, he died from lung cancer several years ago.

Our full-time Ops officer (the position I would one day occupy) was Captain Steve Hepburn. He had been an active duty Weapons Controller in the Air Force and ended up in the Arizona Air National Guard. He seemed like a real character.

I loved it. I cleared about $125 each drill and it was just enough to keep my nose above water, with no other weekend work or Saturdays spent at Park 'n Swap selling my possessions. I liked the people I drilled with and was comfortable.

I had easily completed the correspondence course to qualify me academically and had also completed all the necessary positional training to achieve my "5-level" skill qualification, which meant I was considered competent.

My former spouse Patty re-married and eventually moved to Camp Verde, about 120 miles north of Phoenix. On the weekends I wasn't drilling I picked Daniel up and had him for the weekend, usually returning him to Patty in Camp Verde by Sunday afternoon.

I had an active social life and felt a contentment. I was still able to get out quail hunting frequently, and got in some fishing, too.

I was starting to get caught up financially. After each drill, I began contemplating how much longer I needed to stay with the Air National Guard in order to make ends meet.

I had enlisted under the "Try One" program. Since I had completed my six-year military obligation with the Marines (1967-1973), the Air National Guard and I agreed I could resign after one year if I so chose.

In 1979 Dad drowned while fishing for common snook in the water off Fort Pierce, Florida during a stay at the place he kept in the retirement park.

My little sister was staying with him down there at the time. When she noted that it was growing late and he hadn't returned, she sounded the alarm. They found him and a guy named Sam who lived in the park dead in the water, both drowned.

They had gone out fishing, while there was a severe storm warning, in a wooden skiff lacking flotation *and* left their life vests behind. Dad, always a risk-taker, had taken his last risk. He was 59 years old.

At that time, I was a Job Developer for Chicanos Por La Causa, Inc. in Phoenix. I told my boss, Art Othon (a good guy) I would need about a week off and headed back to Syracuse on the first flight I could catch, spending nearly every cent I had.

My brother Brian and I went down to Fort Pierce and met with the coroner who described the autopsy and answered all our questions. We arranged for Dad's cremation. Then we checked and secured Dad's double-wide and drove his Cadillac back to Syracuse.

My dear sister Kerry fished out two one-hundred-dollar bills from a hiding spot on the spice rack in Dad's kitchen and gave them to me so I could get back to Phoenix. I have loved her for as long as I can remember.

14

FROM GREEN TO BLUE

The conversion from Marine Corps to Air Force was easy. I can't imagine anyone trying to convert from Air Force to Marines with the level of comfort I felt.

I mentioned earlier that I liked the people I worked with. One of them was a former Marine named Israel Campa. He worked for the U.S. Postal Service and had served in combat, been wounded in Vietnam and awarded a disability.

He arranged to suspend his disability because he believed he could pass the physical and wanted to join and serve in the Arizona Air National Guard.

I had worked in his unit's area of operation near An Hoa. I remembered quite well the tough terrain, razor-sharp elephant grass and the red dirt that turned to red mud during the monsoon, and knew the tough combat environment he had been immersed in—where he was eventually wounded seriously enough that he needed to be medevacked. He was a good, solid, level-headed guy.

Another was a former Marine named Bill Baizel. Bill had served with Lima Company, 3rd Battalion, 26th Marine Regiment (3/26) during the same time frame I was with 1/26. He was an infantry rifleman and one hell of a tough guy.

He was awarded the Navy Commendation Medal with a "V" (denoting valor), Bronze Star, also with a "V," and a couple of Purple Hearts. His unit was awarded the Presidential Unit Citation as well.

Bill served as a drill instructor, made it all the way to Gunnery Sergeant, and then left the Corps and subsequently joined the Air National Guard.

Bill and I put together a superior paint ball team in 1984, with my girlfriend, Angie, being the only non-military member on our team. She demonstrated stealth and was a steady shot. In fact, she proved to be a dead-eye, and saved one of our games single-handedly while defending our flag.

She spotted two opponents crawling toward our bunker, and heard one of them whisper, "There's nobody here," just before she shot both nearly point-blank!

Most of our games were played in the National Forest near Mayer, Arizona. Both teams walked the field in advance to view the field, and we swapped fortifications after each round (seven rounds of play).

We developed a winning strategy that involved three fire teams. One team defended the flag, led by Angie. One team led by Bill made the assault to capture our opponent's flag and one team led by me roamed the field engaging our opponents anywhere we found them—quite often in route to our flag base or trying to get back to their base with our flag in hand.

My team would engage the opposing team until they were dispersed, then support the assault to snatch our opponent's flag and successfully fight our way back to our base. It proved to be a highly effective strategy. On our final day of play, we retired from the field 7-0.

It had been more than seven years since I had worn a uniform, and I had no lingering bias. It was all new to me, and I did not take it too seriously.

Since I didn't do Airman Basic Training, I needed to ask around, observe, figure out how to configure my uniform, and meet all Air Force standards, such as reporting/departing from the presence of an officer. In the Marine Corps there were specific requirements. In the Air Guard it was a little looser.

Whenever I started feeling down about spending a drill weekend at the unit, I reminded myself of the hassle it had been, generating that extra little bit of cash I'd needed to ensure that I paid my bills, including my child support every month.

No more crazy side-jobs or Park 'n Swap! I never gave the possibility of a military retirement a single thought.

My unit was in an armory that had once been part of the prisoner of war compound at Papago Park during World War II.

At the time, the prisoners, mostly German U-boat enlisted and officers, lived with some comfort within the prisoner of war camp, located on the eastern edge of Phoenix and southwest Scottsdale. Papago was considered to be quite unusual in its casual treatment of the incarcerated enemy.

There were five camps, and as soon as the war ended, four of the camps began to dissolve back into the civilian domain. A central part of the camp system, Papago Military Reservation, was converted to State property for use by the National Guard.

Four of the five camps were for the enlisted U-boaters. The U-Boat officers were somewhat local celebrities. Few prisoners were uncomfortable.

However, led by a rabble-rousing troublemaker named Captain Jurgen Wattenberg who had been transferred from another POW camp in Tennessee because he was caught planning an escape there, 25 prisoners staged an escape into the Arizona desert on December 23, 1944.

It was one of those cold, rainy Decembers in Arizona, like the Decembers and Januarys during which I served on flood duty while I was a Senior Airman, and again, as a second lieutenant.

The escapees quickly started to realize what a bad idea it was to risk their lives in a desperate, dangerous plot that was, unbeknownst to them, fatally flawed.

The Gila River that they planned to float down to the Colorado River, then on to Mexico in a 3-man kayak they had constructed, was dry.

They had based their escape plan on an outdated road map stolen from a gas station that depicted the Gila River with a solid blue line.

The Arizona desert can be extremely dangerous in any season. In addition, I can't help but believe that in the back of many of their minds, as they huddled in whatever shelter they could find from the cold rain, hungry, wet, and chilled to the bone, they had already started to understand that Germany was going to lose the war.

D-Day had happened six months prior, and they had all heard that the U.S. was victorious time and time again, as the war moved closer and closer to the German populace.

One of the prisoners turned himself in after just 17 hours, remembering what the Christmas dinner was going to be. This was the first notice to the POW camp staff that an escape had occurred.

Unlike the mass executions the Germans conducted as a result of the "Great Escape," as each of the Papago prisoners was caught or surrendered voluntarily, they were treated humanely, and sentenced to one day of bread and water for every day they had been on the loose.

Wattenberg was the last one captured after hiding out for 36 days and living in a small cave.

After the war, Captain Wattenberg returned to Germany and became a beer distributor. He lived to the age of 94.

The main structure was an interesting building. Built like a garrison, it was referred to as "The Fort." There is a fascinating museum inside the base that is sometimes open to the public. If you have an interest in military history, I highly recommend it.

I managed to pull myself together for my first uniformed drill. I was pleased to see that the local clothing store had Marine Corps ribbons.

I sewed on my Airman First Class stripes, my name tag, and a "U.S. Air Force" patch on my fatigues.

We began every drill by standing formation for inspection. I had the opportunity to observe how the officers addressed the senior NCOs, and how the senior NCOs addressed the officers.

I was a little surprised at how much control of the leadership process had been ceded to enlisted leadership. I did not find that disturbing in the least.

I watched as two enlisted personnel, Carol Zimmerman, and Wayne Bryan, became commissioned officers.

Carol was a computer programmer and was involved in engineering with Honeywell: a super smart, fun, attractive lady who retired as a Major.

Wayne was a teacher. He loved what he did and exuded it. Wayne also retired as a Major, and we have had many great quail hunts together in Arizona over the years.

He is the most clean-cut, rock-solid individual you can imagine. The kind of man you absolutely want your children to be around. He later retired as a teacher and continued driving a school bus.

I felt no need to gain authority, and was perfectly content as an A1C, not responsible for anyone else's performance and conduct.

107th Paintball Team. From second row far right-t-left: Bill Baizel, me and Angie (arm around me)

15

TRY ONE

By October, 1978, I was starting to see some daylight financially, and began thinking about ending my part-time gig with the Air National Guard. Nothing personal, I was just starting to enjoy my free weekends.

I had a brand-new green Datsun pickup truck with a 5-speed transmission that I loved driving all over the state hunting, fishing, and touring. My live-in girl-friend, Sam, was proving to be a fun partner. I found her to be very exotic and attractive. As the French might say, she had a certain *je ne sais quoi*. There was something about her that made her stand out and be interesting to me.

She had brought an infant boy, Robert, into the relationship; he was a good little, light-brown-haired, and blue-eyed boy with a million-dollar smile and a personality to match it. She was wild and seemed to lack any maternal instincts, but I encouraged her to try. She left Robbie with her mom at times. Her mom was an overweight blond alcoholic, who once dropped Robbie, scaring him more than hurting him. I encouraged Sam to stop leaving Robbie with her, and for a while she followed my advice.

Sam identified Robbi's dad as a Phoenix firefighter named Aaron, who had no interest in the boy. He had engaged in a brief and dangerous liaison with Sammi (she was seventeen at the time) and ended the relationship as soon as he found out she was pregnant. For her reasons, she chose to not pursue any legal remedies such as child support.

Sam and I met at the laundry-mat near the house. We struck up a conversation, and I found myself attracted to her flawless olive skin, dark brown eyes, long black eyelashes, bright smile, and cocky attitude.

She agreed to come over for dinner. She spent the night, and then stayed.

All three of us lived in my two-bedroom brick English Tudor style house (built in 1925) with its massive fireplace, hardwood floors, and a big garage.

I had bought this house just prior to my divorce, and it was in a nice little neighborhood on 10th Street, just north of McDowell Road, which was later designated as an historic neighborhood.

I now had two motorcycles: a Yamaha 100cc dirt bike, and a Suzuki 380GT—that was a fun crotch-rocket!

I also had a very light-weight aluminum 10-foot skiff (no flotation) with oars and an ancient, rather cranky, 3 horse power motor, both of which I could carry and load in the truck by myself, and easily carry to the shore of the lake.

I am a strong swimmer and had no fear of sinking the boat. I kept an empty Clorox bottle in the prow, tied to 100 feet of clothes line, on the theory that if I ever sank the boat close enough to shore, I'd be able to find and salvage it just by locating the floating bottle.

My favorite fishing hole was on Roosevelt Lake, next to a patch of submerged reeds that was teeming with large-mouth bass and crappies.

One time my brother Bruce came out to Arizona, and I took him fishing at my favorite spot on Roosevelt Lake.

Bruce was very unimpressed with my boat locator system, and as a mean-looking storm began rolling in over the lake, he reminded me what had just happened to Dad. To no avail, I pointed out the seat cushions with flotation.

Nonetheless, we enjoyed fantastic fishing. We took quite a haul of large-mouth bass and crappie and had a great fish-fry at my friend Linda's house. Linda was a good friend. Sammi, at that point, was becoming more distant after she enlisted in the Army and was assigned to Intelligence.

Linda tearfully told me that she had fallen in love with Bruce after he headed back to Syracuse. I understood completely and held her as she wept.

I was pleased to find that my employer, Chicanos Por La Causa, Inc. fully supported my reserve activity. They were unhesitatingly cooperative when I needed to complete "summer camp," even paying me the difference between my salary and active duty pay, long before it was required by law!

My director, Art Othon, expressed a real interest in what I was doing. He had been a Nike Missile radar operator in the Army, so I could talk radar and missiles with him.

One day when I went into the office following a drill weekend, I sat down and typed a letter to the Air National Guard, addressed to the Operations Officer, Captain Steve Hepburn, letting him know that I had enjoyed my time with the 107th, but would now be moving on, under the provisions of "Try One."

The following week, I got a call from Captain Hepburn. He seemed surprised by my resignation. He let me know that when I came to the next drill, I was scheduled to meet the board for Senior Airman. I couldn't resist the easy stripe. I told him I'd be there.

After that, I never considered resigning again. One year later I was promoted to Sergeant, then Staff Sergeant, followed by Technical Sergeant, before being commissioned as a Second Lieutenant in June 1982.

Brother Bruce and me after some great bass & crappie fishing on Roosevelt Lake

16

BALANCING ACT

My part-time work with the Air National Guard which had started when I was at the State Job Service, continued to be a regular part of my life during my employment at Chicanos Por La Causa, and even after I had resigned from Chicanos Por La Causa for my motorcycle road trip.

I began getting more active with the Guard. I took short deployments for various assignments. This was known as "guard bumming."

I picked up active duty wherever I could find it—when I wanted to work. I was selected for training as an Air Weapons Controller Technician, working as a right-hand person for the Weapons Controllers.

This was quite a bit more interesting than doing Surveillance as a radar operator, where I simply tracked the movement and status of airborne objects and other data.

It was a lot of fun assisting in the control of fighter aircraft, aerial refueling tankers (mostly KC-135s), and a variety of ground attack aircraft (mostly A-7 Corsairs from Tucson).

The controllers were all characters. It could be very fast-paced, and competitive. At times, it got wild in the dark room or controller van! As the Controllers and weapons techs sat shoulder to shoulder controlling fighter aircraft against each other;

yelling, cursing, making fake, deceptive calls in an attempt to confuse or disorient the other controller was common.

I also started pulling short tours with the Air Force, working as a weapons controller technician, or other odd assignments that came my way, including a gig at the Pentagon, contributing to a pamphlet entitled, "Making Your Community Guard Aware."

I was a Staff Sergeant. I was currently advertising myself as a writer, mostly writing college papers and resumes.

My Commander, Lt Col Jim Hagenson called me into his office one day and let me know the Guard Bureau was looking for a writer. Was I interested? I was, and orders were cut for me.

The Public Affairs Officer spoke with me briefly and let me know that I had reservations at the Crystal City Marriott. This was my first job in D.C., but not my last.

I caught a flight to Andrews Air Force Base on a KC-135 flown by the 161st Air Refueling Group (later a Wing).

On board, I noted several general officers and then-Senator Dennis DeConcini. They had a raucous card game going, with great laughter and back and forth jokes. I enjoyed watching these senior leaders letting their hair down.

After we landed at Andrews, I got off the plane with my bags, and weighed my options. I'd studied a map before I left Phoenix, and had a general idea where I was headed in Washington, D.C.

I decided to go into the terminal and learn more about available ground transportation.

As I approached the terminal, a cab pulled up in front of me and stopped. Our Adjutant General, John Smith, Jr. leaned out of the rear passenger window and said, "Hey Sarge, where are you headed?" I told him I had a reservation at the Pentagon City Marriott, and he said, "We're going right past there, hop in."

I climbed in the front seat, and looked back at Major General Smith, and Army Brigadier General Pettycrew, a tall, handsome officer. They were also going to be working in the Pentagon.

Years later, after becoming involved in Scottsdale city politics, I got to know General Pettycrew's son Robert quite well. Robert was seated on City Council before I was.

He is a genuinely nice guy, a talented musician, and looks a lot like his dad. I thought he was an exceptional council member, and I supported his campaign.

The two generals and I talked briefly about what I was going to be doing at the Pentagon. They gave me some ideas and would not take any money toward the cab fare. I tipped the driver and got out.

I stood in front of the Marriott and contemplated my current situation. I couldn't believe I had just spent a half hour in a cab with two generals, chatting like amigos.

I looked around and let the fact that I was standing in Washington, D.C. for the first time—and everything else that had transpired—sink in.

I checked into a nice room. My view was of the roadway I'd be navigating on my daily walk to and from the Pentagon.

While working in the Pentagon, I often had time to wander the various rings and corridors, looking at many interesting displays, sometimes picking up a colorful lithograph or meeting people.

One day while I was wandering around the Marine Corps area in the Pentagon, I came across the display for recipients of the Medal of Honor and Navy Cross.

I had been told that one of the Marines I had served with, Corporal Thomas L. Blevins, Jr., a hero who was killed on Go Noi Island during an ambush Charlie Company walked into, had been nominated for the Medal of Honor.

I was disappointed to not find him amongst the Medal of Honor recipients, then I discovered him listed as a recipient of the Navy Cross.

He was a squad leader, and he was killed during Operation Pipestone Canyon while dragging his men who had been wounded in an ambush to safety, fighting as he went, one Marine at a time, while under continuous machine gun and AK-47 fire.

I've never known a braver man, or a more solid, reliable leader in my life. He was a good man. His squad members already knew they could count on him, and he proved it to his last breath.

I spent my time when not "bumming" riding around on a Honda 550, and I had been spending an increasing amount of time with a very engaging woman I had met named Fran. Fran was a gorgeous red head with two boys.

Fran had the misfortune of being thrown from her horse shortly before high school graduation, which resulted in her being paralyzed from the waist down.

Later, her horse was struck by lightning and died while grazing in the pasture.

Her injury didn't impede her beauty or slow her down at all. She drove through life aggressively, had her two boys, graduated from Arizona State University with an MSW, and she was beautiful.

When I met her, she was working for a local bank and was my point-of-contact. Fran started Law School in Tucson, and I stayed with her frequently between my ramblings, including right after my motorcycle accident. Fran, I'm deeply grateful for your support and assistance.

While on a deployment to the Gila Bend USAF Air Facility as a Weapons Controller Technician and staying at the American 6 in Gila Bend, Fran came to visit me, and we decided to have dinner in the motel restaurant.

We sat down for dinner. I looked across the table at her and admired her tall, slender beauty. I studied her and loved everything about how she looked, especially her clear blue eyes, perfect nose, and radiant smile.

The restaurant was about half-full, and service seemed good. A few other unit members were seated in the booths, also still in their fatigues.

It was a relatively quiet assemblage of patrons, and a soft buzz of conversation pervaded the atmosphere with an occasional clatter of dishes and silverware, or a waitress repeating an order to diners. Our waitress brought our meal, and I took my first few bites.

Just as I leaned across the table to share a humorous story, I noticed a glint of light out of the corner of my left eye. I noticed another brief flicker of light and turned to look just as a huge tongue of flame licked from the kitchen through the service window. The place was on fire! I quickly stood and asked Fran to hop into her wheelchair and go outside.

I looked around at the diners surrounding me, who seemed oblivious to what was happening. I thought, this is not good, and could get much worse, quickly.

As I began moving toward the swinging gates that entered the kitchen, I told patrons that they should get out immediately.

I pushed through the gates anticipating my next move. I need to find a fire extinguisher, I thought to myself as I got my first good look at the fire. This is not a good situation. Maybe I should just get everybody out of here, including myself.

I spotted the cook holding a fire extinguisher, standing as still as a statue. Great, I thought, as I ran forward and wrenched the extinguisher from his hands, aimed it at the fire, and squeezed the trigger.

To my surprise only a small amount of chemical dribbled out. I threw it away and yelled to anyone within ear shot to bring me another extinguisher before spotting one on the wall.

Grabbing it, I yanked it from the wall, and I began working on extinguishing the flames. After the fire was out, employees were still bringing me fire extinguishers.

More than a year after the fire, shortly after I had been commissioned as a Second Lieutenant, I received the Arizona Medal of Valor. Not a bad way to start off my career as an officer!

In June, 1980 I was rear-ended on my motorcycle out near Roosevelt Lake. I have no memory of it, only the deputy's assessment when I spoke with him later, just before I drove out to Apache Junction to pick up my wrecked motorcycle and camping gear. I was still pretty banged up and it was a real effort getting my Honda into the back of the rented pickup truck.

Whoever hit me left me for dead on the roadside, placing a towel over my face as I lay on my back, face quite torn up, and out cold. A patrolling sheriff's deputy found me laying on the side of the road unconscious near my bike.

He called an ambulance for me, and initially they took me to Globe. Admissions at Globe Hospital quickly determined that I was indigent, and sought another medical venue better suited to my current financial means.

At Fran's suggestion, I had named her as an "in case of emergency" contact in my wallet, and I ended up at the V.A. Hospital in Tucson, delivered in the same ambulance that I had arrived in at the hospital in Globe. I was still mostly unconscious, and I received both excellent inpatient and outpatient treatment, including an excellent job of putting my face back together.

The VA accepted me simply based on my Marine Corps service with no further documentation. My ambulance bill was somewhere around $650. I paid it.

As soon as I was released as a patient, I got my motorcycle back in working order, and, in serious need of money, rode to Phoenix, then joined a military convoy to Camp Pendleton, California to spend two weeks of active duty at Red Beach with the 107th.

They were a little surprised to see me, but my orders had already been cut prior to the accident.

I was a real mess, with stitches still in my face, broken and missing teeth, broken ribs, and a broken wrist with a brace on my right forearm—well concealed under my BDU (battle dress uniform–fatigues) jacket sleeve.

My broken ribs still had not healed, and one of them still made a clicking noise and hurt like hell when I sat up too quickly! I did the most I could to disguise my injuries, but I was an obvious mess. I completed two weeks of annual training and headed back to Tucson on my self-repaired motorcycle.

The Tucson Urban League hired me as a Recruiter/Counselor, and I spent most of my time working to create apprenticeship opportunities with the local unions. Fran introduced me to her good friend Darwin Aycock, President of the Arizona American Federation of Labor. We met for lunch and discussed my position with the Urban League. Darwin was a Marine Corps veteran and served as a rifleman with the First Marine Division at the battle of the Chosin Reservoir in Korea.

He was very responsive and went out of his way to be helpful in placing my clients in apprentice positions. My director, Rod Hoyle, was a good guy, and I enjoyed working with the friendly folks at the Urban League.

I had used the Urban League in Phoenix to develop jobs under the Work Experience Program along with my very good and beautiful friend, Linda Olsen, while working for CPLC, so the Tucson job was an easy fit.

I was no longer staying with Fran and kept an apartment close to the office on 6th Avenue in Tucson.

I applied for a position and was hired back with the State of Arizona, Department of Economic Security Job Service as a Job Developer for the Indo-Chinese Refugee Assistance Program (IRAP).

150

My job was to develop employment opportunities for the refugees pouring in from Vietnam, Thailand, Cambodia, and Laos. I was out stationed with Catholic Social Services at 19th Avenue and Northern, and had interpreters working with me.

I moved back up to Phoenix and got a studio apartment on West Indian School Road. While working for the IRAP, I was enticed into going on a 30-day deployment to Korea with the 107th.

We billeted in the Osan AFB Tent City and controlled U.S. fighter aircraft cruising the DMZ—with North Korean MIGs doing the same—in an annual saber-rattling exercise involving the U.S. and South Korean forces, called "Team Spirit."

When we first arrived at Osan, our tent city was still being erected, and when we went into the shower tent and many of us had already stripped down, we discovered that there was no hot water. We had just finished a 23-hour flight in a C-5 Galaxy, and I felt grimy.

It was late December, and the weather in Korea was much like Upstate New York, with not quite as much snow.

I jumped under the ice-cold shower while being observed by dozens of fellow unit members standing naked and shivering around the shower, making comments about my apparent lack of sensation as I washed.

As you might imagine, with North Korean MIG aircraft, South Korean fighters, and U.S. fighters cruising in awfully close proximity to each other along the DMZ, we were controlling fully armed fighter aircraft in some pretty tense airspace!

While in Vietnam, I worked for a significant amount of time (2 operations) with the Korean Marines and even traded fatigues with a Korean Marine Sergeant. I found them to be extremely tough fighters. I would hate to ever need to face off against them.

While visiting Panmunjom, where the treaty was signed that ended the major armed conflict underway between South Korea, North Korea, U.S., and China, I had the opportunity to step into the building where the treaty was signed.

There was a large conference table with a line painted down the center of it. One side of the table and building belongs to North Korea and is heavily patrolled. I had the chance to look directly into the eyes of an AK-47-carrying North Korean soldier as he looked in at me through the window. We held that gaze for about five seconds and then both moved on.

I must say I saw a steely determination much akin to the eye-to-eye contact I had with North Vietnamese prisoners.

I believe that they're no match for the South Korean Marines, but I'd avoid getting into a fight with them unless it's absolutely necessary.

When I returned to Phoenix, I found myself itching for something a little more challenging. I resigned from the IRAP and began guard bumming nearly full time.

Sam continued to briefly skip in and out of my life. Her son, Robert, had been adopted, she had joined the Army and served in Desert Storm. We were never able to make it work, and I felt broken-hearted.

The balancing act continued between my increasingly meaningful work with the Guard and Air Force, my relationships, and time with my son, Daniel.

Shortly after being promoted to Technical Sergeant, I met the board for a possible commission, and I was selected. I began getting all of my paperwork in order.

At the time, there was a federal required minimum of sixty college credit hours to be commissioned as an officer by the Air Force. I sat down and carefully added all my credit hours. I had 58!

I went to our Training NCOIC, Joe Rummell and explained my predicament. He recommended that I join the Community College of the Air Force. I was awarded an additional twelve credit hours for various military training and activities. Problem solved.

My next hurdle was to pass a Class One flight physical, required for controller positions, and because I had been knocked unconscious, I was required to also be cleared by a neurologist.

I got myself started on a rigorous physical fitness program and practiced controlling some troublesome tremors and other damaging physical maladies that I knew would seriously jeopardize my chances of passing an examination or physical.

I learned self-hypnosis and I still use the techniques I developed when I need to learn something quickly and completely or memorize a speech.

While still a Staff Sergeant, I had been selected to attend a twelve-week Manual Weapons Controller/Technician Instructor Course at Tyndall Air Force Base, Florida. When I arrived, I found out I was required to have a working knowledge of trigonometry as a pre-requisite of training!

I went to the Base Library, got some material on trig, settled into my quarters, and went to work. My self-hypnosis techniques worked wonders here as well.

The beach on Tyndall was amazing. The sand had a very unusual texture, as if it was round or oval, and bright white. The training was superior. Our two officers-in-charge had nicknames. The American Air Force Captain was "Wombat," and the Australian Air Force Officer was "Barney Rubble," both nicknames purely based on appearance.

I had a wonderful time, and, fortunately, I would return to Tyndall AFB a couple more times in the future.

A few of my neighbors in billeting were from the Canadian Air Force. They introduced me to Dee's Oyster Bar in Panama City and were all-around good guys.

We got pretty drunk once and started trading badges and ribbons off of our uniforms. I still have them and smile every time I come across them tucked in with other special mementoes.

One of their favorite activities was Sunday morning service. We'd all sit around the T.V. on Sunday morning watching one of the many hellfire and brimstone preachers rant as we drank beer, heartily agreeing with him, and occasionally yelling, "Amen!"

It was an extraordinary experience. When I returned to my unit, my commander called me into his office and asked me about the training.

He asked me if I thought I could conduct a two-week course to qualify controllers and controller technicians during summer camp. I told him I was sure I could.

The training went great. Weapons Controllers and Technicians attended, and I put them through the paces.

By course completion, the unit had enough qualified control teams to achieve the highest readiness rating with the Air Force—ten fully qualified control teams. I received an Air Force Commendation Medal.

One morning, while working in Operations as the Operations Training NCOIC, I got a call from Headquarters Air Guard wanting to know if I could be available to begin the Officers Academy at McGhee-Tyson Air Guard Base in Tennessee the following week.

To buy a little time, I informed the sergeant that I was completing an important project for the unit and would get back to him within the hour to let him know if I could wrap up what I was working on and be there by the start date.

I still wasn't sure I wanted to be an officer.

I was a Technical Sergeant with very reasonable expectations placed upon me. I felt secure, I was enjoying what I was doing, and getting a little respect.

I also, at the time, dreaded the prospect of being at the bottom of the food chain again as a 2nd lieutenant.

Another consideration was the fact that I was making a decent living as a guard bum and had lots of free time to play hard!

On the flip side, it would be uncharted territory. What the hell! I called him back and took the academy date.

The officer's academy was good. I learned everything I needed to know on how to dress like and act like an officer, and made a good friend, and running partner, Jim Yeagley.

One night we were dropped in on unexpectedly by a small cadre of yelling and threatening officers and taken out for a kind of "hell night," filled with more yelled threats and running in the dark.

We scampered to the side of the road when a group of armed military police appeared firing blanks in the air and doing their level best to frighten us.

I was mightily pissed, and my friend Jim Yeagley, who had injured his ankle while dodging the SPs, cooled me down just as I was getting ready to blow up. Jim's injury made passing the physical training test a challenge for him, and I wondered if punching that cop would have been worth it just to shine a light on what I thought was a stupid dangerous event.

We were returned to our dorms and given permission to open the bar as a reward for "surviving." The beer cooler was locked, and not a single faculty member could be found to unlock the cooler. We were all fit to be tied.

But the joke was on them. In civilian life, Jim was a locksmith and owned and operated a lock and bike shop in Great Falls, Montana. He easily picked the lock, and the beer flowed!

I came back from the Academy and went right to work as the squadron Intelligence Officer. Within a couple of months, I had a date for controller school, and as quickly as possible, prepared for my positional evaluation to become qualified as a Weapons Controller.

Shortly after I returned from my controller training at Tyndall AFB, our unit had a Standardization and Evaluation Inspection from Group. I was selected to receive a positional evaluation and passed comfortably.

I did what appeared to be a sweet job of swinging a flight of four A-7s behind a KC-135 for an aerial refueling. I prepared an Air Mass Positioning Indicator (AMPI), demonstrated its use, and made all the right calls. It looked beautiful on the radar scope and sounded smooth on the radio. It was mentioned in the out-briefing when we received an excellent rating for the inspection.

The KC-135 was from Sky Harbor in Phoenix, and the A-7s from the Tucson Air Guard. It is quite possible that they all went out of their way to make me look as good as possible just out of loyalty.

I soon found myself in demand and was working as a temporary federal employee, too. Within a year, I was designated instructor qualified. In 1985, I was hired as the full-time Operations Officer, dual hatted as a federal employee and a uniformed military officer.

I maintained additional duties as the Squadron Intelligence Officer. My NCOIC, Laurie Enright, made it a fun assignment, and Laurie later went on to be a commissioned officer, flying as a crew member on the C-130. We are friended on Facebook and I enjoy her frequent updates. Her daughter Mollie is now in the Air Force and just made Senior Airman.

I was also assigned as the Squadron OPSEC Monitor, Squadron Site Defense Officer, and as an Instructor Weapons Director. In addition, I completed the altitude chamber a couple of times and had an interesting F-15 backseat ride in a two versus one against two F-16s. My pilot had a nickname of something like "hotrod." I think he and the other pilots who got stuck taking us for a ride had a bet going on how many times they could sucker their back-seater into quickly looking to the right, saying, "Check your 3-o-clock," just as they yank the stick to the left and bounce your head off the canopy. Or, how many they could make sick. I can imagine the tales as they gathered around their little bar in the pilot's lounge.

My son's situation at home was deteriorating. His mother was going through some difficult times, and Dan and his siblings by another father were not faring well. I finally felt the need to actively pursue custody of my son, and I did, successfully.

It was not an easy transition for either of us. I had been single for eight years and had a budding career as a full-time officer with the Air National Guard. He felt a strong loyalty to his mother and wanted to return to her fulltime badly.

I was blessed to have a sweet, attractive, and deeply religious young lady named Joan Klosterman in my apartment complex who was willing to watch Daniel early in the morning before school started, and later in the afternoon after Daniel got out of school.

She was reliable, good, honest, responsible, and affordable.

Kudos for my former brother-in-law, Dennis, and his wife's willingness to watch Daniel for me when I deployed to Germany twice.

Daniel and I danced that dance for five years, then at his insistence, he returned to his mother. He would come back to me briefly two years later and has remained in my life ever since.

After I had been the full-time Ops Officer for a few years, including two deployments to Germany for Central Enterprise, and with an Excellent Operational Readiness Inspection under my belt, I received a visit from a former 107th officer, Major Mary Cox, who had moved to Headquarters several years previously.

She was a slender, attractive brunette, her hair hanging nearly to her waist when she let it down; she wore little or no makeup and didn't need it.

Based on my past work with minority organizations, she wanted me to consider taking a position in Human Resources as the State Equal Employment Manager.

I told her that I wasn't interested. She asked why. I explained to her that I had no interest in being the most unpopular officer in the state of Arizona. She asked me to please sleep on it and get back to her in the morning, and I did.

17

EDUCATION

On my Marine Corps DD 214, my listed education level is 10th grade. I had not even been inspired to receive documentation of my successful G.E.D. testing until I decided to take advantage of the G.I. Bill.

I held formal education in extremely low esteem. I hadn't enjoyed or appreciated high school, although my last year there had been incident-free—except for my fistfight outside the convent on Court Street.

I viewed college students as children in adult bodies, trapped in the never-never land of academia. I had only known a few college girls and, other than Murphy in Yellowstone Park, they generally seemed pretty self-centered, not very interesting to me, nor interested in me.

While I was walking through the San Francisco airport terminal in uniform after returning from Viet Nam, I was greeted by a small clutch of yowling miscreants casting invectives in my direction.

They were led by a particularly scummy-looking, long-haired creep, holding a sign stating some college name and "students against the war," and yelling something at me about "murdering the innocent." I'd done a lot of things in Vietnam, but that wasn't one of them.

I took the airport confrontation very personally, and silently seethed for quite some time over that experience.

Throughout my time in the Marines, it appeared to me that, with the exception of the officers I served under, one of the purposes of higher education was to provide sanctuary for children not yet prepared for the real world, and I felt that college students generally seemed to go out of their way to cast aspersions on the work I had done as a Marine.

Every time I thought of college, I would flash back to my confrontation in the airport and feel a burning anger.

Once I figured out that, like it or not, education was essential to personal growth and development, I pursued it, and grew to enjoy some of the classes.

I still had no interest in a degree. I took as many electives as I could at Phoenix College, and even changed my major when I could no longer take any more electives under my current program of study. I never participated in any college social activities outside of the classroom.

When I took Psychology 101, one of my course assignments was to select a book and complete a book report. I selected Victor E. Frankl's, *Man's Search for Meaning*. As I read the book and began preparing my report, I actually had an "Ah-ha" moment.

I learned the concept of existentialism and found myself fully embracing it. His quote: "Everything can be taken from a man but one thing: the last of the human freedoms—to choose one's attitude in any given set of circumstances; to choose one's own way." That resonated deeply within me.

Nobody else could make me feel any particular way; only I could do that.

One of the electives I took, and thoroughly enjoyed, was Ground School. At the time, I had about seven hours in a glider (at the Turf glider strip near Lake Pleasant), and no real interest in pursuing aviation as a career or hobby, but flying a glider was entertaining and turned out to be great experience.

It's a good idea to learn how to fly a plane with no engine, first. When your engine quits on you (as mine did, once), you are flying a glider. I found the course instructive and remembered what I learned.

Shortly after I returned from the officer's academy, a brand-new Second Lieutenant, my commander, Lieutenant Colonel Jim Hagenson sat me down and explained to me that if I wanted to succeed as an officer, I would need a bachelor's degree. He explained that I would be lucky to make Captain and would certainly proceed no further without one.

Colonel James Hagenson had selected me for the commissioning opportunity and endorsed me as a worthy candidate, so I listened to him. As a result of his good advice, I completed a bachelor's and master's program, and eventually retired as a Lieutenant Colonel.

I set out seeking the fastest bachelor's degree I could get. I knew I would have to do it at night and be able to work around multiple deployments.

I had no experience as a full-time daytime student on campus. In the Fall of 1982, I started taking classes at the University of Phoenix in the evening.

Each class was six weeks in duration, usually one class per week, lasting at least four hours. And lots of writing and presentations. We were divided into study groups of four, and I lucked out.

Study groups were expected to meet at least once every week, and usually needed to prepare and give a presentation on their assigned project.

My group was excellent and supportive. I stayed with the same group throughout the program and ended up living briefly with one of my team members, Betsy.

Betsy was fun, attractive, intelligent, supportive, and had a quality not seen often; she was damned cute! She helped me to develop an interest in classical music, and her family was genuinely nice.

When it became obvious that I had no interest in taking our relationship to the next level, we parted. I will always treasure the time I spent with her.

I discovered that there were additional options for accumulating college credits as quickly as possible. I learned about the College Level Examination Program (C.L.E.P.) and began testing on subjects.

When I was on a deployment or working in the Phoenix area with access to Luke AFB's Base Education office, I would check out videos and other materials on the selected subject, spend the weekend studying hard, and then take the test as soon as I could schedule it.

I took and passed four exams: History, Math, English, and Science. I was able to use those C.L.E.P. credit hours toward my degree.

I was also able to write essays based on life experience for college credit. I found a course listed in a college catalogue from an accredited university and wrote about how I had learned the course content through my various experiences.

I picked up additional college credits in my forced march toward a bachelor's degree.

As I continued working toward my degree at the speed of heat, I also completed Squadron Officer School by correspondence.

I had made a decision that if I decided I wanted to continue with the Air Guard, I wasn't going to allow any unnecessary barriers toward promotion.

Control what you can and accept what you cannot.

I completed my bachelor's program by the Summer of 1984. Unfortunately, I had a deployment, and I had to skip the graduation ceremony, instead receiving my diploma in the mail.

Mission accomplished. I felt no real interest in a graduation ceremony, even though I had already sprung for the cap and gown. I had never walked the stage for a diploma and didn't until I earned my master's degree.

Betsy had let me know that she intended to continue into her master's program. I had no interest at the time, but it planted the seed. I knew I could do it if I wanted to.

I continued to acquire necessary certifications. I attended training at Tyndall AFB for the third time, attending a two-week program in "dissimilar air combat tactics" (DACT) designed to make me more skillful at controlling fighters against enemy aircraft with dissimilar flight and weapons characteristics, such as the tight-turning MIG 19. Its performance was in many ways comparable to the F-5.

This relatively old Soviet fighter was pretty fast and maneuverable—designed so it could get inside the turn of a U.S. fighter under certain circumstances, with deadly consequences.

I was a Manual Weapons Controller at the top of my game.

I also tackled all my professional military education requirements, such as Air Command and Staff and Air War College (the highest level of professional military education at the time).

Later, I served as an adjunct instructor for the Air Command and Staff program at Maxwell AFB. I completed Air War College in seminar at Luke Air Force Base in the evenings.

Meanwhile, I got the urge to go to the next level and began a master's program with the University of Phoenix.

For both of my degrees, I took advantage of any financial assistance I could secure, or I paid out of pocket as I attended.

One time, I took a student loan for the maximum allowable amount and re-invested it in a Farm Credit Security. I got a 14% return, immediately paid off the loan and pocketed the balance.

Once again, as I pursued my master's degree, I was truly fortunate to be part of a very supportive study group. I pulled my weight, despite my frequent deployments, and they were wonderful to work with.

While completing my Master of Arts in Organizational Management, I also completed Air Command and Staff College, and had a special opportunity fall in my lap, which I seized.

I was approached by Chief Master Sergeant Dan Cochran with a proposal. Arizona State University had made an offer. They had a program entitled, "Advanced Public Executive Program," and wanted to get the Arizona National Guard involved.

They were looking for a volunteer to give it a try. I jumped on it!

It was an excellent growth opportunity. The program walked us through a number of very realistic scenarios, including one segment on dealing with the media.

Each student had the opportunity to walk into a very realistic ambush interview that included reporters yelling questions, sound and light technicians scurrying around, and the ever-present mic shoved in my face by yelling reporters.

After completing the program, I thanked Dan profusely.

I started my position as the Operations Officer with the Joint Counter Narcotics Task Force (JCNTF) in July 1994.

I completed my master's degree program, Air Command and Staff, and the ASU program simultaneously in the summer of 1994.

I also married my wife Karyn in the Spring of 1994. Quite a year!

18

CAREER

After sleeping on Mary's proposal that I lateral to the position in Human Resources as the State Equal Employment Manager, and after weighing the pros and cons, I decided it looked like an interesting job. I agreed to interview for it.

I quickly boned up on Title VII, the ADA, ADEA and EPA, and the various National Guard Bureau and Federal regulations.

The job was offered to me, and I accepted the offer. I transferred to the new position but kept drilling with the 107th for a couple more months until they got past a Standardization and Evaluation (STAN/EVAL) visit from Group Headquarters that was already on the books.

We got a rating of "Excellent". I never controlled any aircraft live or simulated again after that.

My new duties were expansive. As the State Equal Employment Manager (SEEM), I had a line-of-sight relationship with the Adjutant General. I could make an appointment with Major General Owens any time I needed to discuss a matter with him and could expect to be scheduled ASAP.

I was one of his key EEO advisors, and I was responsible for managing a state-wide program over both the Army and the Air National Guard.

I developed and cultivated a robust cadre of collateral staff members to include EEO Counselors, Technician Assistance Program Counselors, and Special Emphasis Program Managers.

I provided a full day of training annually for all staff members and constantly circulated around the state, providing training, guidance, and conducting investigations.

Down in Tucson, I had the opportunity to work with some wonderful folks, both Army and Air.

I worked especially closely with Master Sergeant Benjamin "Benny" Riesgo and Technical Sergeant Susan Rohr. Benny was a fun, wise-cracking Senior NCO, who really knew his way around the unit.

Susan was smart, attractive, professional, and a great help to the program, serving in multiple capacities as a counselor, investigator, advisor, and friend.

I wrote and staffed our annual report to the National Guard Bureau and EEOC, and continuously updated our statistics for internal use.

I noted that a significant number of discrimination allegations were raised because of flaws in our current hiring and promotion process.

I informed General Owens and offered a proposed solution. Once in the past he had scolded me by saying, "Don't just bring me problems. Bring me solutions, Captain!"

I recommended a set of hiring guidelines, which I had already prepared for him to review. He accepted my analysis and my proposed solution.

The Adjutant General mandated in a letter to staff that all National Guard personnel—Army, Air, Federal civilian employees, and State employees—had to have my training before they could interview anyone, for anything.

I developed a full set of guidelines, published a pamphlet, and began the training. Complaints based on the interview process were nearly eliminated.

Almost immediately after starting as SEEM, I recognized that I didn't have any effective tools at my disposal to routinely deal with and resolve complaints at the lowest possible level.

I spoke with a fellow officer in the Army Guard, and he suggested that I contact someone he knew at the Little Rock Professional Military Education Center and see if they had any information on something he'd heard about called "mediation."

I called my friend's contact and asked him about mediation.

Although he didn't have anything on mediating individual complaints, he did have some material for addressing group complaints. He faxed a one-page information sheet to me.

I modified it and began using the modified format for mediating complaints. It worked.

I also learned some dispute resolution techniques while attending the Defense Equal Opportunity Management Institute (DEOMI) at Patrick Air Force Base in Florida. I found DEOMI to be quite informative.

I caught on early that the DEOMI faculty seemed to be encouraging the minority students to be a little abusive and I decided to just roll with the punches.

I assumed that faculty felt that white folks needed to experience some harsh, irrational, abusive conduct. I also understood that the minorities, especially the blacks, had a bone to pick, and many felt they had been abused most of their adult lives. I never took it personally.

The Defense Equal Opportunity Management Institute program was divided into three phases. I attended Phase One in late 1989. Phase Two was at home, on the computer.

This was the early age of the internet, when almost all internet activity was still confined to the military. At the time, I had just upgraded my Tandy TRS-80 Color Computer 2 to a home-built 186 with a dial-up modem.

I wrote two lesson plans in Phase Two and presented one of them in Phase Three back on Patrick Air Force Base, addressing steps to eliminate use of the "N" word in American society.

Phase Three was a breeze. I had joined the Patrick Air Force Base Aero Club as soon as I got there in 1989 for Phase One. I'd been a licensed pilot for about four years, got checked out in one of their Piper Warriors and started renting whenever I could during both Phase One and Phase Three.

At the end of Phase Three, just for the hell of it, I flew my roommate to Orlando so he could catch an earlier flight home. I was cleared to taxi to the Executive Terminal, where he jumped out with his bags and caught a cab. It was great fun and a new experience for me.

I was running a little later than expected on my return flight. I noted that the tower was closing in ten minutes, and I couldn't land without clearance from the tower. The S.P.s would have been all over me! I was still about twenty minutes out.

I called tower with my location and estimated time of arrival (ETA). The tower controller seemed mildly agitated when I landed but taxied me line-of-sight to the flying club hangar.

I would continue to provide mediation services even after I left the SEEM position.

Being the State Equal Employment Manager was a tough job, but after a couple of years on the job, it became routine. After about three years I began to feel worn down and found myself watching for the next opportunity.

I had grown weary of the constant pushback I received at all levels of the organization, and one experience pushed me over the edge.

The Army had a very pretty little sergeant who was performing well as a recruiter. She had been featured in numerous articles. She was a miniature beauty; adored and admired by many in the organization, including me.

The Army had just started conducting HIV testing, and sadly, she tested positive. The process of informing her of the results, re-testing her, and confirming her infection was handled as poorly as it could have been. In a blink, she went from revered to reviled.

Long story short, the Army initially removed her from her recruiting duties, which meant the loss of "pro pay," a considerable portion of her monthly income.

She was a single parent at the time and really struggling to make ends meet while snarled in a bureaucratic nightmare that had her on a one-way path out of the Army, with no benefits.

A large, aggressive law firm took her case "pro-bono," and I was the point-of-contact they dealt with for quite some time.

This was in the early days of HIV, and her legal representatives raised some very valid points on the mishandling of her case.

Both I and the JAG Officer doubted that they would be able to get a military legal issue into the civilian courts, but it looked like we were headed for a long, drawn out legal fight that we could potentially lose with the public.

I conducted a thorough investigation, as did Lt Col Don Campbell. Too many mistakes had been made, some of them appearing to be cruel.

An agreement was reached, and she retired with benefits.

I woke up tired one morning and realized that I had lost all passion for the job. I was tired of being the most unpopular officer in the Arizona National Guard.

I saw an opportunity to move into the Military Personnel Management Officer position in Headquarters, and I took it.

My supervisor, Colonel Dick Drinen was an exceptionally good officer who had a long and distinguished career leading people and managing resources.

I trusted him, and I really liked the Headquarters staff. Chief Master Sergeant Eddie Ong, and Chief Master Sergeant Yolanda Flores were old pros. And Master Sergeant Bonnie Krentler was top-notch at organizing retirements and events—and man, could she sing!

Bonnie did a rousing performance of "I'm Proud to be an American" by Lee Greenwood and was in great demand around the State!

As the Military Personnel Management Officer, I did a little bit of everything. I supervised the office. I kept things moving. I managed all senior non-commissioned officer promotions, and all officer promotions up to full colonel.

I also worked with the National Guard Bureau to facilitate General Officer promotions. I wrote Officer Performance Reports (OPRs), awards and decorations, monitored a myriad of programs, provided counsel, mediated complaints, and ran the Officers Club.

I did anything the ESSO, Air Commander, or Adjutant General (TAG) directed me to do. One day, I got a call to come to the TAG's office. Major General Van Dyke had a job for me. Our then Governor, Rose Mofford required an escort for a luncheon she would be attending in Tucson. He wanted me to take her. I asked him how to contact her. He told me that she was listed in the phone book, along with her address. She was.

I called her and made arrangements to come by at about 9:00 a.m. to pick her up and had an absolutely wonderful day. I learned all about her. She was a major character! I expressed surprise that her phone number and home address were published in the phone book.

She told me she'd never had a problem with that, "Except one time when some drunk called me." She told me about her time as an All-American softball champ, and her near-career as a professional athlete that was nixed by her dad. She grew up in Globe. Her maiden name was Perica.

She also spoke fondly of her ex-husband, "Lefty," a retired Phoenix P.D. Captain.

I sat with her over lunch at a reception honoring her work as Governor.

At her suggestion, we stopped at the Dairy Queen just off the I-10 Picacho Peak exit heading back toward Phoenix. I went in to get us both a cone.

When I came out holding two cones, she was holding court with a half-dozen people who had spotted her trade-mark beehive hairdo and approached her in the staff car. She was a wonderful person, and a real Arizona treasure.

In 1993, the Arizona National Guard became involved in the State Partnership Program (SPP) and began a collaborative effort with Kazakhstan.

The first delegation of representatives for the Kazakhstan military arrived in Phoenix. The Adjutant General assigned Lieutenant Colonel Mike Reichling and me to escort them.

About the second or third day they were in Phoenix, Mike and I got wind that they were planning a "boy's night out." We decided to be proactive and take them out for a night they wouldn't forget!

We identified a club we thought they might enjoy and contacted the manager to let him know our intentions. When we arrived, the manager came to the lobby and provided the rules of the road.

We proceeded into the club, surrounded by tall, beautiful, nearly naked women. Mike and I took turns buying lap dances for our charges and had a fun night.

After we left the club, we returned to the hotel where they were staying, and the vodka came out. Mike and I learned how to toast, Russian style.

The Kazakhstan military had a problem, and our charges began talking about it. Up until a couple years before, they had been entirely subsidized, trained, and equipped by the Soviet Union. Although it had been an uneasy alliance, it had worked.

If you were anybody in the Kazakhstan hierarchy, you spoke Russian, and military officers were trained by the Soviets. Soviet soldiers often supervised and trained enlisted personnel. When the Soviet Union imploded and the Soviet military advisors pulled out, they took everything of any value with them, their technical knowledge and expertise being of the greatest value.

Due to the Soviet military influence, Kazakhstan had not developed a professional enlisted cadre. They had no effective enlisted leadership in place. They staffed their military enlisted force almost entirely through two-year conscription.

The conditions were brutal. As new conscripts entered the enlisted ranks, they were typically set upon by the senior conscripts who seized their new uniforms, boots and other equipment.

Technical expertise in the enlisted ranks was almost non-existent. There were few trained mechanics, electricians, or carpenters.

All work requiring significant skills was performed under the strict supervision of officers. They needed our expertise in building an all-volunteer, trained, enlisted force—like the one we had.

We drank vodka into the early morning hours, making long-winded toasts to this, that, and whatever.

I found a translator through ASU to translate a compact ratifying the State Partnership Program (SPP) initiative between Kazakhstan and the Arizona National Guard. Unfortunately, she lived in Paradise Valley. When the translated document was complete and I picked it up, I had just about twenty-five minutes to get back to Tempe at the Arizona State University President's Club, before dinner started followed by the planned signing of the accord.

As I weaved through traffic on Tatum Boulevard southbound, I got flashed by a radar van (one of the first ever deployed). I just made the dinner on time—and for whatever the reason, never received the ticket. I arrived at the President's Club with the completed document just as dinner was being served.

My military career continued, with occasionally interesting assignments.

At the end of April, 2000, Major General David Rataczak called me into his office.

He had committed to a speaking engagement in Payson to dedicate the Vietnam War Memorial replica wall and now had a scheduling conflict.

He was aware that I was a Vietnam veteran, and asked me to replace him. I gladly accepted the assignment and contacted the person coordinating the celebration planned for May 6, 2000 at Green Valley Park. I drove up prior to the event and had a good meeting with her.

On the morning of May 6th, I was flown into the Park on a Blackhawk helicopter, gave my dedication speech to approximately 7,000 attendees, and then departed again on the Blackhawk. (My speech is contained in the Appendix of this book.)

As the Military Personnel Management Officer, I had a rapidly developing problem—my new in-coming supervisor openly despised me.

We had been quite close at one time but had since moved in different directions as we continued to develop our leadership and management styles and I had recently married Karyn.

Mary would be starting her new position as the Executive Staff Support Officer (ESSO), and she was not happy about it. She referred to her new position as "the queen of nothing."

Under the direction of Colonel Drinen I prepared a briefing for her in his office. She treated me with extreme rudeness and cut me off repeatedly. I understood that I needed to take some immediate action.

Lieutenant Colonel Gary Smith, Coordinator for the Joint Counter-Narcotics Task Force (JCNTF) popped his head in my office door the following morning. I had just finished helping him with a complex personnel issue. He said, "I want you to come to work for me."

I accepted the offer and let him know I was available immediately. Problem solved.

I was wrapping up my Master of Arts in Organizational Management, Air Command and Staff, and the ASU Advanced Public Executive Program simultaneously.

I had just gotten married. I would be on active duty as a Major, and I would be on "military leave" from my federal employment as a GS-11 Military Personnel Management Officer.

When I decided to leave active duty, I would be reinstated in an available position, matching my qualifications, and it needed to be in the Phoenix area.

As a personnel officer, I knew the rules under the Uniformed Services Employment and Reemployment Rights Act (USERRA) quite well. I was required to renew my leave status annually, which I did.

As Operations Officer, I worked closely with seventy-nine law enforcement agencies, bureaus, departments, coalitions, and task forces—from the F.B.I. to Nogales P.D. We provided them with Military Support to Civil Authorities (MSCA).

I normally had approximately 190 personnel assigned or attached to Operations, supporting five functions: Case Support, Intelligence Analysis, Special Operations (aka: "snake eaters"), Cargo Inspection, and Aviation Support.

Part of my aviation support consisted of four RAID unit Bell OH-58 Kiowa helicopters assigned to Operations and equipped with Forward Looking Infrared (FLIR) pods. I got checked out in the left seat as a "safety pilot."

The aviators and crew members were terrific. They were real pros. During our MSCA to U.S. Customs for an operation in the Coronado National Forest, they, in concert with our Special Operations personnel, assisted in the interdiction of 28 pack horses fully loaded with cocaine.

They also were able to assist in the capture of the wrangler who was leading the horses on a dirt forest road through the National Forest approximately seven miles northwest of Nogales on that dark night.

When he tried to flee south on foot, the Customs guys pulled him out of a tree in the dark—with our assistance from the air, constantly tracking him with our FLIR equipped OH-58s.

We later watched a video shot from one of the OH-58s of the wrangler running full-bore—throwing equipment and his weapon as he ran in the dark right into a barbed-wire fence. He was pretty torn up when Customs arrested him.

I spent a great deal of time on the border. I also worked closely with the California task force and with Joint Task Force (JTF) Six over in Fort Bliss, Texas.

Prior to a visit, Headquarters was required to provide JTF-6 with documentation of my security clearance. I held a Top Secret/SCI DCID 6/4 security clearance for many years.

When I arrived, I would be issued an identification badge, and seemed to continuously pass through checkpoints where I needed to show it. I jokingly referred to their headquarters as "The Fortress of Solitude."

JTF-6 was comprised of a mishmash of Title 10 Active Duty personnel, mostly Army and Marine Corps supporting all types of MSCA, and often working closely with our Title 32 Active Duty National Guard personnel. I was de-conflicting operations on the border continuously.

One of the major projects I was responsible for was building the first six miles of wall on the Arizona-Mexican border. The project NCOIC, Chief Master Sergeant Johnny Burk, who was also a former Marine, superintended.

He was responsible in part for the design of the wall, assembling the necessary materials, equipment, and training of personnel once they'd been assigned to the wall project.

He supervised the personnel assigned to this major construction feat under quite undesirable conditions—and did an extraordinary job.

Johnny also served as superintendent for the Thunder Mountain project, during which equipment designed for deep-penetration examination of tractor-trailers and other equipment was designed, developed and tested. A very small package of anything could be detected amongst full loads of agricultural products or other shipped goods, quickly and effectively.

For the wall project, we started by digging a deep trench. Starting the wall well beneath ground level made tunneling under it considerably more difficult.

The wall was constructed of sections of military aircraft landing mat welded together, with a two-foot lip on the top angled toward Arizona. This meant that climbing over the wall to come into the U.S. was relatively easy in comparison with going back to Mexico.

One mile of wall extended in both directions from three ports of entry: Nogales, Douglas and Naco, forcing illegal entrants and smugglers to walk out into the desert for a mile in either direction, which significantly reduced the ease of crossing the border into the U.S. and returning home when they were ready.

Many of the illegal entrants entering the U.S. intended to work for a season and return home with a pocket full of money. The typical illegal entrant also routinely wired cash home to support their family and loved ones.

The Border Patrol was able to concentrate their personnel in some frequent crossing locations, with a light patrol of the wall, and great visibility in either direction.

The Chief of Police in Nogales noted that he wasn't sure that the wall had much of an impact on drug trafficking or illegal immigration, but it certainly had a significant impact on burglaries.

When I asked him why, he pointed at the lip on the wall and said, "How would you like to try getting a color TV over that?"

It was a back-breaking project, and the personnel assigned to it earned every penny they were paid on active duty.

The Mexicans despised the wall and showed their contempt openly. They would sometimes climb to the top of the wall, throw things at the JCNTF personnel, and yell obscenities.

The Mexican authorities demonstrated no support for our interdiction efforts and did nothing to enforce our alleged border sovereignty either to keep out illegal immigrants or drugs.

Their entire focus was on controlling what came back into Mexico—especially cash, weapons, and ammunition.

Most interesting was the low-tech solution to counter the wall. With some minor coordination, a Mexican could climb to the top of the wall with a ladder and lower a rope ladder down the American side.

Their pal would reel the ladder up, and when they were signaled at a future time or day, would throw it back over for the return trip home.

They anticipated little to no interference from Mexican law enforcement other than perhaps paying a bribe.

One very interesting project I became involved in was a comprehensive review of all the Southwest Ports of Entry (POEs) into the United States.

From April 16, to July 9, 1996 I visited each POE and met with the directors, beginning with Rudy Cole and Team Supervisor Roger Cutler in Nogales.

Equipped with a twelve-question checklist I determined how inspection personnel were organized, how contraband seizures were tracked, the percentage of seizures our personnel were involved in, and demographic information on personnel ages, average pay grades, and seniority.

I did a comparison of the average age and military grade of JCNTF personnel, and their overall effectiveness. I also observed how vehicles were selected for inspection, how the inspections were conducted (extensively), and observed numerous drug and other contraband seizures.

Inspections ranged from asking questions and taking a quick look in the vehicle, sometimes with a trained canine, to a significant disassembly of the vehicle, with tires removed and broken down, gas tanks pulled, seats and door panels removed, and more.

Trained canines played a significant role in the selection process, and as I would learn, the more experienced and trained the agent or JCNTF person and the canine, the greater their overall effectiveness.

I inspected the Nogales, Douglas, and San Luis POEs in Arizona first. I then proceeded to the POEs in San Ysidro, Otay Mesa, Tecate, and Calexico, California. I wrapped up the review at the El Paso POE in Texas. I found National Guard personnel to be highly effective at all the POEs.

A Marine Corporal assigned to a JTF-6 observation team shot and killed a Mexican American teenaged sheep herder who was out plinking with his .22 rifle. Believing he had come under fire, the corporal fired back with deadly accuracy. There was a public outcry.

Suddenly, our Coordinator felt great pressure to throttle back our armed presence on the border, and I needed to develop a strategy playbook that addressed this heightened concern.

I was employed in a "dual status." I was always a Federal employee, usually on unpaid military leave (I received federal pay 30 days per year in addition to my military pay).

I always had the option to pay a percentage of my military pay and buy back Federal retirement. This was a smart thing to do. I was surprised how few Federal Technicians serving on active duty seemed to do that.

One of the best pieces of advice I ever received was from my previous supervisor Col. Austin Graton (Army) who was serving as the HRO. While a Captain serving as SEEM, he showed me calculations on a white board in his office, demonstrating what a smart investment it was to always buy back my active duty for federal retirement.

I listened, and immediately bought back my Marine Corps time, at a small interest penalty for being "late," based on a calculation of years served and taxable base salary received. I picked up almost three years in the service calculation of lifetime federal retirement benefits for less than $500.

I bought back all military duty from that point on, wisely, and it applied directly to my later-received federal pension.

Had I not bought back my military time, I wouldn't have been eligible for an unreduced federal retirement annuity when I reached age 55 and was mandatorily separated and retired from military service.

I benefit every month from the wonderful advice he gave me. Thank you, Austin.

When you think you might be hearing valuable advice, listen.

Sometime in January 1995, when I was 45 years-old, it occurred to me that I had completed twenty creditable years of service, and at age 60 would be eligible for some sort of military retirement.

I calculated the number of "points" I had accumulated. I also researched the retirement formula and was impressed!

It was a little hard to imagine me attaining the ripe-old age of sixty, but I kept in mind that I'd been surprised when I made twenty, so anything seemed possible.

In the Fall of 1997, I decided I'd had enough active duty and requested reinstatement to federal employment. I was returned to the exact position I had left:

Headquarters Military Personnel Management Officer, where I was immediately promoted to Lieutenant Colonel.

I remained in that position until moving back to the Human Resources Office in 1999 after being gone from the HRO for more than seven years.

I learned staffing, and labor relations—and working with the unions to solve problems. I mediated issues routinely.

I also became directly involved in negotiations with the unions, negotiating the collective bargaining agreement (CBA) as a management representative with both unions, and introduced interest-based negotiation.

I supervised Human Resource office staff. My military assignment on the Joint Staff was Director of Human Resources.

Several officers and enlisted personnel had approached me with an idea. They wondered why the Arizona National Guard didn't have a state ribbon that reflected outstanding community service.

I worked closely with Chief Master Sergeant Eddie Ong, and Master Sergeant Bonnie Krentler to design and describe the Arizona National Guard Community Service Ribbon.

This ribbon would be awarded to any Arizona National Guard member who provided qualifying community service.

I made a presentation to the General Officers at their quarterly meeting, pointing out that this beneficial award was fully aligned with the mission of the Arizona National Guard, and it was approved.

By that time, I had the opportunity to attend both a private, forty-hour in-residence mediation training program with Ann Yellott and Associates in Tucson, a forty-hour mediation training program with the Arizona Attorney General's Office in Phoenix, and I had been mediating for the Attorney General since September, 1997 as a volunteer.

Over the course of almost thirteen years, thanks in part to my compressed work schedule which gave me every other Monday off, I conducted two-hundred and thirty volunteer mediations before starting as a staff mediator with the EEOC.

While still with the Guard, I planned, organized and implemented an internal mediation program, and began conducting a forty-hour mediation training program.

Soon, the State of Arizona, and then other State National Guards started requesting slots in my training.

Our program continued to gain attention, until finally, in September 2002 James C. Hise, Chief Counsel for the National Guard Bureau, reached out to me and I agreed to conduct mediation training at the national level in Washington, D.C. Staff Sergeant William "Bill" Aragon, then President of the union representing Army National Guard technician personnel in Arizona, agreed to join me and assist in the training.

My class had representation from twenty-four JAG offices in States and Territories, and we certified thirty-eight participants as mediators for the National Guard. It went well. My highest-ranking student was a Brigadier General. The mediation program was thus launched nationwide.

While providing training, program development, and mediation conferences for the National Guard, I was also developing a relationship with the City of Scottsdale.

I worked closely with Molly Edwards and Amy Lieberman to start a mediation program and conducted Scottsdale's first mediation under the new program based on a barking dog complaint.

MAJOR
KEVIN J. OSTERMAN

MILITARY PERSONNEL MANAGEMENT OFFICER
HEADQUARTERS
ARIZONA AIR NATIONAL GUARD

5636 EAST McDOWELL RD.
PHOENIX, AZ 85008-3495

(602) 267-2757
DSN: 853-2757
FAX: 267-2337

CAPT KEVIN J. OSTERMAN
Air Traffic Control Specialist

Arizona Air National Guard

Office Phone
(602) 267-2666
Autovon 853-2666

107th Tactical Control Squadron
2025 N. 52nd Street
Phoenix, Arizona 85008-3404

CAPTAIN
KEVIN J .OSTERMAN

EQUAL EMPLOYMENT MANAGER
SUPPORT PERSONNEL MANAGEMENT OFFICE
NATIONAL GUARD OF ARIZONA

5636 EAST McDOWELL RD.
PHOENIX, AZ 85008-3495

(602) 267-2786
DSN: 853-2786
FAX: 267-2688

ARIZONA NATIONAL GUARD
JOINT COUNTER
NARCOTICS TASK FORCE

KEVIN J. OSTERMAN
MAJOR
DIRECTOR OF OPERATIONS

5636 EAST McDOWELL ROAD
PHOENIX, ARIZONA 85008-3495
INTERNET: AZANGMAJOR@aol.com

PAGER: (602) 240-1332
(602) 267-2491/2503
DSN: 853-2491/2503
FAX: (602) 267-2474

Arizona National Guard
Joint Task Force

Lt Col KEVIN OSTERMAN
Director of Human Resources (DHR)

5636 E. McDowell Road
Phoenix, AZ 85008-3495
kevin.osterman@az.ngb.army.mil

602-267-2792
DSN: 853-2792
Fax: 602-267-2782

My last official photo taken in 2004

19

KARYN

In May 1989, I had been serving as the State Equal Employment Manager for three months. I had now fully sculpted my workplace plan of action with the National Guard and was in the process of implementing it.

I had a significant increase in speaking requests and decided to work on my public speaking skills. I signed up for a one-day program put on by Fred Pryor Seminars, entitled: "Making a Powerful Presentation" being conducted in a downtown Phoenix hotel.

I got to the hotel ballroom a little early, found a good seat, and put my garrison cap and course materials on the table. The huge ballroom was filling quickly.

I found some coffee and sat at the table, waiting for whatever was going to happen that morning. A very pretty reddish brunette sat down next to me and began reviewing her course materials. I did the same as I watched our table fill up.

Over the course of the day, we got to know each other. Her name was Karyn, and she worked as a legal assistant at the Attorney General's office in Phoenix. She had a nice smile and laughed when I joked.

The presenter asked if anyone had a funny speaking experience they wanted to share. I got up and told a story about when I took instructor training at Tyndall Air Force Base.

I had carefully prepared for a 1 ½ hour presentation on "setting up an intercept" for a class of young fighter pilots. This was my first class, and I was quite nervous.

I ended up teaching the entire program in forty-five minutes, and when I asked if there were any questions, was mostly met with a roomful of stupefied stares. Not a good first performance! I was video-taped.

For the next few years, every-once-in-a-while I would bump into a controller who would say that he or she, "knew me from somewhere." We'd do the usual overview of where we'd been assigned, and often drew a blank.

Once, while I was back at Tyndall Air Force Base for some advanced training, I paid a visit to the Fighter Weapons School where I'd received my instructor training. One of the NCOs I knew was still there and we got to talking.

He burst into laughter and told me that for at least a year, they had shown excerpts from the video of me racing through my course materials in a bumbling performance, complete with the dumbfounded pilot's expressions carefully captured on video.

This video was shown to provide an example of what *not* to do! As I told this story, I got a good laugh from the other participants, including Karyn.

Karyn and I talked a little about what I did for the Guard. I told her that I was currently trying to put some training together for a Communications Flight that was experiencing considerable turmoil, primarily due to internal communication difficulties.

They were riddled with anger, hostility and animosity over multiple perceived slights spanning the chain of command. Rumors, gossip, and the grapevine had them in near paralysis as they continued trying to accomplish their mission—and top leadership was considering replacing the commander.

I had been called in by the Group Commander and asked if there was anything I could do to help. Thus, I struggled trying to plan my approach and training.

Karyn told me that she had recently completed a college paper on *Gossip, Rumors and the Grapevine*. Her study analyzed how gossip and rumors were generated, their intended purpose, and how to counter them.

Her paper also included a good analysis on how the Grapevine worked. It sounded perfect. I asked her if she would share it, and she said she would be glad to. I gave her my address.

I received a manila envelope from her in the mail within a week. Inside was a copy of her excellent paper. Just exactly what I needed!

There was also a note attached asking me to not be confused by the name on the paper, that was her married name before she divorced.

She was newly divorced, single and wanted to make sure I knew it!

I sat and read the paper. It was very useable. I would be able to convert this into a training program for the unit, and it was an ideal approach for their current situation.

Using this material would enable me to approach and talk to them without any finger-pointing, and hopefully help them become functional again.

I called Karyn and asked her if she'd be interested in meeting me for dinner so we could discuss her research. She said she'd be glad to!

In October, 1989 we moved in together.

Amazingly, we were able to rent a big U-Haul truck, swing by my apartment in north Phoenix and empty it into the truck, swing by her apartment in central Phoenix and do the same with her apartment.

We then proceeded to the new apartment we had both selected on 52nd Street and Oak in Phoenix and unloaded the truck.

We finished at about midnight, dirty and exhausted, and needed to be back to work the following morning. Welcome to my world! Karyn must have been wondering what she had gotten herself into.

We started a joint-checking account, and every month we both deposited enough money to cover half the cost of rent, utilities, phone, and incidentals, plus a small surplus.

I was still feeling the effects of a previous relationship that had ended rather abruptly when I would not discuss marriage and in which we had no clear plan for sharing expenses.

I told Karyn that if we were still together in a year, I would be glad to at least discuss whether there was any potential.

I'd been single for twelve years and not looking to re-marry, but I'd learned that this could be the "third-rail" in a relationship. She nodded her assent, obviously not in a hurry either.

She had been married for about twelve years, and it hadn't been a good experience. She had left L.A., her health in tatters, with only what she could fit into her little Chevy Sprint and drove back to Arizona.

Her ex-husband had agreed that instead of selling everything and splitting the proceeds, he would provide her with a stipend for three years so she could complete her undergraduate degree and enter law school.

He made a few payments, met another woman, sold everything, and took off for Thailand.

Karyn had worked for a while in Prescott as a paralegal, then moved back to Phoenix where she went to work for the Attorney General's Office starting as a legal secretary and later moving up to a paralegal position.

She owed her Mom for a year's worth of utility payments and was still making payments on the Chevy. She was a trooper, making steady progress toward her goal of completing college, despite her set-backs. She was working during the day and taking college classes at night.

We had a lot of fun together. She had no exposure to the military and asked many questions. We spent time at Hannagan's Meadow up in the White Mountains and had a wild experience on the Black River. We also travelled together and enjoyed preparing numerous delicious and fun meals, including several "naked dinners" by candlelight.

Early in our relationship, she attended several military dining out events with me. Anyone who has ever attended a Military Dining Out knows that it's a formal event with a lot of ritual. For our first Dining Out, she selected a beautiful gown.

I purchased her some earrings and a necklace made with silver and black onyx that complimented her gown perfectly. I assembled my mess dress for the event.

She was beautiful and I was presentable.

On a lark, I decided to get a good professional photo of us dressed in our finest. I made a reservation at Duke Studios over on 7th Avenue just south of McDowell Road, and we swung by there to get our picture taken.

It was one of the best ideas I ever had. I still treasure that picture and smile every time I look at it!

She pursued her bachelor's in communication with Arizona State University while continuing her work at the Attorney General's office, and I continued to try resolving the plethora of EEO issues at the Guard.

Time went by quickly, and enjoyably!

Karyn had a Tarot deck, and we spent a fair number of evenings walking through the deck with her interpretations of the various cards played.

She knew of a fellow named Roger von Oech from Menlo Park, California who was considered to be one of the leading gurus of creative thinking at the time and purchased a new product he had just released called the *Creative Whack Pack*. It was based on the theory explained by Roger that sometimes you needed a "whack on the side of the head" to jolt you out of habitual thought patterns that prevent you from looking at what you're doing in a fresh way.

Soon after being exposed to Roger's "Pack," it occurred to me that maybe the good whack I'd gotten on my head when I was run over while driving my motorcycle near Roosevelt Lake back in 1980 might have actually been a good thing.

The deck contained 64 cards divided into four 16-card suits: Explorer, Artist, Judge, and Warrior. He felt that these four suits represented the four roles or ways of thinking in the creative process. He had written two interesting books entitled: *A Whack on the Side of the Head* and *A Kick in the Seat of the Pants*. We spent many evenings randomly selecting a card from the deck, reading it, and answering the challenging question it posed.

For example, one of the Warrior cards (#54) was entitled: *Put a Lion in Your Heart*. It briefly quoted a well-known bull fighter who opined on courage, noting that it takes no courage to fight a bull when you're not afraid, but when you are afraid and face the bull anyhow, that takes courage. The question was posed: "What puts a lion in your heart? I looked Karyn in the eye and said, "At this moment, you."

This deck of cards occupied several of our evenings, was quite interesting, and we continually learned more about each other.

I looked at the calendar one morning and realized that we'd been living together for more than a year! I had made a commitment to discuss the possibility of marriage if we were still together.

That night when she came home from school, I reminded her of my pledge. She responded without any excitement as she unpacked her school stuff. She was in no hurry to consider marriage as she struggled to work and go to school. I understood, having been there myself.

A couple of days later when I walked into the apartment, I spotted several apartment brochures laying on the table. Someone was moving! When she came in that night, I asked her who.

She explained that she really needed her space right now. She had enjoyed living with me but wanted to be able to focus more on school. I understood.

She found the apartment she wanted, we split the money in the joint account, and I helped her move. Her car was now paid off, she had a small IRA started, and she had settled her debt with her mom. We continued to date.

Then she came down with mono. I suppose that would have been a perfectly good time to distance myself, but instead I made her some soup and babied her a little bit.

We continued dating, and sometime after her lease was up and she had accomplished her goal of graduating from ASU, she moved back in with me.

I still had the apartment on 52nd Street. My landlords, a husband and wife, were wonderful, and the apartment was within an easy bicycle ride to my office. The 52nd Street gate into Papago Military Reservation was open then, and it was almost a straight shot from my place at Oak and 52nd Street to my office in the Headquarters Building.

Major General Owens also rode his bike to work sometimes, and we rode together several times to or from the office, always joining up by coincidence.

The move back was quick and easy for Karyn. Much easier than our initial blending of the two apartments!

We both wanted a dog and set out studying the breeds. Once we decided on a Labrador, we learned about how to select a puppy and found a breeder who appealed to us, located on the Bar-K Ranch way out on the west side of town, so we drove out and talked with the owner, Barbara.

We really liked two of her adult labs, both with lovely dispositions; a male named Cubby Bear who was a champion several times over, and a female named Terra Bear.

Terra Bear was medium-sized, had a pretty face, and was gentle. Cubby Bear was bigger, with a square face, direct gaze, and an even disposition. He was all boy and seemed very intelligent—playful and able to open the latch on the gate at will!

The breeder told us she had just bred them and believed the female to be pregnant. I gave her a deposit of $200 and asked her for first pick of a female. She agreed.

Terra Bear was indeed pregnant, and as soon as she had her litter, the breeder contacted us. We began driving out to her place every Saturday and playing with the puppies.

Terra Bear tolerated us fine, and by the seventh week we had selected our girl, named her Ayla Bear, and took her home.

Around that time, I started to notice that home prices were dropping, as were interest rates. Although after I had sold my first house, I didn't think I ever wanted to own a house again, but it seemed foolish not to. I thought it would be nice to have a yard again, too.

We decided to first look for the neighborhood we wanted to live in. We selected the "Hy-View" area in south-west Scottsdale and began watching for a house.

We spotted a 1,500-square foot brick, 3-bedroom ranch-style house with a pool in the back yard. It needed considerable work from top-to-bottom, and we struck a good deal.

The couple who owned it were going through some tough times, and we elected to look the other way when they remained in the house for a full week after the closing.

They left us a considerable mess when they did leave, including a large, cheap trash bag filled with rotting food in the back yard, that tore and spilled the putrid contents when I tried picking it up!

As Clare Boothe Luce once said: "No good deed goes unpunished."

We moved in, and I immediately installed a doggie-door to the backyard. We gradually repaired or renovated everything, starting with the pool.

We removed the grass and put quartz-gravel in the backyard, planted cactus, and dug a pond, which we stocked with goldfish that grew and reproduced. They would eat fish pellets from our hands.

We also stocked our pond with mosquito fish and lily pads. We installed a covered swinging bench and misting system. Our own little paradise.

I asked Karyn to marry me and she accepted my proposal. We set the date for April 16th, the day after tax-day, joking that we'd never forget our anniversary date. We started shopping for the venue we wanted for the wedding.

One of the churches we visited, a Unity Church in Tempe with a lovely female pastor named Kathy McCall, appealed to us the most. We secured her services, planned a lunch for twenty-five of our friends and family, and reserved a room at the Tempe Mission Palms.

My brother Brian flew out to be my best man, along with my mom and sister, Wendy.

My friend from the officer's academy, Jim Yeagley, and his wife Sharee drove down from Great Falls, Montana, and several of our friends in the valley also joined us, including my friend Ron Marusiak and his wife Barbara, and Dick Drinen and his wife Sue. Karyn's father Tod and his wife Beverley, my son Daniel, Karyn's brother and sister-in-law Rick and Annette, her cousin Linda, and step-sister Ryndi also attended.

When Reverend McCall pronounced us, "Man and wife," Karyn and I kissed, turned to step off the raised alter, and Karyn skipped for several feet as she held my hand. What a wonderful ceremony; what a great day!

That night, Karyn and I settled into our honeymoon suite at the hotel. We had fun wandering around downtown Tempe, had a nice dinner, and returned to the room, ready to lounge in the large jacuzzi-style tub.

I poured a bath, and Karyn dumped a small bottle of bubble-bath into the whirring water. Within seconds, the bathroom was filled with bubbles nearly to the ceiling before we noticed, and I ran to shut it off!

We both stood naked in the bathroom doorway waiting for the bubbles to subside, laughing so hard that it hurt!

On our first date at the Fish Market, Karyn had told me about her desire to someday attend law school. After we married, I had gone on active duty as a Major, and was making fairly good money. We talked about law school again and began saving money toward it.

One day, she came home complaining about a brand-new "baby" attorney who was barking orders. She was a competent paralegal by then and felt a certain resentment. She did not want to be the one always taking orders, especially from someone younger and less experienced in certain matters. It was time for her to advance. I said, "Ok, let's get you in law school."

We knew we could only afford for her to attend Arizona State University on a pay-go basis, and at the time, only 25% of the starting class were in-state, resident students.

She took a course designed to help her do well on the LSAT, which she did, then we assembled her application, to include a wonderful letter of recommendation from the then-Attorney General, Grant Woods, an alumnus of the ASU School of Law. When Karyn approached him with her request, he suggested that she draft some ideas for him, so I happily assisted her in writing, editing and polishing a letter for Grant's signature.

She received a letter back from the school congratulating her on being accepted to the class of 2000. She resigned her position with the Attorney General's office and started law school in the Fall of 1997.

At the same time, I took mediation training with the Attorney General's Office, and began mediating for them as a volunteer.

Karyn's legal career included working for a well-established patent attorney, and more than five years at the Frank Lloyd Wright Foundation in Taliesin West serving as in-house counsel.

She also took the reins of my mediation business after I went to work for the EEOC and operated Hy-View Mediation Services, LLC.

In addition, she served on the board of the Yavapai County Bar Association, ultimately serving as President in 2015. She is now a retired member of the Arizona State Bar.

Our relationship and our love for each other has developed and deepened over the years. We have grown to love each other madly, deeply, and passionately.

She is my friend, lover, muse—an excellent planner and executor of plans, and my best and kindest critic. She is totally reliable. I trust her in every way and want only the best for her.

On rare occasion, I am miserable as she justifiably applies the silken lash of her displeasure.

Her household responsibilities include: House Commander, Operations Officer, Spender-in-Chief, In-House Counsel, I.T. and Security Manager, Editor-in-Chief, and Household Standardization and Evaluation Officer.

She takes very good care of herself and has learned to be a good shot with rifle, shotgun, and pistol. She is also skilled on horseback and with a fishing rod.

She enjoys the outdoors and is tremendously fun to hunt and camp with. She skillfully flew both planes we owned, is an exceptional mediator, and a world-class playmate. Most importantly, she is my most trusted advisor, and she makes me want to be the man I ought to be.

In April 2019, we celebrated our 25th anniversary and threw a party for 50 of our closest friends at the Clubhouse here in Mountain Club. Sister Kerry and daughter Tori put it together for us.

Karyn and me headed for our first dining out

20

VOCATION

I had a calling. I suppose you could call it an epiphany.

The exact time or date eludes me and seems indistinguishable within the timeline of my life.

The last fight I was involved in was at a bar in Great Falls, Montana shortly after graduating from the officer's academy.

I was driving cross-country with my son and then girlfriend Angie and stopped to visit my friend and running partner from the officer's academy, Jim Yeagley. We went out for pizza in a local bar.

Two guys got into a fist fight. They were throwing punches and kicking each other, and it looked like they were fighting in our direction.

My girlfriend Angie and my son Daniel were seated at my table with Jim and his wife Sharee. When one of the fighters bumped the chair next to me, I jumped up and threw myself between the two combatants.

I pushed them apart and ordered both to sit, which they did. I looked at both and pointedly said, "Knock it off."

The bartender sent a pitcher of beer to our table, and a glass of root beer for my son. This was a significant event in my transition from warrior to peace maker.

My time mediating disputes at the Guard, and my volunteer mediations at the Attorney General's Office led me to a point where I realized I drew significant satisfaction from assisting people in resolving disputes.

I realized that, somehow, I had transitioned from warrior to peacemaker. I liked how it felt.

My professional reason for mediating had originally been based on desperation. My reason for mediating as a volunteer was purely for personal satisfaction.

It was not until I applied for and got selected as a staff mediator for the Equal Employment Opportunity Commission that I came to realize how significant those many professional and volunteer mediation conferences had been.

As I began to realize the important role that mediation had in my professional life, and the world around me, I discussed it with Karyn. At the time, Karyn was interning with the Legal Department for the City of Scottsdale, in her third year of law school.

She started talking to me about the need for a mediation program for the City of Scottsdale. She encouraged me to help.

That was the first time I met Amy Lieberman, an up-and-coming attorney (and gorgeous red head) working for the City in the Legal Department.

Amy was also extremely interested in the potential benefits of a robust mediation program. I worked closely with Molly Edwards in the Planning Department while I was a Planning Commissioner, and it was Molly who worked with City leadership and launched the program.

My first mediation for the City involved a barking dog complaint. A young man contacted Molly in the Planning Department and asked what the remedies were for a barking dog next door that was disrupting his sleep.

Molly invited him to try mediation, and his next-door neighbor (who he had never met) agreed as well. They met me at a small police precinct building after hours. We all arrived at the same time, and I spotted them both talking at the base of the front doorsteps.

The young guy was handsome and seemed pleasant, and the dog's owner was an attractive young lady. I sensed something developing between them.

The agreement that I facilitated included him coming over for dinner to get to know the dog better and walking the neighborhood together with the dog to meet their neighbors, to let them know the barking dog situation was being dealt with.

This seemed like a reasonable thing for them to do, as other neighbors had just started to complain. There was an obvious attraction between the two of them, and I've always wondered how well the agreement worked out for them, and for their neighbors.

Since that time, I have assisted numerous organizations in developing and implementing conciliation and mediation programs, and trained hundreds of mediators.

Mediation was not "second nature" to me. As a young man I believed that the best tools for resolution involved either a hasty retreat, my fists and feet, whatever weapon I was carrying, or explosives.

I stopped fighting and started listening.

Listening is key. So is love.

As a mediator, I recommend remaining flexible, and being prepared to realize that you may be the only adult in the room.

Don't get fixated on what you think the best outcome is and take whatever happens in stride.

My three cardinal rules for mediation are:

1. Maintain control of the mediation process.

2. Remember that your purpose as a mediator is to assist the parties in achieving a mutually acceptable and achievable agreement.

3. Get the parties out of their positions, into their issues, interests, and concerns, and keep them there.

21

COMMUNITY

One of the National Guard projects that I became involved in at its inception was "Project Challenge."

I was working as the Headquarters Military Personnel Management Officer and learned that a concept was afoot and building within the National Guard to deal with dropouts early and snatch them from the jaws of iniquity.

As the discussion resulted in funding, and the States started to receive funds, the Arizona National Guard began organizing a program called *Project Challenge*. I decided to become involved.

As various officers with strong academic backgrounds rotated through the leadership position as Commandant, I played differing roles, including sitting on the student elimination board.

When students committed grievous infractions that could result in being expelled, a board was conducted.

Some kids got kicked out, and some were disciplined, mostly for using drugs, stealing, and fighting.

The primary intent of the program was to work with "at risk" dropouts, and assist them in getting a high school diploma or G.E.D.

I believe that many legislators looked to the military as the best possible solution for this burgeoning problem, and they launched funding for this purpose.

Not only did our Project Challenge succeed in assisting dropouts to achieve the primary intent of the program, this project also helped these kids in their transition to adulthood, learning how to live and work with respect for those around them.

I didn't feel that being a dropout myself was helpful. The rules had changed dramatically. When I dropped out of high school, I went right into the Marines, and ultimately received a lifetime of benefits. I've never regretted my decision to be a Marine.

The current requirement for enlistment into any of the services was a high school diploma, or a G.E.D. plus fifteen college credit hours.

Being a high school dropout had become a serious impediment to any future development more than ever, and certainly not something to be held as an example. I rarely shared the fact that I was a high school dropout with anyone.

I received a phone call from Scottsdale Mayor Sam Campana. She wanted to learn more about Project Challenge and had been provided with my name. I took her on a tour of the campus and introduced her to the Commandant.

I really liked Sam, and we "clicked." She was inquisitive, artistic, articulate, well educated, and fun to be around.

The students at Project Challenge were nearing graduation and were a sight to behold. These former "at risk" kids who had originally wandered into the project a mess, were marching, singing, and performing well in the classroom.

They all looked clean, healthy, groomed, and well-rested. Many had received their G.E.D. or high school diploma or were on the verge of getting it—and they all seemed ready to take on the world! Sam was very impressed.

We got to know each other better.

After Sam was reelected, she contacted me and asked me to serve on a new task force that had been formed by City Council, and I agreed.

There was a growing problem with gang activity in Scottsdale, and City Council wanted a better assessment of the problem, as well as some recommendations to combat this burgeoning issue proactively.

The "Mayors Gang Task Force" was a very good experience.

Almost immediately after we wrapped up the task force, Sam called me and asked me to serve on the Citizens Budget and Bond Review Commission. I agreed.

The Budget and Bond Review Commission provided me the opportunity to really learn about the financial innards of Scottsdale.

We reviewed past bond performance, financials, ratings, current and projected debt, and recommended a good bond proposal to the City Council.

I made the observation that the cost of a properly structured bond proposal designed to improve and maintain a major infrastructure project, such as flood control or a needed road-widening, is best shared amongst all beneficiaries.

It was approved by the voters.

As we were wrapping up our work on the Commission, Sam approached me again and suggested that I sit on the Planning Commission.

In the course of my time on the Budget and Bond Commission, I felt I had learned a considerable amount about planning and zoning and agreed to serve on the Planning Commission.

Sam nominated me. At the next City Council meeting, the proposed Planning Commission candidates were reviewed and discussed. Only one Council member, George Zracket objected vociferously to my nomination.

Fortunately, George was thought to be a "bomb-thrower," and seemed to have little if any support on the Council. In fact, several Council members had taken a dislike to George and tended to oppose any of his proposed legislation or notions outright for that reason alone.

He had his own candidate for the vacant position on the Commission. His argument, that I was already seated on a Commission and therefore ineligible, fell on deaf ears.

The Council knew that the current Citizens Budget and Bond Review Commission was coming to an end after we presented our bond proposal and supporting information.

I was appointed to a three-year term, which I completed. I got to know George better later, and actually liked him. He had his opinions, but his intentions were good.

Meanwhile, an issue was brewing in South Scottsdale, involving the former Los Arcos shopping mall that got my attention.

A growing discontent was looming over the proposed use of the rapidly deteriorating mall, and future development proposed by a developer, Steve Ellman.

Steve was extremely wealthy and successful. No matter how this deal ended up going, he seemed confident that he was going to make money.

It started with a plan to build a new hockey arena for the Phoenix Coyotes. As a member of the Planning Commission, I voted for approval of the arena.

Numerous citizens came to the Commission meeting and raised holy hell against this proposed use. I sympathized with them, not being a hockey or sports fan, but still felt the need to support a legitimate use of this miserable deteriorating property.

At this point in time, it was my perception that Ellman was starting to get in over his head, as costs soared, and this original investment started to look like an overreach. Los Arcos Mall continued to deteriorate.

The Coyotes tired of the controversy and struck a last-minute "midnight" deal with the City of Glendale to build the arena there instead. Scottsdale really dodged a bullet on that one!

Ultimately, I believe that the arena deal cost the City of Glendale huge gobs of revenue that I felt could have been used much more effectively elsewhere.

Ellman began tantalizing many residents in South Scottsdale with the thought that he was in the process of attracting a Walmart to the site of the crumbling Los Arcos mall.

My research led me to believe that Walmart didn't build on property owned by others, and there was no way they were going to purchase that land from Steve Ellman based on the amount he apparently now needed just to break even.

I didn't like or dislike Ellman; I recognized that this wasn't personal, as a developer he simply wanted to make as much from this deal as he could.

As the deal swung from a hockey arena to a Walmart, people who had stated publicly how much they despised Ellman started supporting him loudly. Citizens wept before the Council. They made threats, and they heartily supported the new plan.

As a Planning Commissioner, my seat on the dais was the farthest to the left as I faced the attendees seated in the Kiva. After I was elected to City Council, I had the exact same seat, and generally found myself looking at the same folks from a different perspective!

All the controversy was captured on Channel 11, the public access channel, for both Planning Commission and City Council meetings.

Los Arcos had become a real liability for seated Council Members as the citizen outcry became louder and louder, magnified many times by the *Arizona Republic* and the *Scottsdale Tribune*. Soon, at least three current council members were "skating on thin ice."

I was recruited into the effort to stop Ellman's latest venture, and I began circulating petitions and speaking to groups of citizens on the subject.

One of the "Stop Ellman" committee members suggested that I run for City Council. I discussed this move with Karyn, and we both agreed I should try it.

There were three projected vacancies on City Council, plus a fourth half-term became available when a seated Council Member, Cynthia Lucas, decided to run for Mayor. I filed my papers and began circulating petitions.

Collecting signatures on petitions is a painful process, most certainly not for the faint of heart. Karyn and I both learned to ignore some of the terrible things people would say to us.

I became aware of how ignorant the average citizen was when it came to how government did its business, and how it operated.

I memorized a 3-minute and 5-minute speech using mnemonic devices and used each speech frequently. I would get up at citizen forums, where I was told, "You have three minutes," and wrap my speech up right at the 3-minute mark. The same for when I had five minutes.

My earlier study of self-hypnosis came into play as I learned my material.

While with the National Guard, a group of us formed a Toastmasters Club we named the "Guard Gambits." It was great fun and an excellent learning experience. Karyn and I both earned our "Competent Toastmaster" qualification, and it was invaluable. I could comfortably get up and speak at an event with truly little preparation.

I was still working fulltime as a National Guard Officer, so I carefully researched the Hatch Act to make sure I would not be in violation. City politics are non-partisan. I never campaigned in uniform or used government equipment.

I raised money and spoke at every event available, including candidate forums organized by various citizen groups, and a forum initiated by the *Scottsdale Republic* newspaper which was shown on Cable Channel Eleven.

It was a wonderful experience, and the vote was close between the top four candidates. I was elected to the 2-year seat.

As a seated Council Member, I supported an agreement formulated between our City Manager Jan Dolan and Arizona State University to create a center where innovation and future technology were aligned with big resources—a place where start-ups could sit shoulder-to-shoulder with Fortune 500 Companies.

Known as "Sky Song," aka: Scottsdale ASU Innovation Center, it was an exceptionally clean industry to be placed at the very important intersection of McDowell and Scottsdale Road.

At the time, I also envisioned a light rail spur from Tempe to the intersection of McDowell and Scottsdale Road.

This idea was loudly booed by a downtown merchant's group who didn't want the "train" anywhere near their businesses, and viewed any expansion of the rail line toward Scottsdale as creeping osmosis. It got no traction.

As a Council Member, I knew the Miracle Mile auto dealerships, and the auto dealerships on Frank Lloyd Wright Boulevard produced a whopping seven percent of the total revenue collected by the City. Talk about a "golden goose!"

I thought that placing thousands of potential customers directly across the street in Sky Song was an excellent idea.

Many citizens had fallen for the story that Walmart was potentially going to be built there (which I knew wasn't true) and howled loudly at the prospect of a major property that offered little or no retail.

These same citizens overlooked the fact that they had long ago taken their shopping dollars elsewhere and were in many ways responsible for the demise of the original mall. They were also slowly killing the only grocery store near that intersection by taking their business elsewhere. Talk about being fickle!

After carefully examining the possible uses of this property, I included stability in my force-field analysis. I wanted to establish a solid foundation for future development.

In the end, Ellman probably broke even, or made a few bucks, but SkySong was launched. So far, since 2005, ASU SkySong has built every proposed phase on or ahead of schedule and has kept its promise to revitalize South Scottsdale.

A couple of Council Members who strongly opposed this important project became supporters.

Being on City Council was a wild ride. I enjoyed it for the most part but grew weary of the mean pettiness I encountered daily. The City Council meetings could get pretty crazy. People could get up and say whatever they wanted to for three minutes at the beginning of the meeting.

During one of the Council meetings, Lyle Wertz, a local activist got up and attacked me for an alleged vote I had participated in for money directed to the Frank Lloyd Wright Foundation, and that my wife directly benefitted from this, as did I.

He was followed by Henry Becker, who repeated the same allegation.

After they had both spoken, I pointed out that the funding they were so upset about occurred before I joined the City Council and provided them with the date of the Council action.

I approached Lyle after the meeting and invited him to come to my office. I asked him who had fed him that line of crap.

Initially he wouldn't divulge the source, stating only that it was another Council Member who was in the know on such matters. I pointed out that the information he had been provided was untrue, putting him in an uncomfortable situation unfairly.

After much prodding and cajoling, he finally told me who it was; it was Jim Lane.

Much later, after I had lost my second election and was up north elk hunting, I walked out of a steak house in Flagstaff and saw Henry Becker admiring my friend's Kings Ranch F-150 pickup truck.

I approached him and offered my hand. He seemed startled, took it, and we spoke. I asked him who had fed him that line of crap about my wife. Without hesitation, he told me it was Jim Lane.

It is one thing to go after me, and quite another to attack my wife's employment. I realized how much I despised Jim Lane's Machiavellian antics that the *Scottsdale Republic* seemed to embrace.

Another Planning Commissioner named Betty Drake had also been elected to City Council. I had greatly admired Betty's work on the Planning Commission. She held the distinction of being a professional, degreed, urban designer, and I believed when it came to urban planning, she was by far and away the most knowledgeable on the council. I had been impressed by her when serving together as Planning Commissioners.

One of the looming issues facing the council was the lack of ethical guidelines, and I fully supported the idea of developing some guidelines for our council, and future councils to work within.

I soon got wind that Jim Lane and several of his supporters were developing a set of standards that would essentially force my friend Betty to resign from the council, based on her professional activities as an urban planner. But Betty was a very ethical person. While on the Planning Commission she had consistently recused herself if she had even slight suspicion that she had a conflict.

I'm not sure exactly why they wanted her off the council, but I generally suspected that it had something to do with her being a woman, a registered Democrat, or both.

Although the council was officially "non-partisan," politics were constantly at play, and the Republican Party wanted desperately to "purify" the council, on the notion that City Council was a stepping-stone to partisan elections, such as the State Legislature.

I approached our mayor, Mary Manross, and shared my concerns with her. She was the only other woman or Democrat on the council and was already feeling back-pressure from the Republicans.

I told her I wanted to be placed on the agenda, to discuss and agree on ethical standard guidelines for council members.

My standards wouldn't prevent someone highly knowledgeable in urban planning such as Betty from serving on council, as they could simply recuse themselves if there was a conflict of interest. She agreed.

Based on my efforts, the draconian language was removed from the proposed ethical standards.

The *Scottsdale Republic* seemed charmed by Lane, and from that point on, any support the newspapers provided seemed to be eroding quickly—especially the Editorial Board.

As my first 2-year term came to an end, I decided to run for reelection. It turned out to be a bitter campaign, and a questionable decision on my part. I encountered a level of viciousness I had never experienced before from a small clutch of embittered ne'er-do-wells, thugs, and bullies who I had refused to support.

One of the candidates running for office, Nan Nesvig had a personal issue that she wanted to tackle from the dais as a Council Member.

The issue was a water treatment facility on the canal close to the home she and her husband owned.

It had been there for years, silently treating water for arsenic removal that, after treatment, went to Paradise Valley. Operators of the facility proposed replacing it with a newer, "greener" facility that had a higher capacity and was much more efficient.

It also had a slightly larger footprint and was a bit taller.

Nan and her husband strongly opposed it because it impacted their view from their property.

A great deal was done to mitigate the impact of the new proposed facility, but nothing the developer did was found acceptable by the Nesvigs.

A website was launched that cast aspersions in many directions, including at seated council members.

A fellow council member, Bob Littlefield, who I would end up pitted against in a bitter runoff election, approached me with the idea of contesting her petitions for council. He was certain that she didn't have enough valid signatures, and I believed he was correct.

I didn't care much one way or the other about Nan. I didn't like her style, and I felt that her position against the water treatment facility was mistaken and petty, but I really didn't think she had a chance of being elected, especially after her performance at her one and only candidate forum.

Bob managed to recruit both Councilman Wayne Ecton and me to challenge her petitions and marshalled a small group to assist. Little did I know what a shit-storm this would create, especially after the *Scottsdale Republic* began viewing this as a major issue for whatever reason.

Rule: newspapers don't care about the mess they help create. Their view is the bigger the mess the greater the opportunity to benefit from it.

We attracted the support of several entities, and I reported everything required under campaign finance law.

Somewhere along the way, Nan began drawing support from some of the ugliest, most awful characters in Scottsdale, several of whom actually participated in a "no integrity" campaign against me during my effort to get reelected.

All candidates had agreed to not erect political signs, and I soon discovered that the hideous signs they had placed in various locations were garnering more votes than they were costing me. In a gesture of good will and chivalry, Bob Littlefield publicly called on the perps to take the signs down, and they were immediately removed. I was profoundly disappointed.

Following the legally prescribed means, we succeeded in having Nan Nesvig removed from the ballot. She was clearly short of valid signatures on her petitions, and, to the best of my knowledge, never able to run successfully in future elections for City Council.

The *Republic* started painting me as the ring leader for kicking Nan off the ballot, and wily Bob did nothing to dispel that growing untrue belief.

I believe that the *Republic* knew otherwise but seemed to like the bounce they were getting. In reality, although Bob had been the "ringleader" amongst the three of

203

us, none of us were the actual organizers of the petition challenge, and neither Wayne nor I ever exposed Bob.

One of their columns actually portrayed Nan as being akin to Joan of Arc! Most surprisingly of all, Nesvig endorsed Littlefield prior to the runoff election! Talk about a patsy.

Bob, Wayne, and I took a pounding from the *Republic* in varying degrees. Ultimately, the *Republic* provided me with an endorsement. Unfortunately, the endorsement was too little, too late. Mail-in ballots had already been mailed to voters, and their endorsement was too late to have much of an influence on the run-off. I lost by less than a thousand votes.

Wayne Ecton was reelected in the primary, and later, over dinner he expressed regret that he hadn't supported me by correcting the record when people started believing the misinformation that Littlefield and the *Republic* seemed to both be dishing out.

Wayne was very worn down by the controversy and just did not want any more drama in his life. I told him I fully understood. Overall, my time on Scottsdale City Council and failed reelection attempt were good experiences.

There is no better way to find out who your friends really are than when you lose an election. When you win, everybody loves you!

Rule: don't ever expect anyone else to fight your fight for you.

I wasn't quite done with getting involved with controversial issues. While seated on Council, I had voted in favor of a dust-control ordinance for the city that put us in compliance with guidance already enacted by both the County of Maricopa and the State of Arizona.

It was a well-crafted ordinance and a necessity if we planned to continue effectively functioning as a well-run city.

I became aware that some local ranchers had begun to take exception to certain provisions in the ordinance that included a signage requirement. They greatly resented that they would be required to either treat their dirt roads for dust control, or place signs that said, "5 mph, please."

This was actually a non-issue. The roads, located on private land, would have not been subject to legal enforcement of the requested speed. The City just wanted them to behave like good neighbors.

They hired young, good looking ladies to circulate petitions, and they had a champion on City Council, Tony Nelssen, who owned land that would be subject to the ordinance.

Tony was a big tall rancher who also taught photography part-time at Scottsdale Community College and had been involved over the years with several business ventures in Scottsdale. He could be seen riding his big mule in city events, such as the Parada del Sol.

He was viewed by many as "Mr. Scottsdale." He had lost his first election, running against me.

As soon as I got wind of what the ranchers were trying to do, I contacted my friend Rick Kidder at the Chamber of Commerce. Although I was no longer on Council, I could see that this proposed recall was a very bad move for the City of Scottsdale, and potentially ruinous.

It would make us pariahs in the eyes of the County and State, and we would be subject to sanctions.

Under current law, if Scottsdale was out of compliance with the State legislation, very significant amounts of revenue would have been withheld. No developer would be allowed to legally turn a spade of soil, because no building permits could be legally issued.

No potholes could be legally repaired on City streets, and no work could legally be done on infrastructure.

I also believed that this ordinance couldn't be legally recalled because it was an administrative, not legislative action. Rick agreed with me, and so did our attorney, Tom Irvine. Ultimately, Judge Peter Swann agreed with us, too.

It was a brutal court fight, and if my name wasn't already dirt, the *Arizona Republic* set out to make sure it was. One editorial bemoaned the fact that once again, I was denying the public their "voice." In a future editorial, they even called me "sleazy."

Later, Tony died in office from an unexpected bout with a blood cancer that killed him quickly, and his term was finished by his wife Marge. The City of Scottsdale voted to name the horse arena at West World after Tony.

While on City Council, I made several close and lasting friendships with some wonderful people to include Mayor Sam Campana, Mayor Mary Manross and Councilwoman Betty Drake.

Working with Jan Dolan was an excellent experience. Her red hair was cut in an interesting fashion, with spikes and highlights, which seemed to disturb other Council members. She was smart, very quick on the uptake, and I thought she was a fantastic City Manager.

Working with her Assistant City Manager, Natalie Lewis, was an equally wonderful experience. Natalie went out of her way to assist me. She had a beauty that radiated from within and she spoke very proudly of her family.

I also enjoyed getting to know one of our local attorneys, John Berry, better. I enjoyed his presentations when I was a planning commissioner and councilman. He was a scotch aficionado, and I am too. We enjoyed many fine scotches together, including my all-time favorite, The Classic Cask of The Millennium Rare Scotch Whiskey Aged 35 years. Thank you, John.

I greatly enjoyed serving on the Planning Commission with Margaret Dunn. She was a fun companion on the dais, and really livened up the meetings. She owns the trolley in Scottsdale, is ultra-smart, and a real wit.

I was totally fed up with Scottsdale after that little fight. Karyn and I decided to sell our house and move on. At that point, I had been retired for a year from the National Guard.

We had a beautiful little Cessna 150, and no other obligations. We owned everything outright. Karyn still worked for the Frank Lloyd Wright Foundation, with her office located at Taliesin West in northern Scottsdale.

I was a lifetime Republican, though I had voted for Democrats or Independents in the past simply because I considered them to be the best candidate.

After an intimate peek into the inner-workings of the Republican party machine in Scottsdale, I began to feel repelled by what seemed like an indifferent view of the less-fortunate—and they had proven to be no friend of mine, clearly and inappropriately siding with Bob during the run-off.

The party leaders appeared to be looking right through a rather significant portion of the population—largely minorities, who were still reaching for the American dream. In many instances it seemed like the Republican Party coldly did not view their wants and needs as legitimate.

Disgusted, I quit the Republican Party and registered as an Independent.

In addition, Karyn and I had already agreed that if we did not see an improvement in air quality within five years, we would move.

There had been no improvement. In fact, the air quality seemed to be slipping even more.

We put our house on the market and sold it for our asking price to the first person who viewed it. Goodbye, Scottsdale, and thank you for the experiences we had while living there.

"When once you have tasted flight, you will forever walk the earth with your eyes turned skyward, for there you have been, and there you will always long to return." (Leonardo da Vince)

22

FLYING

The best decision I have ever made was to marry Karyn. The second best was to learn how to fly. There is nothing else quite like it in this world.

I hope that as I transition from this mortal coil to whatever awaits me, I feel the sense of flight—my wheels lifting from the ground one last time as I pull the yoke back gently. I have loved it that much.

I never wanted to make flying a career. My eyesight wasn't good enough to qualify for military pilot or aviator. But I was able to pass the Class One medical with eyesight correction when I was a controller and never had a problem with the Class Three medical as a pilot.

As a Close Air Support Controller and Weapons Controller, I'd controlled thousands of military aircraft in numerous different scenarios, but other than a brief period where I'd flown gliders, I didn't fly—until I met Captain Tom Braswell.

Tom was a former Air Force Flight Instructor who ended up serving with me in the Arizona Air Guard for a brief period of time.

I was sitting at a radar scope in the darkroom of the 107th one day, just wrapping up a mission, when Tom and I got to talking about flying. Tom said, "You need to learn how to fly!" He then made a good case.

I'd been a Weapons Controller for a little more than a year. Being a pilot in my career field could be an asset. He was a licensed instructor pilot, and he'd teach me how to fly, cheap. We started flying, and he soloed me quickly.

We went out one morning to do take offs and landings again at Falcon Field. I was at the point where he usually didn't need to say much. He might ask me a question, such as, "Ok, when you turn final, what will your airspeed be?"

I'd answer the question and he'd talk about airspeed briefly or tell me a flying story that involved airspeed, often while we were on "final," with the runway ahead of us.

After my first touch and go that morning, he said, "This time let's do something different. Call tower and let them know we'd like to do a full stop with a taxi-back to the base of the tower."

No problem. The thought occurred to me that Tom was going to request a tour of the tower for us. He had spoken of that previously. As we pulled up to the tower, Tom turned to me and said, "Don't kill the engine!" He unplugged his headset, jumped out, and looked at me with a grin.

"You ready?" he yelled over the sound of the engine.

I immediately realized what was happening.

"Yes," I said.

He said, "Good," then proceeded to give me instructions on what to tell the tower. "When you get done, taxi back on over here."

I sat in the plane listening to the engine idle, waiting what I thought was a minute, called the tower as instructed and said, "First solo." I got clearance to taxi to the active runway and off I went.

I was cleared for takeoff. I turned out onto the runway and pushed the throttle full forward. I looked over at the empty right seat and laughed hard!

I sped down the runway in the Cessna 150, watching my airspeed indicator, and began gently easing back the yoke at 60 mph. I felt my wheels leave the ground and gave a Cajun yell!

My first touch and go was good. I enjoyed it so much that I stayed in the pattern for three more before I decided I better stop playing, request a full stop, and pick up Tom.

I soloed in N3034S, a beautiful, well-maintained green-on-white Cessna 150G.

The first airplane that Karyn and I bought was a 1977 Cessna 150M, N714JT (aka: "714 Juliett Tango"). What a fabulous airplane. We loved our "Juliett." Karyn did her first solo in Juliett.

Amongst the many flights we took in our 150 was a long cross-county to Syracuse, New York to visit my family. We stopped first in Spring Green, Wisconsin. That was the closest airport to Taliesin.

At the time, Karyn was serving as In-House Counsel for the Frank Lloyd Wright Foundation. I had not been outside Arizona on a long cross-country, and Karyn was just barely licensed. She had never been to Taliesin before, so we decided to stop there first. We proceeded across the U.S. heading for Santa Fe from Saint Johns when I started feeling uncomfortable. I thought I knew where Santa Fe should be, and it wasn't.

Long story short, there was a belief that I had overflown Los Alamos.

I was instructed by tower to park and meet. The meeting was with a couple of very professional Blackhawk pilots who discussed our flight with us and noted that I was a retired Lieutenant Colonel.

No further action required. They bid us farewell and Karyn and I headed for the plane and continued on with our planned flight.

Otherwise, our flight was wonderful. Karyn's Annie Oakley fantasy was fulfilled when we stayed at the Annie Oakley Motel in Oakley, Kansas while in route.

Karyn was an awesome co-pilot both going east and returning west.

We learned that some small airports had a loaner car with the keys under the mat (such as Oakley), and a little sticker on the dash that said, "Leave it like you find it," which we did. I filled the tank.

Our stay at Taliesin was almost beyond description. The grounds were absolutely beautiful! After the tours stopped at 5:00 p.m. we had complete run of Taliesin for two evenings, and the weather was perfect.

We stayed in a bedroom designed by Frank Lloyd Wright for his daughter. We were treated with the utmost courtesy by the staff and Fellowship Members and made to feel at home. They provided us with a vintage AMC Pacer for transportation, and we enjoyed driving around the grounds in it.

Then, all too soon, our wonderful stay came to an end. We got dropped off at the Spring Green Airport, strapped Juliett back on, and proceeded to Syracuse.

I felt elated as we approached Syracuse from the west and flew over Camillus and Fairmount inbound to Syracuse Airport.

I couldn't recognize many of the things I saw on the ground but knew about where I was. We had a good view of Onondaga Lake, the source of carp for the Huck Finn contests.

The 150 is so easy to fly. It is a very forgiving airplane. Even though I have flown many other types and models, I still feel a deep fondness for the 150. The Cessna 150 is the Curtiss Jenny of the 1960s, 70s, and 80s. Many pilots learned to fly in both.

After owning her for ten years, we decided to sell Juliett, and a year later, we so missed owning an airplane that we decided to buy another.

The joke between Karyn and I is that first, you buy a knee-board. That gets you on the Sporty's mailing list, and eventually, you buy your first headset. It's just a matter of time after that before you're going to buy an airplane. The second plane is even easier.

We shopped very carefully for our first plane. We were originally going to build our own, then, on the advice of Karyn's flight instructor, decided to find a nice Cessna 150 or 152 instead.

That's what we did. I found a nice little 1977 Cessna 150M. 1977 was the last year they were produced, and arguably the best 150 ever made.

I travelled to San Diego, examined the airplane, flew it, liked it, reviewed the log books carefully, then called Karyn, and conferred. She said, "Buy it," and I did.

This time was different. Both Karyn and I flew "Piper" first, before making an offer of purchase. We asked a lot of questions.

We had a really comprehensive pre-sale inspection done on the three planes we seriously considered; the Piper Warrior we selected (aka: "Piper") still had the original 1981 paint job and interior.

We knew it would need some work. The engine compression was outstanding, and there was no corrosion. It had never been owned by a flight school, had less than 3,000 hours on the airframe, and had "good bones." We negotiated a price we were satisfied with and bought it.

We redid the interior, had micro-vortex generators installed on the flight surfaces, and re-painted Piper. We also installed ADS-B In/Out and made a wonderful upgrade on our mags to make cold starts much easier!

We used ForeFlight on our iPad, and as a backup, we kept a battery-powered Garmin snapped onto the pilot-in-charge's yoke.

Our first long flight in Piper was to French Valley, California to visit Karyn's sister, Ryndi and her brother-in-law, John. What a fantastic 22nd anniversary we had!

We had an awesomely wonderful time as guests at their beautiful estate in Temecula. It was just about the most spectacular long weekend you can imagine, filled with gourmet meals, swimming, and a Padres game in San Diego with John.

John and I drove to downtown San Diego and found parking near the ball park stadium. It was Jackie Robinson Day, and all players wore the number 42 on their jerseys. Not a baseball fan, I was surprised and puzzled by it.

As I pondered the players from both teams all wearing the number 42, my first thought was back to *The Hitchhikers' Guide to the Galaxy* In which the Super Computer Deep Thought declares that the answer to the Ultimate Question of Life, The Universe, and Everything is: 42.

After a while I collected enough data-points to correctly make an educated guess that it was all about Jackie Robinson.

Karyn and I also lavished in leisure, totally spoiled by the end of the weekend, and fizzing with excitement by the time we got back to Piper for our flight home.

We departed with about forty pounds of Haas avocados we had harvested in John and Ryndi's avocado orchard.

We flew back to Prescott, passing over Palm Springs, and on to our home field. Once again, Karyn served as a magnificent pilot, navigator, and co-pilot.

One of our favorite fun flights was to Sedona. It was an easy twenty-minute hop over Mingus Mountain, with Jerome and Cottonwood just off to our right, then a slow, easy descent onto the mesa Sedona airport is nestled on.

Pilots jokingly refer to Sedona as, "U.S.S. Sedona," because of the shape of the mesa. It's kind of like landing on a gigantic, stationary, aircraft carrier.

Once on the ground, we had options. We greatly enjoyed the airport restaurant, with its million-dollar panoramic view of the red rocks; and we often split one of their sumptuous breakfasts.

We are also owners at Los Abrigados, and often grabbed a cab to the resort for a swim and spa to our hearts content, or spend a long weekend there.

We enjoy strolling the grounds of Los Abrigados, and through Tlaquepaque Arts & Crafts Village where we browse the art galleries and craft shops as we follow cobblestone paths under decorative arches and enjoy the unequaled environment.

Just a wonderful, peaceful experience for the soul!

A significant part of my flying experience has been sharing the fun and freedom of flight with others. Over the years I have carried numerous passengers experiencing their first flight in a small plane.

I helped Karyn become a licensed pilot. Her landings were better than mine. Since flying many times with us, our daughter Tori has begun taking flying lessons and I look forward to her taking me for a flight after she gets her license. In May of 2019 she sat for the grueling 5-hour AFOQT (Air Force Officer Qualification Test) and scored a 98% on Navigation. I'm confident that she'll be a very capable pilot.

One of my former co-workers from the EEOC, Julia Darby, has a son named Noel. I had the opportunity to take him for a couple of flights out of Deer Valley Airport in Piper and we had some good conversations about Noel joining the Air Force after he graduated from high school.

In 2017 I received an official Air Force photo of Airman Noel E. King with an attached note: "I can't thank you enough for your love and support." I wrote him back and thanked him for sharing his accomplishment with me.

We advertised Piper for sale in April 2018 and sold her in a week for our asking price to a nice couple named Jay and Ginger, who immediately jumped in and flew her back to Dayton, Ohio in two days. Ginger is a retired Air Force Colonel, and Jay retired as an Air Force Brigadier General.

On to our next adventure!

After we sold Piper, I continued renting a Cessna 150 to stay current and play. I'm spoiled. I concluded that I no longer enjoyed flying other people's airplanes.

It was with considerable thought that I decided, at age 69, to hang up my wings for now.

"Juliett" parked in our hangar in Stellar Air Park, Chandler, AZ

"Piper"

23

KINGMAN

At times when you fly a plane, you'll have some minor issue occur that requires additional attention.

It could be that one of your radios in the stack starts to grow dim or flicker. Or, it could be a surprise burp of the engine, and you turn your attention to all the gauges, hoping you don't have a real problem.

Back in 1984 while I was still a student pilot on a solo flight to Prescott in a Cessna 150, my radio went silent. Dead silent. No radio!

I immediately dialed 7600 into my transponder, followed no radio procedures, and landed uneventfully.

At the time, there was a Flight Service Station located on the airport, and as soon as I secured the airplane, I walked over there and talked to them about what had just happened.

All was good. I messed around with the radio and fuses, and managed to get it working again, and flew back to Falcon Field in Mesa, Arizona.

On another occasion while flying the same Cessna 150 (N3034S) in 1991, just as I flew over the Mazatzal Wilderness, my engine abruptly quit.

I did everything I could think of to re-start the engine, and finally got it to grudgingly cough to life with enough rpm to get me directly to the airport in Payson.

I kicked hard left rudder just before the Payson Runway 24 threshold and touched my wheels about two seconds later. It turned out to be a problem with carbon build up on the engine valves due to the recent conversion of General Aviation from 80 octane leaded fuel to 100 octane low-lead, which initially created problems such as this.

In May 2017 on a "practice flight" for our planned Yellowstone flight, Karyn and I decided to fly over to Kingman, Arizona and have breakfast.

We departed Prescott at about 07:00, flew to Kingman uneventfully, and had a nice breakfast at the airport. On a scale of one-to-ten, I would rate their biscuits and gravy about "eight" (very good).

Sometime around 09:00 we lifted off from Kingman on runway 3, with a right turn back toward Prescott. About ten miles out of Kingman, as the landscape became more rugged, we started to notice a hum on the radio.

I commented on it, and Karyn confirmed that she could hear it too, and that it was new. Our KLN 94 (GPS) quit three times in as many minutes, and I started getting an external power message on the Garmin.

I noted that our amp meter was showing zero charge and anticipated that we were soon going to lose all electrical. I tried recycling the master switch twice. No luck.

We agreed that since we had a compass, a Garmin Aero 510 on my yoke, and Foreflight on Karyn's iPAD (still with a 63% charge) mounted on her yoke and linked to an independent battery-powered-antennae sitting on the dash, plus some familiarity with the route (since we had just flown it from the other direction), navigation wouldn't be an issue.

I called L.A. Center, and asked them to advise Prescott Tower that they might need to use the light gun on me since I'd soon be losing all electrical, and they acknowledged my request.

That was my last communication with L.A. Center on that flight.

This wasn't the first time we'd lost our electrical. One time in 2004 we were transitioning the Phoenix north-south corridor in our Cessna 150 (N714JT), heading south, on a flight path that took us directly over Sky Harbor Airport.

Just as we passed Piestewa Peak (still shown as Squaw Peak on aeronautical sectionals), we lost all electrical power.

We had noted our amp meter had gone flat about twenty minutes earlier, and I had tried re-cycling the master switch, with negative results.

We immediately dug out our handheld radio and communicated effectively until we reached Stellar Airpark and landed.

As we continued toward Prescott from Kingman on our May 2017 adventure, the radio quit, and everything started to go blank on the console.

Karyn had already dug out the handheld radio, and as I started fiddling with everything, including re-cycling the master switch and double checking the fuses again without success, Karyn spoke loudly over the roar of the engine, "My airplane."

I let go of the yoke, took my feet off the rudder pedals, and yelled back, "Your airplane." I tried calling L.A. Center on the handheld. Nada. I tried Phoenix Approach. Nada. I dialed in the Prescott ATIS, put the radio on the dash, and yelled, "My airplane." She acknowledged me and relinquished control of Piper back to me.

Soon we started to hear the ATIS (Automatic Terminal Information Service), which provides current altimeter, winds, runway in use, and more) on the handheld.

We set our altimeter and planned our approach. I called Prescott Tower at ten miles out, and tower heard me and responded. Kudos to my Sporty's handheld!

The controller gave me my assigned runway followed by my landing clearance and checked with me to make sure everything else was okay. I advised tower that I was using a handheld radio.

Tower directed me to remain on their frequency and taxi to our hangar in the "Bottlenecks." After we landed and taxied toward the Bottleneck Hangars, Karyn and I both looked at each other with a big grin and gave a loud "whoop," then turned Piper toward our hangar row.

Amazingly, our two mechanics were standing in one of the neighboring hangers talking as we swung to the right, slowly taxiing toward our hangar. Karyn signaled them and yelled that we wanted to talk to them.

I finished the taxi to the hangar, stepped on my left rudder, swinging the plane left, and killed the engine.

Pete and Ericka walked over to us. They both looked remarkable, and we learned why soon. They had just returned from re-assembling a Cessna 182 for a wealthy Sri Lankan airline pilot—in Sri Lanka.

It is the first privately-owned airplane officially registered in Sri Lanka! The owner paid all expenses, and generously compensated both.

One day, Pete's acquaintance suggested that while they were there Pete should pay a visit to a very well-known medicine man for an examination and possible treatment of anything that ailed him.

Pete told us that it was an amazing experience. He gained significant improvements to long-term ailments on the spot! They both were treated by the same medicine man, and Ericka benefited equally well from the visit, resolving a long-time skin issue. They both loved Sri Lanka.

They expect to return there to re-assemble more planes in the future and can hardly wait!

Pete walked over to our plane, held his hands above the engine cowl, then turned and took on a mystical quality. "I think it's a disconnected wire on the alternator." We popped open the cowling, peered down into the engine compartment, and sure enough, there was a wire dangling next to the alternator.

Karyn had been an exemplary co-pilot, cool as a cucumber, and "spot on" as she helped navigate, fly, and dial frequencies into the radio.

24

GAMBEL'S QUAIL

Growing up, I had a number of good experiences hunting pheasant with my Dad. I also hunted several times with a petite 5' 1" model Dad was dating who I called "Little Jean."

Jean was a tough strawberry-blonde, gimlet-eyed, baby-doll-pretty young woman; a real country girl, great on horseback, and a crack shot with her .20-gauge side-by-side.

She would come over to the motel on early Saturday mornings after I got off work, and we'd head out back into the fields to hunt pheasant, and we became friends.

We would hunt for a couple of hours, get cleaned up, and grab a late breakfast together, before I showered, slept and readied for my Saturday night shift in the office.

I shot my first pheasant using my father's Model B Fox, .16-gauge side-by-side opening day +3, in 1964. The bird flushed explosively ten yards in front of me, with our Golden Retriever hot on its tail.

The pheasant made a steep, climbing right turn, flying back past my right side, cackling as it went.

I shouldered the unfamiliar gun my father had just handed me that morning. I had missed two birds in the past two days shooting a clunky .12 gauge, full-choke, single-shot, long-barreled hammer gun on the first and second day of the season. Frustrated on our third day in the field, he swapped guns with me, briefly instructed me on what the sight picture should look like, and I took a few moments to practice throwing it into my shoulder and getting a sight picture after he handed it to me.

As the pheasant swung past me, I pivoted, and the gun slipped comfortably into my shoulder—a perfect fit that seemed like an extension to my arm. I snapped off the safety, led the bird, and dropped it with my first shot—using the improved cylinder barrel (first trigger).

I still have the Fox, and have shot innumerable pheasant, chukar, quail, doves, and rabbits with it over the years.

And I still hunt with it on occasion, and it brings back fond memories of many great hunts over the years.

My favorite quail gun is my .12-gauge Winchester Ranger, Model 120. I bought it in 1979 at the K-Mart on McDowell Road in Scottsdale. I carried it strapped to my motorcycle for quite some time when I rode out into the desert to hunt rabbit, dove, and quail. It has served me faithfully and has been a very dependable shotgun.

In 1974, while sitting on the cab stand at Sky Harbor's East Wing, I struck up a conversation with another cabbie named Andrew Wilkes about his dog, a Chesapeake Bay retriever named Damien.

He told me how difficult Damien could be, and how he had to discipline him sometimes. I made the mistake of asking exactly how he disciplined his "Chessie." He yanked his right shoe off and whammed it on the fender of my cab, and said, "Just like that!" I was shocked.

I said, "You just dinged my fender!" He responded, "Who cares... You have dings, dents, and scuffs all over your cab. What's one more?" Thus, spawned my friendship with Andy.

Andy was my first quail hunting partner. My quail gun at the time was a Mossberg .16-gauge pump that I had a gunsmith bore to an improved cylinder.

Andy and I hunted quail and dove together for a couple of seasons quite successfully. We hunted many areas now covered with homes, all around Cave Creek and Carefree. One area we frequented was just north of the Carefree Highway where 16th

Street dead ended. We would park and climb down the embankment into a nearly endless stretch of Sonoran Desert spreading to the north.

Those hillsides and open fields of cactus were heavily populated with Gambel's Quail, and we had some fantastic hunts.

One time when Andy and I were tracing a hillside, and I was on what appeared to be a game trail, Andy just below me, I flushed a bird that made a fast, low-level flight straight up the trail.

I brought my gun up, lined up quickly, and snapped off a shot.

The bird tumbled on the trail about 15 yards in front of me. When I walked up and bent to pick it up, there was a perfect little bird-point arrowhead laying in an indentation on the side of a rock, right next to the bird.

I picked up my bird and stood there, imagining some young native-American hundreds of years before me, hitting and losing a bird, or missing and losing the arrow right where I stood on that hillside.

Damien displayed a strong dislike for me on several occasions, including when he swallowed a dove whole rather than hand it to me, snarling as he gulped it down!

In the second year, Andy's Brittany Spaniel named Sally joined Andy, Damien, and me. She was a sweet dog, loved to run, and accidentally on occasion produced some shooting opportunities.

Andy and I have remained friends throughout the years. I loved his first wife, Betty, dearly. She was smart and pretty with a twinkle of mischief in her eyes. She was an LPN (working at Saint Joseph's in Phoenix), had a wicked sense of humor, and seemed to like me quite well too. Tragically, she died of a brain hemorrhage after collapsing on the kitchen floor while nobody else was home. Her two young boys came home from school and found her, dead.

Andy had studied and practiced T'ai Chi since the late 1960's, and wrote a very interesting essay entitled "The Soulful Warrior," which I have read and reread several times.

He married again, this time to a lovely lady named Patricia, and his sons have grown to be good men. We trade Christmas letters every year.

I have hunted by myself many times over the years, infrequently taking someone new out with me. I began hunting the Waterman's Wash area in the mid-1970s, and still do. I have hunted quail all over Arizona, and especially have enjoyed some of the areas I've found near Oracle Junction, and off of Cherry Road. I have found spots that I believe won't be eliminated due to encroachment plus the expanding population and subsequent development.

My first real quail dog was Eve. She was a Border Collie mix left with me by my former lover and roommate Carol when she moved out.

"Evie" was about three or four years old and had always been a house dog. She had rarely been walked on a leash and had never heard gunfire or been in the desert, but she enjoyed playing fetch with me in the back yard very much.

I took Evie out with me right in the beginning of the season down in Waterman's Wash, and she did well. She flushed, retrieved, managed to avoid the cactus, and listened to me. She was a good dog and we hunted together for two seasons.

My four all-time favorite quail hunting partners are Andrew Wilkes, Wayne Bryan, Michael Colangelo, and my wife Karyn.

Wayne served with me in the 107th Tactical Control Squadron. He was a talented Weapons Controller and an all-around good guy. He accurately fires a pump shotgun fast enough to make you wonder if he's carrying a semi. He retired as a Major.

Mike transferred to the Arizona Air National Guard from Connecticut to take the helm as Commander of the 107th after I had already transferred to Headquarters. We had been contemporaries when he worked as the full-time Operations Officer for a mobile radar unit in Connecticut.

We struck up a conversation about hunting, and as soon as the season started, I took him to a spot I knew of down near Oracle Junction, and we had a great hunt. He's an excellent shot with both shotgun and rifle. He retired as a Brigadier General.

Mike, Wayne and I have enjoyed many great quail, chukar, and pheasant hunts together over the years.

Once, while Mike, Wayne and I were hunting one of our favorite spots near Oracle Junction, I heard Wayne yell, "Hey Mike and Kevin, I just found what looks like a .25 caliber pistol!

I immediately knew it was the handgun I'd lost the week before after it slipped out of its holster as I tromped through the thick underbrush and didn't notice it missing until I got back to my truck and was unloading birds and gear.

I called back to Wayne, "It's a .22 caliber long-rifle Jennings semi-automatic." Wayne asked how I could possibly know that, and I told him. I still had the box it came in.

That is one of the most remarkable finds I've ever seen anyone make!

Karyn has hunted with me many times over the years. She is a good shot with rifle, pistol and shotgun, and very good at spotting game. She is also good on horseback and uncomplaining, no matter how awful the conditions are.

I have hunted numerous species large and small over the years and have never enjoyed hunting anything as much as I enjoy Gambel's Quail. This is an unusual bird. Described as "Arizona's most popular game bird," in David E. Brown's *Arizona Game Birds*, they can be found in a variety of habitats.

I have found many coveys along mesquite-lined rivers, creeks, and the many arroyos that fan across the desert. Although they seem to like the upland desert the best, they can be found as far north as the Colorado River in north-west Arizona.

If you're willing to walk distances in the wash-laced *bajadas* (cone-shaped deposits of sediment flowing from hill-sides), other drainages, dense scrub, and scrub-invaded semi-desert grasslands early-to-mid morning, or the last couple hours of the day, you're bound to flush quail. I typically walk 8-10 miles during a hunt.

There is almost always cactus involved, and I have often spent a week getting all the stickers out of me after a hunt.

ATTENTION: There are many places where you simply don't want to take your dog and be careful about snakes if you're going to take your dog out in the early part of the season.

When hunting alone, I will walk along the edge of the selected wash or arroyo, often swinging around and walking the other side, and sometimes right up the middle, too. When walking in or near heavy cover, my shooting opportunities are generally brief, and I hit most birds inside twenty-five yards.

Two birds are a perfectly good day for me. If I have a dog with me, I'll keep her within fifteen yards of me if possible. My Labrador, Ayla was exceptionally good at staying close, but not too close. She was a good girl. Karyn and I decided to see how many tricks we could teach her, and how extensive we could make her vocabulary.

We documented more than 100 words that she clearly understood the meaning of (many involving objects), and when we would leave her with somebody, we'd provide them with a list of her known vocabulary.

She loved retrieving the newspaper in the morning. Every dog should have a job, and fetching the newspaper was her primary duty assignment. She took her assignment seriously.

When she heard the newspaper hit the drive early in the morning, she ran to the door in great excitement. She tackled her job with happy enthusiasm every morning. I'd open the door and out she'd go. She'd race to the paper and brake herself, toenails on all four feet screeching as she scooped up the paper and spun back toward the door. On several occasions she dropped our paper at the doorstep and retrieved one of our neighbor's newspapers next. I'd quickly get dressed and figure out which driveway the errant newspaper belonged.

We also taught her to recognize a bird call from a clock our son gave us. At five-o'clock when the tufted titmouse called, she knew it was time to eat! We jokingly referred to it as the "food bird."

She was also a strong swimmer and loved our pool.

In the field, Ayla was uncomplaining, usually at least initially enthusiastic, and smart. She had a good nose, decent instincts, and a sense of humor.

She was fun to hunt with and hunted fairly well up until she was ten. That was the first time she turned and started walking back towards the truck halfway through the hunt. As a result, I shortened the hunts.

Ayla loved early morning rides in the truck, her chin on my right leg, while I sipped coffee and listened to the radio. The ride home would be similar, me sipping a beverage, both of us pooped out, and ready to get home.

When she would start hugging my pant leg and glancing up at me, I knew she was done hunting for the day.

Our next dog is going to be a Labrador.

Note: I stop frequently and make sure my dog partner has plenty of water.

Our adopted daughter Tori owns a Golden Retriever named Honey.

I took Honey hunting for a couple of seasons with success before Tori divorced and Honey relocated to her Mom's ranch in New Mexico. Honey came back to live with Tori for a while before reuniting with Andreas and his grandma, Peggy, in New Mexico.

I took her out for a fun hunt in early-February 2019 just before the season ended and she headed back to New Mexico.

Without question, the best dog hunts I've had have been with Mike Colangelo's Brittany Spaniels, Allie and Maggie.

Allie was good but could be a little difficult to keep track of. She worked the tough brush areas like a pro and produced innumerable flushes over the years.

Maggie is a bird-crazy champion hunter. Beyond the fact that she points, flushes birds like a little maniac, and has made some miraculous bird retrievals, she has a pleasant disposition and is full of energy. I have greatly enjoyed hunting with Maggie.

You'll usually find Gambel's Quail moving around in the morning and late-afternoon, or lounging during mid-day in coveys, although I have stumbled onto singles many times over the years.

They are gregarious, and monogamous. The males will take responsibility for managing the nest if the female disappears. Over the years in late spring I've seen many little chicks following their mom or dad in a line as they travel to food, water, or a lounging spot.

I've flushed many small, early-season coveys and flushed many large late-season coveys that numbered in the hundreds of birds. As the season progresses, the easier-to-find small coveys seem to coalesce into harder-to-find large coveys.

They also flush sooner, and at longer distances as the season gets later. There is nothing quite like a covey of quail flushing to make your heart skip a beat.

The males have more colorful plumage with a distinctive, jaunty-looking black top-knot atop their head, and a distinctive three tone call, that sounds like: cha-kee-tah (with "kee" being the high note).

When I hunt them, I walk in the direction of the calls, with success. The hens, who are slightly smaller (and maybe smarter, based on my take over the years) have more subtle plumage. They also have a top-knot, not as big, and not as jaunty looking.

When agitated, the females will make a muffled, rapid two or three note complaining sound, and the males a deeper one or two-tone sound. At that point, they're already moving through the foliage to another location, or getting ready to flush.

The desert has its perils: cactus, various thorny brush and trees, and rattlesnakes. I have had numerous snake encounters over the years, including a few very close calls. It's rare that I encounter a snake after the terrain starts to cool down (mid-November, or earlier, depending on the weather) unless it's unseasonably warm.

If you're new to hunting in the Sonoran Desert, and hunting early in the season, watch your step.

It's hard to believe that Gambel's Quail will ever become extinct even though their numbers have diminished significantly over the years. They are plentiful, smart, hardy, have good instincts, work well together, and are mostly hunted by licensed hunters in a well-regulated state.

Unfortunately, I'm certain that there was a time when nobody would have believed the carrier pigeon, an unbelievably plentiful bird whose flocks were noted as "blackening the sky" and were hunted hard, would ever become extinct.

Little Jean mounted on her friend Herbie

Honey, our first-year hunting together

Evie and me after a quick quail hunt

25

THE FRANK LLOYD WRIGHT FOUNDATION

My relationship with the Frank Lloyd Wright Foundation began in October 2004 after Karyn spotted an ad in the *Scottsdale Republic* and applied for a position as their Licensing Assistant.

Since graduating from law school, she had worked as an associate with an intellectual property lawyer who practiced in the area of patents, copyrights, and trademarks.

He was winding down his practice, and when it was time to transition, Karyn continued working as an attorney with the firm that took over most of his remaining files.

The patent side of the practice was robust, but there was insufficient work in the trademark arena to keep her busy full time, so she began looking for other opportunities.

When she saw the ad in the *Scottsdale Republic* for a Licensing Assistant with the Frank Lloyd Wright Foundation, she was intrigued and decided to investigate further.

We both took a tour at Taliesin West to better acquaint her with the Foundation before her scheduled interview.

On tour, I wondered about the obvious adoration exuded by students and faculty and decided that Frank Lloyd Wright had been quite an intriguing fellow. Someone you might enjoy having a drink or two with.

He fostered organic architecture and liked to build low ceilings and doorways; he was a lady's man, a bit of a dandy, and his roofs leaked. He also often insisted that his patrons use only his furniture in the homes he designed and built, and at times inspected them.

The buildings at Taliesin West have a good sampling of his architecture and furniture.

Over the ensuing five plus years, I learned that he had been a force to be reckoned with and had left an enduring legacy.

Karyn's qualifications were impressive. She was a licensed Arizona Attorney with three years of experience working on matters involving trademarks, copyrights, and patents.

She had gotten some of her continuing legal education credits at the U.S. Patent and Trademark office, during a fantastic trip we made together to Washington, D.C.

I was going to D.C. on official business and had a nice government rate room at the Ritz-Carlton in Pentagon City. She spotted a useful 2-day program at the USPTO and decided to join me.

She flew to D.C. on a separate flight the day after I got there, and we met under the huge American Flag in the large open area at Reagan National Airport. We rode the Metro back to our hotel and made it a honeymoon!

Her interview went well, and she was quite excited. She would be working for and learning from the Director of Licensing, and there were many intellectual property issues.

Based on her background and interview, Karyn was hired. She went right to work learning the scope of her work, the legal landscape, and the many personalities she'd be working with.

About one week after Karyn started in her new position with the Foundation, her supervisor, the Director of Licensing, was terminated. Karyn was instructed to take over the director's responsibilities.

In addition to absorbing the duties and responsibilities of her very briefly former boss, she was immediately elevated to the position of attorney. She was informed that the reason they had made the decision to hire her was based heavily on her obvious legal expertise and qualifications.

Also, the Foundation was looking for ways to minimize the high cost of outside legal assistance. She now reported to the two Co-CEO's that were holding down the CEO position until a new one was named. Karyn was initially overwhelmed and wondered if she had made a mistake by accepting the position.

It reminded her of the time she took a position as a paralegal before attending law school, thinking she would be mentored by the current very experienced paralegal.

Shortly after she started her new employment, she was informed that the paralegal was re-locating out of state. Her new employer knew this when she was hired but failed to let this key piece of information be known to Karyn until it was officially announced.

She wondered at the time whether she should stay or leave, and ultimately decided to take on the challenges. She was glad she did as it provided exceptional work experience.

Now she had a similar situation. If she stayed, this might be a wonderful opportunity for professional growth. I told her she could always quit any time she wanted to. That's all she needed to hear from me, so she bucked up and started taking on the challenges.

The Foundation had never had in-house counsel before. They didn't know, what they didn't know, as Karyn discovered during her tenure at the Foundation.

Her ability to view the Foundation's business through a lawyer's eyes, and a penchant for identifying current and potential issues, kept the Foundation out of a good number of lawsuits. Few people at the Foundation appreciated her accomplishments in this arena since the lawsuits never materialized.

She set in place several preventive measures, negotiated new and existing licensing agreements and other contracts; provided training, got their insurance issues straightened out, dealt with infringers, and more.

Being associated with the Foundation was not all work. Karyn had the opportunity to get to know Fellowship members (former Frank Lloyd Wright apprentices).

The stories they told about their adventures with Frank Lloyd Wright and the Taliesin Architects gave Karyn an insider's view that could not have been achieved any other way.

Initially, Karyn's office was in a newly renovated area, spacious, and located right next to the Director of Licensing.

That office was later to become a conference area for the Chief Executive Officer. When Karyn was told that the director was being terminated, she was also informed she would be re-locating to an office next to the licensing staff.

It was felt that the poor communication between the Director of Licensing and the licensing staff was aggravated by the physical distance. Karyn had to wave good-bye to her luxurious digs.

As it turned out, she was moved to a trailer where she had more privacy and better views. She needed to get past the thought of being in a trailer as opposed to a Frank Lloyd Wright-designed office.

She found the working environment to be quite comfortable, and she occupied that office for about the next four years.

I greatly enjoyed driving out to her trailer. I learned desert shortcuts and had the combination to the gate. It was isolated enough that many critters walked right beneath Karyn's window with some frequency. Sometimes I'd be talking with her on the phone and she would interrupt me to tell me about a coyote, bobcat, road runner, deer, or a covey of quail moseying by.

She spent her last year with the Foundation in a nice secluded office that at one time had housed Frank Lloyd Wright's personal physician, Dr. Joe Rorke, for many years. The building and grounds were remarkable. Her view was spectacular, looking out over pristine desert toward Scottsdale—and the roof leaked. I never stopped pinching myself that I had the virtual run of such a very architecturally significant property.

I struck up a friendship with Dr. Joe. We both collected stamps, and for many years he passed along interesting stamps to me as he came across them.

I found the Taliesin Fellowship members to be quite engaging and eccentric as well.

The Foundation found a new CEO while Karyn continued to handle primarily licensing issues. With the new CEO in place, she began to take on additional legal duties, which again expanded her exposure and enhanced her experience. She worked well with him.

The new CEO, Phil Allsopp terminated the 3 top executive positions—which included the HR person responsible for hiring Karyn. It also included the two Co-CEO's who had supported Karyn's selection for the position and fired her supervisor.

The terminations came as a complete surprise to everyone, including Karyn. She called me and told me what had just happened. She suggested that my extensive experience in Human Resources might be useful and encouraged me to volunteer my services. I agreed with her and offered my assistance during this time of transition, while the Foundation put other staff in place.

Karyn suggested I call Phil and talk to him directly. I did just that. In my conversation with Phil, he indicated that he needed immediate assistance getting HR sorted out.

At the time he was at Taliesin in Wisconsin, and he felt that a positive on-site presence was also greatly needed at Taliesin West until he got back.

I was retired from the Air National Guard, had recently finished my last year on City Council, and had just wrapped up a one-year contract as the Chief Operations Officer for Y-2 Ultrafilters.

I agreed to come out to Taliesin West for a couple of weeks and cover Human Resources. As soon as I walked into the office, I realized I had taken on a considerable challenge.

The first thing I recommended was that all the senior leadership office doors be re-keyed. In addition, payday was just around the corner, and there were no time records or payroll information in place.

The former HR person had done it all. She kept her own spreadsheets, calculated leave usage and balances, advanced pay balances, raises and more.

She did all the computations and submitted payroll data directly to the finance guy, Dan Nesbitt (a good guy) who cut the checks.

I could not access her computer.

A very real disaster was looming, and I needed to move quickly. There was no way I was going to try unscrambling hard-copy documents and data, leave usage, and everything else—and submit a payroll request to Dan in the following week.

With Phil's consent, I engaged a Professional Employment Organization (PEO). They cost less than half the price of a full-time HR person, and performed flawlessly. Nobody other than Karyn, Dan and Phil knew there had been a problem, and I kept it that way. Everyone was paid as expected, and in the correct amount. Basically, I kept the "trains" running on time.

After a couple of weeks, I had everything pretty much straightened out and began coming out one day every week to deal with any odds and ends, all as a volunteer.

Phil is a good man. I had the opportunity to quail hunt with him a couple of times. He is an excellent shot. We went to our local range and shot skeet. Frankly, he did better than I did. I hit my usual 21 out of 25 more or less, and Phil nailed nearly every clay pigeon with his Barretta over-and-under.

Frank Lloyd Wright had greatly enjoyed the many cocktail parties thrown at Taliesin and Taliesin West. They were gala affairs designed primarily to teach his students how to conduct themselves during social events and cultivate patrons.

Someone would always be playing the baby grand, and quite often there would be other musicians playing and singing as well.

There were poetry readings, conversation, plentiful and delicious hors d'oeuvres, and of course, good wines and cocktails.

This tradition continued long after his death in 1959, and Karyn and I had the privilege to attend many of these events. What beautiful evenings we enjoyed strolling under the stars, on those very romantic nights on the grounds of Taliesin West.

I had many memorable conversations with former apprentices who had served under Mr. Wright, such as Cornelia Brierly and John Rattenbury.

John was quite a character, and Karyn, John and I enjoyed some great quality time together, including a couple of fun flights in our Cessna 150.

I took him on a flight over the Superstitions and the lakes east of Phoenix: Saguaro, Canyon, Apache and Roosevelt.

While flying over Roosevelt Lake, I pointed out the small cove where I had fished frequently, and my brother Bruce and I once murdered the crappie and large-mouth Bass.

John flew the plane a little bit and told me a fun flying story about when he was a young man flying with an acquaintance who without notice handed the controls over to him and disappeared into the back of the plane to look for something. It was the first time John had ever flown a plane!

Karyn flew John to Payson for breakfast and shortly afterward, John gave her a framed photo of his cousin, 24-year-old Bentley Beauman, behind the wheel of a Deperdussin Monocoque, and annotated: "Self in 35 H.P. Deperdussin on which I took Royal Aero Club Flying Certificate June 1913. Bentley Beauman."

What a fine man he was. After doing a little research I learned that Brigadier Archibald Bentley Beauman, CBE DSO and Bar, served heroically and with distinction as a British Officer in two World Wars, and was an early flying pioneer. I smile every time I look at it.

Karyn and I attended many social events to include Easter breakfasts, parties, and invitation-only dinners. We never hesitated to accept an invitation.

The dinners were warm and inviting and the special events were presented with the same high degree of splendor as in days past. It was all about quality of experience.

One of my favorite dinners was where they served lobster that had been shipped in from Maine. The students did most of the setup, cooking and presentation. We paid $15 apiece for some very fine, well-prepared lobsters, and a bottomless glass of some decent reds and whites.

Just as dinner was served, a group of tourists were guided past our building. Many of them peered in through the windows at us as they went by. Karyn and I joked that it might be difficult to convince any of them that the Frank Lloyd Wright Foundation needed donations.

Every year there was an Easter breakfast, and there were many kids there. They did an Easter egg hunt, and there was great pageantry in decorating the May Pole. The kids and adults had a blast.

Students would also release a large helium-filled balloon with a message attached, asking whoever found the balloon to contact the Foundation with the location and date it was found.

The students had a map with many pins and dates of Easter balloons that had been found in the past, and a collection of postcards and letters from the finders.

As part of our planned flight to Syracuse in our Cessna, we stopped at Spring Green, Wisconsin to visit Taliesin for a couple of days. We landed at the Spring Green airport in the early afternoon and tied down Juliett on the ramp in front of the small terminal building.

The airport was scenic with a well-maintained runway and taxiways, spacious hangars, and manicured grounds.

We wandered into the unoccupied terminal building, which including a nice pilot's lounge with a recliner and an "honor system" snack bar.

The weather was gorgeous. Unfortunately, there was no cab or shuttle service to or from the airport.

I called one of the motels in town to ask about a room and potential dining. One of the restaurant employees agreed to drive out and get us for $5. I gave her ten.

We continued trying to contact someone at Taliesin and decided to stay in Spring Green for the night, then head out to Taliesin in the morning.

We had a great Italian dinner and our room was nice. As it turned out, the same woman who picked us up at the airport was our server that night for dinner, and shared tidbits with us about Taliesin.

Taliesin had been having trouble with their phone system. That explained why we could not reach anyone. Stephen Nemtin, one of the Fellowship members, picked us up in the morning and got us safely tucked into the bedroom once inhabited by Frank Lloyd Wright's daughter, Svetlana.

It was a cozy little room on the second floor with a comfy bed and a balcony and an impressive view down onto the property.

We spent the next two days being treated well by the entire staff. We were lent a vintage AMC Pacer that was clean, seemed well-maintained, and was fun to drive. We took a tour and wandered the spacious acres. We had complete run of the property, including the house after closing time.

We were informed that Eric Lloyd Wright, Frank Lloyd Wright's grandson, was also staying there, but we never crossed paths.

We loved Minerva Montooth's garden. She was a gracious hostess, and from that time on, I have always referred to her as "The hostess with the mostest." In addition to our wonderful visit to Taliesin, we visited some other buildings and properties built by Frank Lloyd Wright.

We hopped back into our plane and headed for Syracuse feeling really jazzed.

On one occasion while visiting family in Syracuse, we drove over to Buffalo to tour the Martin House complex with my sister Kerry and her then husband Rick. What a great day!

We had great timing with a special event for the Frank Lloyd Wright Foundation. The Guggenheim Museum and the Foundation worked together for over a year to prepare for an exhibition of a selection of Frank Lloyd Wright's work.

The Guggenheim Museum building itself had been designed by Frank Lloyd Wright.

We had a family wedding on Long Island that coincided with the exhibition. Karyn had worked on the necessary contracts between the Foundation and the Guggenheim Museum.

When we arrived in New York we rented a car with a GPS. As I zipped through the streets, staying with traffic, I joked that the GPS let me drive like a native!

On our way to the Guggenheim, we found a single parking space on a street within easy walking distance of the Museum just as a parked car pulled out.

During the exhibition most of the museum was dedicated to the works of Frank Lloyd Wright, and it was excellent. Karyn and I pored over all the displays, drawings, and models and marveled at the building itself.

John Rattenbury had been quietly spirited to the Guggenheim by staff to make the necessary architectural corrections during the actual construction of the Guggenheim. He initially lived almost as a pauper until he got established. He had some great stories.

While our house in Scottsdale was undergoing renovations, we arranged to rent the Frank Lloyd Wright-designed Desert House at Taliesin West for a couple of weeks.

The Desert House is isolated, and spending time there was a beautiful experience. We had the opportunity to explore the many acres encompassing the campus and surrounding grounds at great length.

We walked out into the desert acreage and looked at the many Taliesin West shelters built by and briefly occupied by architectural students over the years. This was the first structure they would build, and they were expected to spend time in them. Some were quite elaborate, others not, and all were quite tiny.

Frank Lloyd Wright had originally purchased the 500+ acres far north of the little town of Scottsdale for $3.50 an acre in 1937. It quickly became his "desert laboratory."

Nearly all the original buildings were constructed with materials found locally, and his students worked without compensation while paying tuition.

I believe that Frank Lloyd Wright possessed genius as an architect, and he was a dynamic force in the field of architecture. He liked the ladies, and the ladies liked him—and the Japanese loved him.

He demonstrated great determination. The more you learn about him, the more enigmatic he becomes.

Karyn had five and a half exciting years at the Foundation as in-house counsel. She is proud of her many contributions to the organization and will always be grateful for and cherish the extraordinary opportunities and experience she had while at the Foundation.

She looks back with a feeling of accomplishment. She knows she brought great value to this somewhat archaic and culturally unique organization.

Phil Allsop moved on, and then the Board of Directors determined the in-house counsel position should be eliminated. Timing is everything. Karyn and I easily relocated to the downtown Phoenix area where I had a "foot" commute to my new position with the Equal Employment Opportunity Commission.

26

THE U.S. EQUAL EMPLOYMENT OPPORTUNITY COMMISSION

After I turned sixty my military retirement kicked in and we wrapped up a lawsuit involving adjoining property owners who had filed an easement through our property without our permission. That bump in the road had sucked about $40,000 cash out of our personal economy.

Karyn and I agreed I could resign my position with the University of Phoenix, which I had started initially to keep up with the legal bills and stop working.

Within a week of that conversation, I received an email from my friend Carol Blackman letting me know that the EEOC was advertising a position for a staff mediator in the Phoenix District Office.

At the time, I was serving as President for the Arizona Association for Conflict Resolution, and Carol was on the Board of Directors.

I had been conducting mediations for the Attorney General's office for almost thirteen-years, and I was operating my own private mediation service: Hy-View Mediation Services, LLC.

Hy-View provided me with a tidy income and gave me a chance to travel around Arizona and the country in general conducting mediations, providing training, and helping organizations build their own alternative dispute resolution programs. While conducting several of the 40-hour mediation training programs offered, I had the good fortune to attract two skilled professional mediators, Denise Blommel and Joy Borum.

Denise was an interesting combination of cerebral and humorous. Her husband Don is literally a rocket scientist and has been directly involved in many aspects of space exploration since the 1970s. She is a talented speaker and is all about preparation.

Joy is a real character and wit. She had spent many years as an attorney practicing family law and had gravitated to conducting mediations only. Like Denise, we got to know each other when I ran for and served on Scottsdale City Council. All three of us belonged to a professional mediation association known as the Arizona Dispute Resolution Association (ADRA) which later morphed into the Arizona Chapter of the Association for Conflict Resolution (AACR).

At one time or another we had all served as officers, and our paths as mediators occasionally crossed. We soon struck a deal to conduct mediation training and conducted numerous week-long training programs together over the period of several years. I greatly enjoyed working with both.

Karyn and I had recently purchased our "Treehouse" in the Mountain Club, just outside of Prescott, Arizona, and our only big expense was our Piper Warrior.

Karyn had just left the Frank Lloyd Wright Foundation, and the timing seemed perfect to retire. I looked at Carol's email, examined the job announcement, and discussed it with Karyn. We agreed I would explore delaying my retirement.

I followed the instructions to apply through USAjobs.gov and launched my application and attachments. Shortly after the announcement closed, I received a call scheduling an interview, and began preparing for it.

As an experienced interviewer, I have learned to enjoy interviews. I anticipate the questions I will be asked and contemplate my best responses.

Several days before the interview, I received a call from Kathy Plitt, who ran the mediation program for the Arizona Attorney General's Office. She was deeply concerned: I was supposed to receive an award from Attorney General Terry Goddard in a couple of days, and it appeared that nobody had contacted me! Was I available?

After the appropriate hemming and hawing, I let her know that I was sure I'd be able to clear my schedule and be there. I submitted my leave request with the University.

The ceremony was in the Capitol Rotunda. I received an Exemplary Service Award from the Attorney General in recognition of my service as a mediator.

Terry is a nice guy. He is a retired Commander from the Navy Reserve. I considered him to be a particularly good mayor, and I thought he did a good job as Attorney General. I have always personally liked him.

My interview was scheduled in two days. I swung by Kinko's and made full-color copies of the award certificate.

I arrived for my interview. The interview scheduled before mine was running a little long, and I was seated in the waiting area, a room packed with charging parties and their entourages, waiting to meet with an investigator.

I was in a suit, alone, and stuck out a little.

I felt a little bored after a few minutes and decided to explore. I let the receptionist know I'd be right back.

I left my folder on the chair and went out to the hallway to look at the rack with all the pamphlets on it in the hallway just outside the door. I plucked one out to read and made a quick trip to the restroom.

I went back into the waiting area, sat down, turned my phone off, and read the brochure. It provided a brief overview of the laws enforced by the EEOC. Right at the very top of the brochure was their Mission Statement. I read it, and thought it might be important, so I memorized it.

About two minutes later, Robin Campbell entered the waiting room to get me. Robin was the director's secretary and had originally called me to schedule the interview.

I already felt like I knew her after our brief conversation on the phone, and I liked her. She escorted me into the conference room for my interview and introduced me to the seated panel.

I took a seat, looked around the room, and propped my tablet on my knee, prepared to start writing names and taking notes.

The panel members introduced themselves, and I repeated back their names in a greeting as we went around the table to aid me in memorizing each name. Each panel member asked me a couple of questions.

The first question I was asked was, "Describe the mission of the EEOC." The recently memorized mission statement of the EEOC just poured from my lips.

Based on the look of the panel members as they studied their notes, I decided my response was good. The rest of the interview went well. I had anticipated nearly all their questions.

As I had also anticipated, the last question asked was, "Is there anything else we should have asked you, or any other information you'd like to make the panel aware of?"

I pulled out the copies of the Exemplary Service Award and handed a copy to each panel member.

I then apologized and explained that I had just received it from the Attorney General a couple of days ago and thought they might find it helpful in making their decision.

As soon as I left the interview, I turned my phone on, called Karyn, told her that the interview had gone well and that if I didn't get the job, it wouldn't be because of the interview.

I received a call from the ADR Coordinator, Yvonne Gloria Johnson offering me the position, and we negotiated a start date. I submitted my resignation to the University and took two weeks off to go back to Syracuse and spend time with my mother, brothers, and sisters.

Mom wasn't doing so well. She would look at me and say, "Help me." I would ask her how I could help her, but she could not explain her request; she would tear up and lapse into a distant gaze.

She was suffering from dementia, at a point in time became completely incontinent, and was unaware of what was going on around her. Old age offers many indignities.

My brothers, sisters and I placed her in a full-care facility with a lovely view of James Street from her bedside, not too far from where she had worked for so many years with WSYR Radio/Television, which for the most part had remained unchanged.

245

It was a good visit with my brothers and sisters, and I was ready to go to work for the EEOC. I jumped right into my position, observing one mediation with Carol, and then co-mediating a second one with her, which went very well.

After the second mediation, I felt confident enough to start scheduling and conducting mediation conferences.

Carol watched me carefully and made corrections whenever necessary. Throughout our relationship, she has never hesitated to correct me, and even scold me when appropriate.

As mediators, we did it all, from when we received the charge, to the day we convened and mediated.

We helped resolve the charge, prepared an agreement, and submitted the fully executed agreement along with the closure documents to our capable program assistant, Mari-Cruz "Maria" Castaneda, a truly beautiful lady and wonderful team player.

Each mediator did all their own correspondence, scheduling, and conducting. We were a one-stop shop for respondents and charging parties to resolve issues at the lowest possible level.

Carol Blackman had started mediating for the EEOC in the Philadelphia District Office in 2001 and was in training the day the World Trade Center towers and Pentagon were struck. She transferred to Phoenix in 2006.

Before she began with the EEOC, Carol completed law school as a single parent, raising her daughter Samantha and working full time as a Paralegal for a large Philadelphia law firm. She worked for six years as an attorney and found herself wearying of the never-ending extraordinary workload and the lack of work-life balance. Life was to be savored and enjoyed, so she sorted out a career that would utilize her negotiation skills and bring her happiness.

Carol sought out mediation training, honed her mediation skills, and began mediating pro-bono at the EEOC. She spotted a position advertised with the EEOC for a mediator, applied, and was hired. She spent almost five years mediating for the EEOC in the Philadelphia office as a staff mediator, noted a vacancy in Phoenix, applied for a transfer to the Phoenix office, and was hired in 2006 replacing two mediators who had just retired.

After about a year, the other mediator in the Phoenix Office retired, and Carol became the sole mediator in her office for about three years before the hiring freeze was lifted. That's when they hired me, and a bi-lingual mediator named Enedina "Dina" Cruz in 2010.

Fluent in Spanish, Dina had served as an investigator for the EEOC before being promoted to the vacant mediator position. Although we were both selected at the same time, she began serving as a mediator one week after me due to her very heavy case load as an investigator that still had to be dealt with before leaving Enforcement. The Enforcement Manager, Berta Echeveste, made it clear to me that Dina was dearly missed in Enforcement.

Dina had an interesting background that included investigating for both the EEOC and the Arizona Attorney General's Office, a bachelor's degree in criminal justice from Arizona State University, running a family business, and modelling.

She received the Chair's Champion of Justice Award in 2015.

She has a beautiful family, a great reputation, is extremely attractive, articulate, and brimming with confidence. Based on my experience, if you want something accomplished quickly, accomplished well, and accomplished appropriately, ask Dina. Three years after I retired from the EEOC, she interviewed for and was selected to fill the vacant ADR Coordinator position.

We all settled into a routine of scheduling mediation conferences, sharing conference room space, and vigorously closing charges through a facilitated mediation process.

Our supervisor, Yvonne Gloria Johnson, the ADR Coordinator—the position I would later assume—gave us plenty of room to learn and perform our duties.

Carol is the consummate professional. She took both of us under her wing and guided us through the development of our skills. I will be eternally grateful for her assistance and warm friendship. She became my "office wife"—with Karyn's consent, of course—and made my transition into the EEOC work culture comfortable and effective.

One time we sat and talked about our dads. I learned that her father served as an infantry sergeant during the Battle of the Bulge, also referred to as the Ardennes Counter Offensive, and was awarded the Bronze Star for his bravery and leadership during a very difficult fight with a desperate enemy. The initial German attack included some 410,000 German troops, 1,400 tanks and other armored assault equipment, 2,600 artillery pieces, 1,000 combat aircraft, and numerous other armored fighting vehicles.

Due to extremely poor weather conditions that kept a good part of U.S. aircraft grounded, the Germans achieved total surprise when they sprang on early morning, December 16, 1944.

Carol's dad witnessed soldiers freeze to death in the deep cold as they repelled attack after attack, and marveled that he survived, for good reason.

By January 25, 1945, of the 610,000 U.S. troops involved, there were 89,000 casualties, and 19,000 dead. This battle turned out to be the largest and bloodiest fight for the U.S. in all of World War II, and the third deadliest campaign in U.S. history. German losses were placed between 80,000 and 100,000 men, and they never recovered. They surrendered on May 7, 1945.

Carol is the best mediator I have ever worked with. She decided to retire at the same time I did.

Generally, facilitative mediation is fun and rewarding. It isn't work. If you feel like you are working while you are mediating, you may be doing something wrong.

As a mediator, all you need is your brain and the ability to communicate effectively. You are responsible for assisting the parties in working toward a mutually acceptable and achievable resolution of *their* dispute. It's a wonderful process when it's done right.

The charge filing process begins in Intake, where I had first sat and waited to be called in for my interview.

Intake is not a happy place. The many aggrieved persons complete an intake questionnaire, then wait to meet with an investigator to discuss their allegations. Quite often, they have family members, friends, or an attorney with them.

Based on the initial interview and documentation, after the interview is completed and the charging party has left, the investigator evaluates the claims and makes a recommendation on the likelihood of a "cause finding" determination based on the alleged harm involving laws enforced by the EEOC and the strength of the charge.

Sometimes the allegation involves laws that the EEOC doesn't enforce, such as wages and overtime, unless possibly covered under the Equal Pay Act.

If the EEOC didn't have jurisdiction, the investigator provided the aggrieved person with contact information for the Department of Labor Wage and Hour Division or the appropriate entity.

No matter what, if the individual wants to file a charge, it is accepted, and sometimes closed almost immediately. This preserves the charging party's right to elevate their issue to the courtroom, or try to.

Often, the charging parties wouldn't be able to produce any usable evidence or witnesses. Enforcement would triage all the charges taken, from the least likely to result in a cause finding, to extremely egregious well-documented allegations.

Sometimes the allegations are accompanied by horrific recordings or even a more shocking video.

I recall one charge where a supervisor was in the process of sexually assaulting a female employee who had an audio/video-recording pen in her pocket and caught him masturbating as he approached her with a leer.

You could hear her begging him to leave her alone and stop.

That charge was deemed ineligible for mediation.

All charges that were evaluated to be in the mid-range, and some that were evaluated to be "A" charges were referred to the ADR mediators, and we'd begin to potentially schedule the charge for mediation.

The EEOC also had a small number of "frequent filers" who filed ten, twenty or even more charges of discrimination. These charges were often so baseless that they were closed soon after the interview.

Often the respondent (employer) would have no interest in mediating. After some discussion, they might agree to try it, with success. They sometimes had extensive documentation of misconduct or theft and felt no need to reach any kind of negotiated agreement with the charging party, represented or otherwise.

Sometimes, the charging party would have such inflated expectations that it would be crystal clear that mediation was not the correct venue. They would clearly state that the only agreement they would possibly enter into involved a hefty six or seven-figure settlement, often including someone's termination as well—both very unlikely results of a mediation—and they would ask that I present their demand to the respondent prior to the mediation!

The respondent would hear the impossible opening demand, and say, "Let's not do this." Mediation was completely voluntary for the respondents, charging parties, and the EEOC.

All charges not mediated would be returned to Enforcement for investigation or closure.

There were times when I listened to the charging party rant about how they were going to really sock it to the respondent, and I would have a strong hunch based on everything I knew that the charge was going to be closed with no cause finding after I returned it to the investigator.

There are some terrible employment attorneys who help create unrealistic expectations, and often demand several thousand dollars up front to represent the charging party, already staggering under the weight of no income and many obligations.

The represented charging party would sometimes march into the mediation in full combat mode, expecting the respondent to immediately capitulate, accompanied by a blustering attorney who threatened to cost the respondent "hundreds of thousands of dollars" if they didn't immediately surrender to the inevitable, only to discover that the employer had mounds of documentation proving all sorts of misconduct, and often accompanied by a wizened attorney who specialized in representing respondents.

Sometimes the respondent would also have a signed arbitration agreement, which significantly dampened the possibility of any full-blown litigation costs for the respondent.

I witnessed some incredible clashes between attorneys.

On rare occasion, the charging party or respondent's attorney would return to the table, striking a more conciliatory tone.

I would meet privately with all parties and attempt to help them identify and select the most effective negotiation posture and discuss their expectations in depth.

I remained facilitative in my approach, usually asking an open-ended question, and listening reflectively.

They might vent for a while, then get down to business. Sometimes I'd pull the attorney out into the hallway for a private conversation if I felt they needed some help out of earshot from their client.

The attorney might admit to me that they were experiencing serious client-control issues, and we'd discuss what would help their client to become effective in resolving the charge.

At times both charging party or respondent and their attorneys would be so lost to emotion and/or misinformation that nothing worked, and sadly the mediation would impasse—sometimes after a long, arduous day of mediating.

There were times as well when the charging party was extremely credible, sometimes well-represented, and produced evidence that was compelling.

As a mediator, I assisted in resolving approximately one-hundred charges per year, and my resolution rate with the EEOC averaged 82% over the more than six years I mediated for the Commission.

I have always believed that no agreement is better than a bad agreement and have at times worked with the parties for months after the mediation to help them reach a mutually acceptable agreement.

One of the very enjoyable activities that Carol Blackman got us involved in was working with the Arizona State University School of Law Mediation Clinic.

Professor Art Hinshaw offered the Clinic to nine lucky students every semester. This prestigious Clinic prepared them to represent clients in mediation—a prized skill that effectively avoids unnecessary or risky litigation.

At the beginning of the semester, we would meet with the class of mostly 2L or 3Ls, (second, or third year students) and provide them with an overview of what we do.

Each student would have the opportunity to observe and participate in mediation conferences with us.

I viewed it as beneficial in many ways, including my impression that the parties generally seemed to behave better when there was a student in the conference room observing or interacting with them!

Carol Blackman was always on the lookout for outreach opportunities. My favorite was the Annual ABA Representation in Mediation Competition, where law students demonstrate their skills in negotiating an agreement for their clients effectively.

I have served as a judge and mediator but prefer mediating. These students are the best and brightest.

As their mediator, my whole purpose is to provide them with a mediation environment where they can most completely demonstrate their skills as a representative, negotiator, mediator and attorney.

The scenarios are complex, with no one right solution. Great fun for me!

In addition to mediating, we often received emails that detailed outreach opportunities from our public affairs person, Krista Watson. When able, I took advantage of these opportunities. I enjoyed the chance to get out of the office, do some public speaking, and promote ADR.

One of the outreach activities I received through Krista was a one-hour presentation on the laws that we enforce, presented to the Catholic Social Services at 19th Avenue and Northern.

This was the first time I had stepped in that building since I resigned my position as a job developer in 1981, and I was still able to find my way around.

The audience was primarily those involved in job placement for the constantly arriving refugees from everywhere in the world. To my delight, one of the job developers had served with me briefly as my Vietnamese interpreter.

I remembered her as a very pretty, slender young refugee newly escaped from Vietnam with a decent command of the English language.

Back then, I had told her that I was hesitant to speak Vietnamese, because I had learned much of it in a combat environment and I was certain that at least some of it was profane.

She asked me to speak to her in Vietnamese, and then confirmed that I should be careful where and when I tried speaking it.

It had been many years since we'd seen each other, and she was still beautiful.

In late spring, 2014 right after I turned 64, the EEOC advertised the position of ADR Coordinator. I needed to make a decision. My original plan after discussing it with Karyn was to retire in 2015. I'd be 65, and we'd have a nice little nest-egg accumulated.

I absolutely wouldn't take a promotion without a personal two-year commitment, and I knew it would involve leadership and management responsibilities, which I was not eager to take on again. On the other hand, I had no idea who would be supervising us if I didn't step up.

In addition to discussing this with Karyn, I sat down and had a good discussion with Carol. I encouraged her to apply for the position. I felt that she would make an ideal ADR Coordinator.

She told me that she would prefer to see me in that position, and she knew enough about me at that point to believe I would be selected if I applied and interviewed for it. I knew in my heart that she was right. After discussing it with Karyn, I decided to apply.

During the interview process, I made it clear to the panel that if selected, I intended to continue mediating, and I told them that if they were looking for a program administrator who didn't mediate, they shouldn't select me.

As per usual, I enjoyed the interview tremendously, and I was selected. I started as the ADR Coordinator in June 2014 over our five-state District. It was a great job, more fulfilling than any other position I have ever held.

The seven mediators, two program assistants, and ten contract mediators I supervised were wonderful, interesting people. I had an office in Phoenix, Arizona; Denver, Colorado; and Albuquerque, New Mexico.

Within a month of starting my new position, I submitted my list of goals that I intended to accomplish, and when each goal would be accomplished.

My first was to make sure everybody in ADR had an Annual Performance Review for all the intervening years between Yvonne's departure, and my arrival. Goal accomplished.

My second goal was to meet with each mediator in the District and observe them in mediation. Goal accomplished.

My goals were designed to leave ADR better than I found it. That's my mantra. Leave things better than I find them. I identified that as a core value in mid-life, at roughly the same time that I embraced servant leadership.

On my first visit to the Denver and Albuquerque offices, I met my fellow District mediators face-to-face for the first time. It was wonderful. I was very impressed with the ADR team Yvonne had assembled.

Yvonne Gloria Johnson rose through the ranks of the EEOC and was the first ADR District Coordinator after formation of the mediation program by the EEOC and the re-formation of the Districts, which elevated Phoenix to District status and reduced Denver to Field status.

Yvonne recommended my selection as a staff mediator. Her leadership and supervisory skills worked quite well with me. I enjoyed working with her.

My routine duties included supervising the three offices and providing any assistance necessary to help the mediators and program assistants be as effective as possible.

I spent a fair amount of time communicating with other members of the management team. I especially enjoyed my many conversations with Diana Chen, who went on to become a judge with the Social Security Administration.

A good portion of my time was also spent supervising the contractors, and I continued to routinely conduct mediation conferences.

The EEOC's premier annual event is TAPS. This is an annual seminar during which the EEOC provides updates and training. This annual event is a "must" for large employers and employment attorneys. Everyone is welcome, for a fee.

As the ADR Coordinator, I established an ambitious ADR outreach plan that included TAPS. I enjoyed speaking at several seminars or providing a panel.

On two occasions, I had the good fortune to serve as master of ceremonies for the Denver TAPS, and enjoyed every minute of it. What a great group of attendees! Patty McMahon, a published author, gave me that opportunity. Thank you, Patty.

Being a contract mediator can be a tough gig. Many of our ten contract mediators that I worked with as the Coordinator had extensive experience working with the EEOC and held contracts with multiple Districts.

Some of them could seemingly perform magic when all indicators were pointed toward an impasse. Some of them, such as Amy Lieberman, owned a thriving mediation service and were constantly in demand.

Two of those magic-performing mediators were Amy Lieberman and Rita Montoya.

Amy is also a published author of a book containing a common-sense approach to mediation. I suggest if you are planning to mediate with Amy, read her book. I greatly admire her professionalism, and entrepreneurship.

In addition to being a damned good mediator, Rita provided much-needed pro-bono coverage for us in the Albuquerque office during a critical period when our staff mediator was absent for an extended period.

Karyn was selected as a contract mediator prior to my selection as the ADR Coordinator. I had no input in the selection process. She was selected based on demonstrated ability, education, and training. She was a licensed Arizona Attorney (now in retired status) and is a very experienced mediator. The contract administrator for the contract ADR mediators is the ADR Coordinator.

After my selection for this position, one of the first things I did was to ask Karyn which she would prefer, being a contract mediator, or me becoming the Coordinator? She preferred me taking the promotion, and I assisted her in resigning her contract.

The running joke in the office was that one of my first official acts as Coordinator was to fire my wife.

I routinely went to the sixth floor first thing in the morning most days that Intake was conducting interviews and spoke to and answered questions for the aggrieved individuals who were waiting to meet with an investigator.

I spoke with them about the benefits of mediation and encouraged them to consider it. I would answer any questions they had to the best of my ability. After my talk, I would often walk past the offices located within Intake, and as I passed the investigators, I would say, "I got them all warmed up for you!"

I especially enjoyed my many conversations with Nancy Draper, typically the first person the aggrieved individual would meet, and Pat Miner, who supervised Intake. Pat was a tough investigator, and applied a firm, steady hand as a supervisor. She ran a very tight Intake unit.

Nancy and her husband own horse-property way out on the west side of Phoenix. Her husband drives an 18-wheeler, and she is a tall, fun, good-natured country gal.

I continued to mediate. Not wanting to impact the staff mediators, I only took mediations in the Prescott area, which would require hiring a contract mediator at $800 a pop, when we suffered from constant limited funding, or to provide coverage during absences. This also meant no travel costs for me working in Prescott because it was my home of record.

By agreement, I also took any mediation the staff mediators felt certain was going to impasse, based on conversations with the charging parties and respondents, and various other valid reasons. By taking these tough ones, I believed I was helping the mediators to continue working at their highest and best level, with no impact on their morale or their statistics. I wanted to make sure they knew that someone had their "six-o-clock" (their back).

Besides, I really enjoyed the challenge, and resolved quite a few of the tough ones. I also provided back-up if for some reason, a staff mediator could not conduct a scheduled mediation due to sudden illness or a family emergency.

I conducted twelve mediations for the EEOC in Prescott, Arizona. If possible, I always scheduled them for a Monday or a Friday, giving me three contiguous days at home. I resolved all of them, several involving multiple charges.

One thing I enjoyed tremendously was mediating federal complaints. I worked on the same floor as three lovely judges, and sharp legal minds: Katherine Kruse, Dianna Chen (then supervisor), and Nancy Griffiths.

I knew that every charge I mediated for them that resulted in an agreement freed many days on their already impossibly packed calendars. I absolutely loved sending them an email to let them know the parties had reached an agreement.

There was no requirement or expectation that ADR mediate for the federal sector administrative judges. I just liked doing it. I only scheduled mediations on days not already booked. They were generally entertaining.

Soon, the other mediators started to get on board with the idea. I enjoy looking back on the many charges our fine District mediators resolved for the A.J.s during my tenure.

Anastasia "Stacy" Sdanowich was a long-time employee who began mediating for the EEOC Denver District Office shortly after the program was established and retired one month after me. She is attractive, accomplished and admired. I greatly enjoyed working with such a polished professional. She has continued mediating for clients in the Denver area.

Much like Stacy, Maria Vela began mediating for the Denver Office as a bi-lingual mediator soon after the mediation program started. She is all business in mediation, but the parties know that she cares about the resolution being mutually acceptable and achievable. She is also an avid reader, and always had a new, interesting book perched next to her desk when I would swing by.

Maria "Valerie" Taylor, also serves as a mediator in the Denver office. As a long-time mediator, this Argentinian native developed a style that provided a positive counterbalance in the office.

She is well-known in the Latino community as an ADR spokesperson for the EEOC, and bravely accompanied me on a whirlwind one-day speaking tour in Denver, during which her assistance was invaluable.

We arrived at my speaking engagement and realized that I had left my thumb-drive in her computer before leaving the office and walking to my next engagement. I was scheduled to provide two hours of negotiation training for the Colorado Attorney General's Office and had just wrapped up a 2-hour program at the Denver EEOC.

She ran multiple blocks through downtown Denver in heels, retrieved my thumb-drive, and returned just as I was being introduced. What a fantastic lady!

Our Albuquerque Office had one assigned mediator, Christopher "Chris" Venegas. Chris was an ambassador for the EEOC. He was absolutely adored in the ADR community.

A former U.S. Air Force Security Policeman, he was awarded the Air Force Achievement Medal, and worked his way up the ranks in the EEOC to bi-lingual ADR Mediator.

A truly talented mediator, I personally observed him perform magic. He also retired a couple of months after I did.

I had the opportunity to select a mediator for the Phoenix office. As always, I enjoyed working with our HR person Ron Davis. My initial selection for the position was Amy Burkholder. Her background with the EEOC was impressive, and she interviewed well.

She also received an offer to become a supervisor in Enforcement and informed me that that was where her heart was. Later, I had the honor of formally mentoring her. I fully expect Amy to one day become a District Director, or beyond.

I next reached out to Julie Armstrong. Julie had also interviewed quite well. She had all the requisite skills, knowledge, and abilities to do the job. She immediately began to far exceed expectations and became a top performer.

She likes to experiment. She introduced aromatherapy to the mediation process, and provided adult coloring books and stress-relievers.

As a former EEOC investigator, and U.S. Air Force OSI Agent (commissioned), she can work with the parties, and help them gain a result that is mutually acceptable and achievable. And, she is a beautiful person.

As my days with the EEOC ended, I labored to assemble a continuity binder I'd been working on since starting as the ADR Coordinator. As I sorted through the many saved documents, reports, and correspondence, I was flooded with numerous memories.

I came across a newsletter I had held onto from Guide Dogs of America, a charity that I contributed to as part of my annual CFC donation and continue to support. Two blind folks I had the good opportunity to work with were Celeste Williams and Allen Hall. At the time I went to work for the EEOC, Celeste had a fantastic Golden Retriever guiding her through the perils of navigating Phoenix to and from work daily. Her Golden's name was Dealer, a sharp-looking Golden with classic features. A truly noble beast.

Getting to know Dealer prompted me to include Guide Dogs of America in my annual splurge, and I strongly recommend you learn more about this honorable organization.

When Dealer retired, he was replaced with a smaller female name Saffi. Saffi was gentle, attentive, and calming to be around.

On my final day, I turned my ID and office key over to Altovise "A.J." Douglas and walked out of the building for the last time as an employee.

The U.S. Equal Employment Opportunity Commission is one-of-a-kind. Before the EEOC, President Kennedy initially formed the Presidential Committee on Equal Opportunity and placed Lyndon B. Johnson in charge of it. This Committee enforced rules against discrimination based on race, creed, color, and national origin with federal contractors only.

Lyndon Johnson became President in late 1963 after President Kennedy was shot and killed in Dallas. One of the first really important pieces of legislation President Johnson signed into law was the 1964 Civil Rights Act.

Since then, there has been little other than the EEOC standing between vulnerable parties and irresponsible cruel employers with, on rare occasion, truly evil motive and intent.

Far from perfect, the Commission has continually re-invented itself since its creation on July 2nd, 1965, shortly after the historic Civil Rights Act of 1964 was enacted.

The first chairperson was Franklin D. Roosevelt, Jr. in 1965, and the chair has been filled with such notables as Supreme Court Justice Clarence Thomas.

When I started as a mediator in June, 2010, the Commission was chaired by Stuart J. Ishimaru. I had had little to do with the political appointees other than my director, Rayford Irvin, hired as an SES (Senior Executive Service) after his promotion to full director.

Shortly after Jacqueline Berrien became the Chair, I had the opportunity to meet her during a speaking engagement at ASU.

She was a big, beautiful, black woman with a keen intellect and a great smile. I enjoyed listening to her presentation and had a chance to chat briefly with her afterwards. A graduate of Harvard Law School and former counsel for the NAACP, she was a consummate professional who believed in what she was doing. Her life was claimed by cancer in 2015.

After Ms. Berrien completed her term as chair and before she died, she was replaced by Jenny Yang. As the newly appointed Phoenix District ADR Coordinator, I admired her work from afar. I liked the way she tackled the big issues and enjoyed her frequent updates.

I had the wonderful opportunity to join her for dinner one night in Denver, along with our Phoenix District Director, Rayford Irvin, and our Regional Attorney, Mary Jo O'Neil, on one of the occasions when I served as master of ceremonies for TAPS.

Both she and Rayford sipped ice-tea and talked baseball, while Mary Jo and I shared a good bottle of Cabernet Sauvignon. The conversation between us was lively and interesting. It cemented my admiration for Jenny.

One of the big initiatives tackled by Ms. Yang was to develop a clearer focus on systemic discrimination and facilitate development of a workable action plan. In our District, one of our top investigators, Anick Flores, was assigned to head up the newly formed task force and did an outstanding job.

This task force brought to clearer focus systemic issues that illegally present barriers to gainful employment.

I believe it's important for anyone who wants to be gainfully employed that they have opportunities commensurate with their skills, knowledge, abilities, and background. Artificial, unnecessary, and illegal barriers need to be eliminated if we are going to raise our society to its highest and best level of productivity.

I had the rewarding opportunity to serve with some of the finest federal employees in the country. Their dedication and professionalism were incomparable.

One of the investigators, John Oare had been a cop in L.A. and was hit in his handcuffs by an AK-47 round while heroically attempting to direct traffic away from a crazy armed robbery that involved two gunmen brazenly walking the streets in body armor, with fully automatic AK-47s, spraying patrol cars with automatic fire as they attempted an unsuccessful escape.

Talk about lucky! He kept the mangled handcuffs hanging in his office. When I complained one time about how tough my day was going, John smirked, pointed at his prized handcuffs, and said, "That's a tough day."

John took the time to complete the 40-hour mediation training with the Attorney General's Office, and there is no doubt in my mind that had he remained with the Phoenix office, he would have been promoted to a mediator position.

The Phoenix District, like all Districts, staggered under the constant burden of a huge charge inventory. I witnessed several years where the total charges taken nationally exceeded 100,000. Those were very difficult years for the EEOC, and grueling years for ADR.

The mediators were constantly busy, typically mediating 3-4 days every week, with just barely enough time to keep up with convening mediations, continuing to work on mediations still in progress, and returning charges to Enforcement for further investigation.

We put a great dent in the standing inventory of charges, and assisted charging parties and respondents in recovering as best possible from a bad situation.

Carol Blackman and I decided to throw a fun party to celebrate our retirements and rented the rooftop of the Clarendon Hotel—the site of Don Bowles' murder. We invited some of our closest friends and people we had enjoyed working with while mediating. It was a beautiful evening, and we had a great time saying thank you, and turning the page to the next chapter in our lives.

I have agreed to continue mediating as a volunteer for the EEOC and the Arizona Attorney General's Office.

Aside from departing from the EEOC as a paid employee, I needed to depart from the best apartment I'd ever rented, and the wonderful swimming pool that I had so many enjoyable evening swims in.

I took the time to go to the office and express my gratitude for the wonderful environment they and the rest of the apartment complex staff had facilitated.

One of my extra-curricular activities while not at work or swimming was taking classes of interest. I am now a life-time student, and it's fun to only take classes I'm interested in.

One of my favorite sources is Great Courses, which has an extensive catalogue of self-paced courses. Right now, I'm trying to learn how to play the guitar.

Many years ago (1970-72) I tried my hand as an artist completing a couple of projects that were rewarding to me. Life had its demands and I was forced to earn a living, which I couldn't do as an artist.

In 2014, I registered for an art class, focusing on the use of charcoals and graphite, which I'd never spent a great deal of time learning. I learned some great techniques for shading, line drawing, adding depth, and more.

For my final project, I asked Karyn to sit for me, and drew a portrait of her. I received an "A." I attempted to capture her beauty and joy for life. I smile every time I look at her picture.

KEVIN J. OSTERMAN
FEDERAL MEDIATOR

UNITED STATES
EQUAL EMPLOYMENT OPPORTUNITY COMMISSION

3300 N. CENTRAL AVENUE
SUITE 690
PHOENIX, AZ 85012

TEL (602) 640-5038
FAX (602) 640-4729
kevin.osterman@eeoc.gov

KEVIN J. OSTERMAN
DISTRICT SUPERVISORY ADR COORDINATOR

UNITED STATES
EQUAL EMPLOYMENT OPPORTUNITY COMMISSION

3300 N. CENTRAL AVENUE
SUITE 2220
PHOENIX, AZ 85012

TEL (602) 640-5038
FAX (602) 640-4729
kevin.osterman@eeoc.gov

KEVIN

My best attempt to capture Karyn's beauty, 2014

27

PRESCOTT

"I'd rather be lucky than good." Lefty Gomez (1908-1989) said that. I agree. There's nothing like luck. Many people don't believe there's such a thing. I do.

When I ran through a burst of machine gun fire, and didn't get hit, I felt lucky. When my airplane engine quit unexpectedly while flying over Mazatzal Peak in route to Payson, and I was able to get it restarted, I felt lucky. I could easily go on and on.

My favorite "luck" cartoon is Ziggy, being informed by a cheery stewardess that he had the whole airplane to himself because a large group heading for a psychic convention cancelled at the last moment. The look on his face is priceless.

Karyn and I purchased some property in Skull Valley, Arizona with the intention of building on it. Plans were prepared, a builder was selected, power was run to the property (we already had a great well!), construction began, and we became entangled in litigation over a road easement through our property that we hadn't agreed to.

A pretty fair amount of money was expended for the land, early construction and litigation; we soured on the idea of living there and we eventually sold the land, but we still longed to get out of the Phoenix metro area and into a place we loved.

One day in 2009 while we were wandering around in Prescott we drove around the area and looked at several properties.

Karyn's cousin Linda recommended checking out Mountain Club. She described it as an interesting eclectic mixture of homes and properties. As we cruised around, we stumbled onto a neat little place that was advertised as the "perfect artist's retreat."

Few had viewed the property because the price was too high. As real estate prices continued to plummet everywhere, the seller decided to reduce the price significantly, and we were the first to look at it after the price reduction.

Karyn and I agree that it would have sold immediately if we hadn't made an on-the-spot offer and settled on a price after a brief negotiation.

It is located in Arizona's first planned community, Mountain Club (established in 1926), just outside of Prescott.

The little retreat was fully furnished, like someone had just locked up and left for the weekend (the dear owner had actually died). We made an offer, negotiated, and sealed the deal.

I noted that there was a nice Afghan on the sleeper sofa and Karyn immediately fell in love with it. I also noted that there was a well-stocked bar, including an unopened half-gallon of decent scotch. When we came up to our new home the weekend following the closing, both were gone.

I called our realtor. He was deeply embarrassed. He explained to me that on the day of the closing, he stopped by the house to make sure all was well. As he approached the door, he noted that the realtor's key box was already open, and when he walked into the house, there was a woman sitting on the sleeper sofa sipping a drink and weeping. He carefully asked her who she was. The weeping woman explained that she had been a friend of the deceased, and that a realtor friend of hers let her in to pay her last respects.

Apparently, paying her last respects included taking a few souvenirs. Our realtor bought me a bottle of 18-year-old Chivas Regal and offered his deepest apology for the lost Afghan.

Sometime later after we told our story to our good friend Lauren Allsopp, she surprised us with two beautiful Afghans she had woven, both which match the interior of the Treehouse perfectly.

We love our little retreat, and have grown to love Prescott, too.

Prescott is a great little city. Of the many places I have lived in my life, this is the best. Our home is up in the trees on a county-maintained road that was recently paved for the first time, just outside the city limits.

Our neighbors include significant numbers of mule deer, javelina, racoons, skunks, ravens, coyotes, and an occasional bobcat or mountain lion. We also have a decent population of garter and king snakes, and a good population of plateau fence lizards (voracious insect eaters). A wide variety of birds migrate or live here too. We're not isolated, but we're surrounded by ponderosa pines, juniper, oak, and manzanita trees on all sides.

We also have a diverse variety of cactus on our property. The weather is mild, and people are friendly.

Our hangar was an easy twenty-minute drive. The airport is well-run, and we loved the location of our hangar in the "Bottlenecks." Karyn and I were also members of the Prescott Airport Users Association.

After I went to work for the EEOC, Karyn and I decided to move from our apartment in Scottsdale and find an apartment in Phoenix.

I wanted something that was affordable, and either within walking distance of my office, or close enough to the light rail, since there was a light rail station directly in front of the office building, located at Osborn and Central.

We first rented a studio at 2nd Avenue and Clarendon, about a half-mile walk to the office, then moved to a condo with a decent pool at 3rd Avenue and Clarendon. The condo was nice; unfortunately, after we'd been there for about 1 ½ years, the owner sold it.

While living in the condo, I met an interesting woman, and fellow swimmer, named Shawna. She was tall, had nice features, was a sculpted bodybuilder, a former Air Force Security Police Sergeant, and had the most elaborate tattoo on her back I'd ever seen—a geisha holding a fan!

We almost always had the pool to ourselves, and she shared some fun stories with me as we swam. She was knowledgeable in martial arts. She made her livelihood travelling around the world wrestling with male customers who were willing to pay a significant amount of money for the tough work out. She also did fitness training and coaching.

Karyn had been living fulltime in the Treehouse after our first year in the condo. I sped up to Prescott every Friday afternoon, right out of the office, working my way through Phoenix traffic, straight up I-17 to SR 69, and in the reverse on Sunday.

I was pulled over twice for speeding and ticketed once.

Nearly every weekend was a honeymoon!

As soon as I received notice that the condo had been sold, I started looking for a new location. The seller explained that the buyers would probably want to keep me as a tenant, and I decided I didn't like my negotiating position, nor did I want the uncertainty.

I shopped around and settled on a one-bedroom in the Forest Park Apartments. They had a very nice heated pool and spa, and I liked the feel of the place. This was the best apartment I've ever rented. It was a bigger one-bedroom, and I liked the layout.

I had my own washer/dryer, a large private balcony, and the pool was right below it. Most importantly, Karyn liked it too.

I had the freedom of walking to work nearly every day I cared to, with a Safeway between me and the office, and a Walgreen's directly across from my office.

I swam daily. Almost every day right after I came back from the office, I'd immediately strip, pull on my suit, and head for the pool. Sometimes I would walk back to my apartment and swim for ½ an hour during my break for lunch. After a difficult morning mediation, this was often quite therapeutic.

I used light rail frequently. I sparsely operated my vehicle in the Phoenix Metro Area unless I was coming from or going to Prescott.

The apartment complex was aptly named. Large trees surrounded and filled open space within, making it an urban enclave identifiable from the air.

One time while Karyn and I were flying the Phoenix transition corridor southbound in Piper during a crisp, clear Fall Saturday morning, we were able to distinguish Forest Park. It was a nice-sized green rectangle bounded by Osborn, Indian School, 4th, and 7th Aves. I first picked out St. Joseph's and then my eyes went right to the forest.

I've never been much of a cat person, but Forest Park had an intriguing cat program. By trapping, neutering, inoculating, otherwise repairing if possible, and

268

releasing feral cats back into Forest Park, they maintained a constant population of about twenty cats, all still quite feral.

There were designated feeders (volunteers), and otherwise, tenants were discouraged from feeding the cats.

I began to recognize many of the cats, as they wandered freely about the large, treed community like small jaguars on the prowl.

Forest Park was rodent-free. I thought that the cat program was part of an overall ambience of Forest Park Apartments.

The staff was friendly, helpful, and dependable. The Park was gated, well-maintained, and had a feeling of relative security. Special kudos to Rene!

The maintenance staff were almost all Romanian, very polite, and helpful, often greeting me with a friendly, "ah-lo!" I received my refund for my security deposit within a week. Forest Park was a particularly good life experience.

When I retired from the EEOC, I vacated my apartment, and became a full-time resident of the Treehouse.

Regularly, a good variety of wildlife here in Mountain Club walk by our front door on a game trail leading to adjoining vacant land. I love sitting on the deck and spotting deer, javelina (also known as collared peccary), and other occasional critters, and sometimes I get a jaw-dropping air show put on by the ravens or the hawks as they wheel and soar above the trees.

The walking is conducive to neighborly interactions and healthy exercise in the pine-fresh air. There's little traffic, and we have great neighbors.

In May 2017 I was appointed to the Board of Directors of Mountain Club to fill a vacancy and complete the rest of the elected term of another Board member no longer able to fulfill his duties and responsibilities.

In July of 2017, during the Annual Mountain Club membership meeting, I was elected as Board President, and immediately established my first nine goals. I was reelected in July 2018 by property owners and I was also reelected to a second term as President by the Board. I established my next five goals. The Board reelected me as President again in July 2019, and I gave them my one-year notice that I would not serve another term as President. I explained that I preferred not staying in any one position for more than three years. I established my last set of annual goals, including identifying my successor and aiding in making their presidency a success.

The Board is a colorful assemblage of good people, including a USMC Vietnam vet who served as a dog handler with the infantry. An interesting man, and a good fellow. We worked many of the same areas at the same times in Vietnam.

I remember watching the dog handlers and being glad I wasn't one. He had one dog partner killed by a booby trap, who died after the company commander he was working with refused to call in a medivac. His dog had been severely wounded by an exploding device placed close to the trail they were following. They were both savvy about booby traps and it was totally unexpected when it happened.

Our prime mandate in accordance with the Mountain Club By-Laws is to:

> " … maintain and improve property values through the upkeep and improvements of the Mountain Club owned amenities including but not exclusively, the clubhouse, parks, water supply system and properties, and to conduct the business of the Mountain Club according to the Bylaws, Rules and Regulations, and Administrative Procedures."

Right up my alley!

We are not an HOA, although we have some semblance to one. The Mountain Club is an eclectic planned community (the oldest in Arizona), occupied by a wide spectrum of residents representing a band of income levels, and occupations.

When we purchased our home, it was not unusual for a multi-million-dollar home to have a two-hundred-thousand-dollar retreat cozily nestled right next to it. We're in the woods outside of Prescott, an easy five-minute drive to the city limits. It's quiet, clean, and comfortable.

In October 2018, I was nominated by District 1 Supervisor Rowle Simmons and appointed to serve as a Planning and Zoning Commissioner beginning in November. It is a four-year appointment. There are five Districts, two Commissioners per District.

After I retired, I immediately joined the Prescott YMCA. Although I feel no religious stirrings, their pool is excellent.

I have deeply enjoyed an early morning swim, and typically swam laps for about ½ hour several days a week and engaged in water aerobics twice a week. It was wonderful exercise and just a great way to start the day! Karyn sometimes joined me for laps and participated with water aerobics with me too.

I picked up an occasional class at Yavapai Community College (YCC) just to exercise my brain or body a little.

Sadly, Karyn and I were taking a water aerobics class at YCC When COVID-19 struck, and class was cancelled for the rest of the semester. This was our fourth semester with Toni. Our instructor Toni Ristich gave us a good workout every Tuesday and Thursday morning. The class was almost all women, and much like Typing 101, I enjoyed it immensely!

28

THE DAVE NETWORK

Probably nearly every community has a network or multiple networks of contractors who know and work with each other frequently, and even refer each other for jobs. In Prescott, we have the Dave Network.

Dave was born and raised in Prescott. His father, Bernie, was a well-known contractor who moved houses, purchased a fair amount of real estate, and built and repaired nearly everything under the sun in Prescott. At an early age, Dave started working with his Dad, and learned a great deal from him—including, most importantly, how to be a problem solver.

After graduating from high school, Dave continued working with his father and eventually took over the business.

Many of his school classmates, friends and acquaintances also ended up working in the trades. Over the years they worked on numerous projects together and learned who could be relied on and trusted, and who they couldn't. There's a lot of tough love in the Dave Network, and great deal of respect.

They sometimes enjoy the outdoors together or join organizations such as the Yavapai County Jeep Posse, or Search and Rescue, which Dave and one of his friends in the network both belong to. They are a group of men who have developed a certain nobility.

While still litigating a right-of-way dispute concerning four and a half acres of undeveloped land we owned in Skull Valley we hired a local attorney, Paul Roberts, to represent us. He did a masterful job of protecting our rights and securing a favorable verdict. He also introduced us to Dave.

We needed some help with a project at our newly acquired Treehouse. When we purchased our little bungalow, it was adorable, but needed a considerable amount of work. The carpet was probably at least 30 years old, and had a tattered area rug over it in the living room that we knew was going to need to be dealt with ASAP. The deck was made of Trex, a composite, wood-alternative, decking product, and was somewhere around 30 years old; it was nearly as unstable as the front porch. The staircase leading up to it was also a concern. Everything that had to come into the upstairs house had to go up that staircase, to include a refrigerator and a freezer, a washer and dryer, a new sleeper sofa and bed, and more.

I had very nervously watched a couple of strong young guys haul our refrigerator up the stairs. One of the workers turned to me and said, "Is this going to hold us?" as he took another step and listened to the stairs creak. After that, Karyn and I agreed the stairs would have a high priority on the repair/replace list.

One day when Karyn and I came home from the store, arms full of groceries, walking up the steps I turned to Karyn and said, "We really need to fix these soon!" She agreed.

Paul mentioned that Dave had done a considerable amount of work over the years for him, and he considered him to be talented, affordable, and dependable. We got Dave's phone number and gave him a call. Thus, began our entry into the Dave Network.

We made arrangements for Dave to come out and talk with us about some of the projects we had in mind. When he arrived, he was an impressive sight. A little over six foot, he had the physique of an athlete, with broad shoulders and a narrow waist. His hands were large and rough looking, with several digits partially lost years ago. He is a tough looking guy, and we came to understand that behind his rough exterior, he was a gentleman, too. Before we could point out the first project (front porch), he had already diagnosed it as a little unsafe, and immediately set in a very workmanlike manner to repair it. The bill he presented was well within the cost we had anticipated.

Next, he installed a new shower and toilet, and tiled the bathroom floor. All was done well, quickly, and inexpensively. His problem-solving abilities came to the fore when the shower assembly would not quite fit through the narrow opening to the bathroom. A buzz saw and shaving ¼ inch off the backside of the unit did the trick.

Duly impressed, we had him remove the extremely worn carpet and install a wooden floor, followed by installing a new stackable washer and dryer in the back room, and a new sliding glass door.

We were inspired to put in a doublewide carport, and we found exactly what we wanted at Home Depot for the right price (10% military discount), and made arrangements for Dave and a helper to construct it for us.

The storage area and workshop under the deck had fallen into disrepair many years before. The roof-deck above it leaked, most of the wooden structure below was rotting, and it was generally a pretty unpleasant work area. The main beam above the front door broke in half, and the front of the deck sagged a bit. The entire structure needed to be replaced/improved. We asked Dave for advice and an estimate. I had already done a rough estimate, and his estimate was a bit lower than mine.

We pulled a permit and upgraded the electrical. Dave and a host of skilled compadres descended on our property with great efficiency. At a very fair price the deck was fully repaired—as were the stairs—and the work area down below was totally transformed!

Our Treehouse now became so much closer to what we had envisioned when we purchased it.

An opportunity fell into our lap to purchase the undeveloped half-acre behind us at a fair price. We now had more space to build onto, and we developed plans, pulled the necessary permits, and as you may have guessed already, we discussed plans with Dave to tack on a bedroom in the back.

And the gentleman who drew our plans is also part of the Dave Network. He came out and talked with us, took measurements, quoted us a very reasonable price, and prepared complete, ready to submit plans.

He worked as a local contractor for many years including working with Dave's dad and has known Dave since he was a kid. He learned how to draw plans over the years. He told us that for a fixed price, he would prepare our plans, re-draft them as necessary, and work with the county as necessary to meet their requirements. He did.

The guy who did the required soil compaction testing is also in the Dave Network and was equally skilled at working with the County Planning Department.

So was the electrician who did the electrical for us.

We still marvel at how beautifully our addition was constructed. We now have a true master bedroom and den, not to mention the million-dollar view outside our bedroom door. As Frank Lloyd Wright stated, the best way to preserve your view is to own it.

I am feeling a growing concern. Over the years I have had many conversations with Dave and his friends. One of the questions that I always asked them was about who would replace them when they retire. Their answer: Nobody.

Few skilled young people seem interested in working the trades as an assistant to an independent contractor. Dave is a hard worker, and a challenge to keep up with.

Most up-and-coming construction workers would much prefer being steadily employed in the trades, drawing a paycheck, and enjoying all the perks of being an employee. Everyone I've met in the Dave Network will be retired in the next 5-10 years with few in the ranks behind them.

29

THE BOAT COMPANY

Karyn and I agreed that we'd like to try taking a cruise. We talked about where we would like to cruise to, and after considerable discussion selected Alaska. Neither of us had an interest in cruising on a giant liner, and we began our search on Google to see what was available in small ship cruises.

After lengthy searching, discussion, and defining our decision points, we settled on The Boat Company. They offer one-week trips between Sitka and Juneau through the Tongass National Forest and operate two ships: Motor Vessel *Liseron* and Motor Vessel *Mist Cove*.

We selected the Motor Vessel *Liseron* ("morning glory" in French and pronounced "lee-sir-on"), cruising from Sitka to Juneau, May 27 to June 2, 2018. The *Liseron* has ten guest quarters, each designed for two-person occupancy, and has twelve crew members quartered below deck. She is 145 feet long, 28 feet wide, with a draft of 8.5 feet.

The *Liseron* was built in 1952 in Seattle and sold to France, serving as a minesweeper. She was constructed completely with non-ferrous metals, making her ideal for potentially wading through mine-dotted waters detecting and removing—or detonating explosive devices often designed with magnetically triggered detonators. She was purchased and restored with great care as a passenger ship in 1989 and has been cruising the Inner Passage ever since.

We agreed it would be fun to build an extra day into our visit to Sitka before the cruise. Our extra day in Sitka would give us time to visit the Fortress of the Bears and the Raptor Recovery Center. In Juneau we had time to take a flight in a float plane over the glaciers and visit a remote lodge for dinner.

As the household's Operations Officer, Karyn immediately leapt to the task of very effectively organizing our trip from start to finish. We had a full year plus before we were scheduled to cruise.

Time whizzed by as we engaged in our many activities. Karyn fell and broke her elbow while getting ready to go play pickleball. I stumbled through my first year as president of The Mountain Club, and Karyn became editor-in-chief of the newsletter. I completed a good portion of the first draft of my book.

Suddenly, it was the end of May, and almost time to head out on our adventure.

I Googled the Sitka and Juneau 10-day weather forecast. It appeared we had a good chance of rain every day but one. We packed our umbrellas and rain suits. We both had a backpack, a carry-on bag, and one duffle-bag we planned to check that contained our boots, warm clothing, rain gear, and additional clothing.

We buttoned up the Treehouse and departed at 03:30 in our Honda Civic Hybrid for Sky Harbor International Airport, Terminal 2. We had a smooth, uneventful two-hour drive all the way to airport parking.

We both have TSA Global Entry, and we eased through the early morning checkpoint quickly. We bought some breakfast and, using our dual-audio jack, listened to our latest Audible book, *Dead Wake*, about the sinking of the Lusitania (a tragic, complex, and fascinating story). The boarding process was quick and easy. We took a quick restroom break and were back and lined up in good time for boarding.

Our seats were window and middle and we had no difficulty stowing our carry-on bags. The passenger seated on the aisle was a native of Sitka who had been at a conference in Phoenix and was returning home. He introduced himself as "Junior."

Junior was headed home and planned to take a canoe trip from Sitka to Juneau with his brother and about fifty other Native American participants. His brother organizes this trip every two years, and Junior decided to join the expedition this year. The group planned to travel in 32-foot canoes and had a permit to camp—plus take fish and game as needed for subsistence. Junior planned to sleep in a hammock with a poncho draped over him at night, gun in hand.

He is part Tlingit and his destination was a gathering of Alaskan Native American tribes for an event referred to as the "Celebration."

In keeping with historic native ways, the individual participants travelled in a manner most closely resembling the ways of their ancestors as they made their way through the Inner Passage to Juneau—in canoes.

As he and Karyn chatted, the subject of chocolate came up. He suggested that she visit the Chocolate Moose in Sitka and ask for his girlfriend Aurora.

After arriving at the Sitka airport, we were greeted by a driver holding a sign with our name on it. She took us to our bed and breakfast. Throughout our time in Alaska, all our transportation needs provided by The Boat Company were flawlessly executed. The preparatory materials and ongoing support they provided can best be described as meticulous, carefully planned, helpful, and quite useful. We agreed that they had thought of everything.

Junior also made recommendations for dining, and after Karyn told him she loved duck, he recommended we dine at the Sitka Hotel that night. Karyn had duck and loved it. I had a particularly good pasta dish.

After our satisfying and delicious meal, we walked over to the Chocolate Moose to look for Junior's girlfriend Aurora. Aurora is a beautiful woman of true warmth, and when Karyn and I walked into her shop and called her by name, she brightened and said, "You must be the folks who spoke with Junior on the plane. I just got off the phone with him." We bought some very tasty chocolates for both of us. Thanks, Junior!

While in Sitka we stayed at the Jamestown Bay Bed and Breakfast. Our accommodations were comfortable and inviting. Our apartment had a heated spa on the deck right outside of our door. It appeared very well maintained with the temperature set at 104 degrees. It was lovely. The view from the spa was of Jamestown Bay, a beautiful expanse of bright blue water surrounded by forest, with an occasional ship or fishing boat slowly crossing it and was soothing and serene.

We visited the Raptor Recovery Center and then the Fortress of the Bears, which is two adjoining enclosures with diameters of about 100 yards each containing black bears on one side and brown on the other. We observed two brown bears on a date (yes, humping). Warning: there was no Saturday or Sunday bus service when we were there.

Our transportation was fully arranged from the bed and breakfast to the Westmark, the gathering place and the usual lodging for those embarking on a Boat Company voyage. Very seamlessly, we stepped out of our room, and as we started down the stairs, the shuttle pulled in, and the driver was a delight.

Our baggage was already tagged and ready for transport to the *Liseron*. We all slowly coalesced into a comfortable meeting area at the Westmark, and Karyn and I found ourselves seated near a couple from California named Trish and Matt Schulz. Trish had beautiful, distinct features (light skin, chestnut hair) that you do not see often, and wore big glasses, giving her a kind of girl-reporter look.

Matt, an attorney had the build and look of a retired athlete and a very direct communication style that helped me understand, based on past experience, that he could be all business if necessary, but was a good guy.

They were fun to talk with and we got to know them better throughout the cruise—as they ended up right next door on the ship. We shared a bulkhead.

Karyn and I were surprised and pleased when we got home, unpacked, and found out that Matt had donated his fish to us. We greatly enjoyed our many subsequent feasts involving Halibut and Rockfish pulled from the clean waters of the Inner Passage.

Captain and crew members introduced themselves and provided us with a quick orientation. It was very nicely done.

After the briefings were completed, we all joined up and walked from the hotel to the North Petro Marine dock. It was fun for Karyn and me because we had already wandered around Sitka and this gave us the opportunity to see even more!

We boarded the *Liseron* early Sunday afternoon. Our luggage had already been transported and placed in our quarters before we arrived. My first impression was how beautiful the *Liseron* was. She is a wooden ship with well-varnished banisters, ladders, gleaming brass rails, and obviously a well-loved ship. Our quarters were clean, comfortable, and had a nice layout. The location was perfect. Our cabin was Located most forward on the starboard side of the skip deck.

A few of us had met and chatted briefly prior to boarding, and we all began introducing ourselves after we boarded. Karyn and I deduced that the Salon (the sign on the door says "Saloon") would be the best place to hang out and went down there. It was welcoming and comfortably seated all of us on couches and over-stuffed chairs. Windowed on both sides and with a beautiful décor, the Salon contained a small informative library and a full bar that included alcoholic and non-alcoholic beverages and a generous variety of snacks—M&Ms, Goldfish crackers, candy bars, orange slices and other fruits, and a pretzel mix. There was a decently tuned guitar sitting in the corner.

Coffee, tea, and cocoa were available on the fantail at 6:30 every morning and throughout the day.

Karyn made a request when we originally booked our trip that they stock coconut water. They provided all the coconut water Karyn could drink, and more. They also maintained a large, enclosed pitcher of cold water with lemon slices floating in it.

A regularly updated map of our cruise through the Inner Passage remained propped upright in one of the corners of the Salon. Katelyn Rennicke routinely added new information, including a growing list of wildlife sightings as we continued through the forest waterways. In addition, she regularly briefed everyone on our progress through the Inner Passage and described the flora and fauna we would encounter.

There is an observation deck fore and aft, and the view from the fantail is wondrous. This is where all twenty of us dined together every day and were able to use as a platform to fish from for a couple of days.

After boarding, the crew fully introduced themselves, facilitated by our Captain, Kirk Rouge of Rockland Maine. He gained our immediate confidence and kept it. We were briefed on and practiced using our life-vests and reporting on deck with life-vests in the event of an emergency.

Over the course of the voyage, we had the opportunity to visit with the Captain on the bridge and learn more about the crew and ship.

Chief Mate Drayton Parker from Charleston, North Carolina performed his duties with great efficiency, and helped keep the ship and all within on course.

Our crew Naturalist and talented videographer, Katelyn Rennicke from Bayfield, Wisconsin provided us with excellent briefings on the surrounding flora and fauna. We were also briefed on the planned fishing excursions.

Our Guest Coordinator, Anna Boone from Toronto, Ontario briefed us on the services offered and who provided each service. The talks and briefings they provided were a highlight of the cruise.

Captain Kirk is an excellent skipper, highly effective communicator, and over the course of our voyage earned our deepest respect.

M/V *Liseron* untied and began cruising from Sitka to Fish Bay through the Kakul Narrows. We powered north and delighted in the passing scenery, and after a couple of hours, we were called from the Salon to the fantail for our first dinner.

We shuffled around the table and took our seats. As a group we quickly identified our preferred dining spots, though we routinely mixed things up and often had new company next to or across from us from meal to meal. Our menu for the first meal was: Caesar salad with poppyseed puff crisps, roasted salmon with a honey-lime glaze, chili-spiced cauliflower, and forbidden rice with baguette.

We were served family-style which enhanced our contact with each other and helped us remember names. Karyn and I would test our name-recalling ability frequently. Karyn had everyone's name memorized by the second day.

As the meal was being brought to us by Steward Ronni Hernandez from Woodland, California, who carries herself with great dignity and has one of the most beautiful and engaging smiles I've ever encountered, and Assistant Steward Sam Vaughan from Vashon Island, Washington, a rainbow showed brightly off of the fantail, appearing to end right where we were anchored.

I proposed a toast. "To us, for being at the end of the rainbow!" My toast was followed by a hearty, table-wide, "Here, here!"

Later in our voyage, we observed a double rainbow, just as bright and clear a rainbow as any I have ever seen, and my first crystal-clear double rainbow ever.

We anchored in Fish Bay for the night. There had been some light rain during the day, but as darkness fell the sky appeared to be clearing.

The meal was, as were all, delicious. Chef Justin Oberg from Wrightwood, California, and Assistant Chef Maggie Haight of Steamboat Springs, Colorado, demonstrated great creativity with the menu and the meal service and presentation were exemplary.

A fellow passenger, Joy, who was seated with her husband Chip, picked up the guitar and started playing in the Salon. After our evening meal we sipped beverages, sang, and laughed as we all forgot the words to a popular song.

Karyn and I noted that it was ten-o-clock and barely dark. We decided that it was time to turn in. We had a big day ahead of us. We returned to our cabin, showered, snuggled up, and talked for a couple of minutes before falling asleep.

Early in the morning I awoke to the rattling of the anchor chain being hoisted and heard the two, big, two-stroke diesel engines come to life. I also began hearing the crew move around as we got underway. Karyn and I got up and looked out our window to see the ship slipping past a multitude of tall pine trees lining the Surgess Narrows as we headed toward Saook Bay.

Breakfast of corned beef hash, mixed potatoes, scrambled eggs with chives and cheddar, oatmeal, and croissants were served at seven on the dot on the fantail. We were briefed on the planned morning activities.

We had our choice between a hike, some stream fishing, or saltwater fishing for halibut and rock fish. Karyn and I raised our hands for saltwater fishing.

We jumped into a skiff skippered by deckhand and guide Dylan Whitney from Kittery, Maine, that carried us out to the Peril Straight. Dylan sported a great handlebar mustache. He provided some lessons on fishing in these waters, and we caught a few nice-sized Rockfish.

We sped back to the *Liseron* powered by a 115 hp outboard motor at a good clip and climbed back onboard ship. The anchor was hoisted, and we headed for Kelp Bay, where we spent the night. Using the carcasses from the Rockfish, we baited five shrimp pots, which five of us, including me, ceremoniously threw overboard as we entered the Bay.

Lunch consisted of seared scallops seasoned to perfection and pasta with cascarilla pesto, hearty focaccia bread, and lemon bars for dessert. As always, the meal was delicious. After lunch, we had a comfortable afternoon on the observation decks, hanging around the Salon and lounging in our cabin.

Dinner was served: broccoli cheddar soup, seared Wagyu steak with chimichurri, roasted red pepper mashed potatoes, and garlic pull-apart buns.

We had another enjoyable evening hanging out in the Salon and talking with our fellow passengers.

Early Tuesday morning, I and the other four passengers who had tossed shrimp pots out the previous afternoon, rose and hopped into a skiff to collect them up. We pulled in five quarts of shrimp. It was kind of my Forest Gump moment as we hauled in the pots and counted the many shrimp, one pot at a time.

Lunch included Chicken Geary with rice and spinach, flatbread, and honey bird nests for dessert.

That afternoon, we tried fishing from the fantail, which turned out to be kind of a fiasco due to the constant wagging of the ship back and forth in the current. Lines got severely tangled several times and no fish were caught. Dinner was again delectable, and we spent another interesting evening in the Salon before turning in. We listened to our audio book for a while and fell asleep.

We enjoyed a hearty breakfast while surrounded by clear calm water and the Tongass National Forest as we headed for Whitewater Bay at a moderate speed.

Karyn and I decided to give saltwater fishing another try, this time guided by Senior Deckhand and Second Mate Jon Ford from Poulsbo, Washington. We caught several big Rockfish and Karyn caught a beautiful 36-inch halibut in Whitewater Bay. It was a lot of fun watching her get that fish to the boat. I dubbed her Ms. Halibut 2018, a title she greatly enjoyed.

Several of our fellow passengers elected to stream fish (catch and release) or take a hike through some old-growth forest.

We then hoisted anchor and crossed Chatham Straight to Takatz Bay, where we anchored for the night. Karyn and I decided to spend our afternoon conducting self-directed activities in our cabin.

After socializing in the Salon for a while we were called to dinner, which featured roasted and seared blackened halibut with a nice dollop of sweet and savory chutney, a side of cranberry quinoa sprinkled with a sweet pea puree and some tasty Hawaiian rolls. Our meal was deliciously paired with the table chardonnay. Desert was a yummy berry cobbler with a nice big dollop of ice-cream on top.

On Wednesday morning we awakened early and went outside to look at the forest and wildlife. After a sumptuous breakfast that included banana pancakes with whipped mascarpone, ham and cheese croissant puffs, a feta and kale scramble, and a big dish of fresh fruit, Karyn and I took a kayak out and explored the bay. It was a perfect morning and we enjoyed taking our time leisurely paddling along the shore line.

After we returned to the ship, the *Liseron* hoisted anchor and our Naturalist and multiple passengers, including Karyn and I, began searching for wildlife in route to the Keku Islands. We spotted numerous humpback whales rising and spouting, sometimes rising out of the water and giving us a good look at them as they flashed their enormous tails and dove back under.

Lunch was Yakisoba stir fry with fried eggs, braised pork belly, sesame rolls, and rice pudding desert.

In the afternoon Karyn opted to take a nature hike, and I joined a handful of fellow passengers in a skiff skippered once again by Senior Deckhand and Second Mate Jon Ford. He took us out for some fun saltwater fishing just off the Keku Islands. We caught several halibut and Rock Fish too small to keep and reeled in several nice-sized Dusky Rock Fish which we deemed to be "keepers."

After returning to the ship, we got cleaned up and headed for the Salon, where I mixed myself a Manhattan and Karyn sipped coconut water. Other guests filtered into the Salon until it appeared, we were all there. A fellow guest, John, asked me to mix him a Manhattan too, and we toasted to the "Nectar of the Gods."

Joy was cajoled into playing some music on the guitar, and we all talked. Karyn and I slipped away for some time alone in our quarters, then got ready for dinner, which included Southwestern corn chowder, grilled Duroc dry-aged pork chops with a fig and honey mustard compote, green beans, sweet potato jojos, and beer bread. The desert was a highly memorable raspberry cheesecake with a white chocolate scone crust.

As we often did while dining, we steamed toward our next destination. This time it was Pybus Bay, where humpback whales gave us a spectacular after-dinner show.

We spent time that evening sitting in the Salon, sipping our beverage of choice, and chatting with our newfound friends before heading for our cabin and snuggling while we listened to our book. As we listened, we sensed that the Cunard ocean liner RMS *Lusitania* was getting closer and closer to being torpedoed and sunk by the German U-boat, U-20, and marveled at all the mistakes and miscommunication that led up to the tragic event.

Thursday morning began bright and sunny, with a delicious breakfast that included broccoli cheddar caramelized onion frittatas, mixed potatoes, fresh fruit, and chocolate almond muffins.

Karyn and I opted for salt-water fishing, and once again, we headed out on a skiff skippered by Senior Deckhand and Second Mate Jon Ford. I caught a 36" halibut (we couldn't keep anything above 38 inches), and several nice Dusky rock fish which were also deemed "keepers." Karyn and I now both had plenty of halibut and rock fish to take home!

We steamed toward the Brother Islands as we ate lunch. Lunch was the best yet, including rockfish tacos with fresh guacamole, salsa, Spanish rice, tortillas, and a raspberry sorbet. The flesh of the rockfish is much like sea bass, and perfect in tacos.

The view from the fantail was drop-dead gorgeous as we dined and slipped past the Brothers Islands.

For dinner we had fresh halibut cioppino that had been caught by fellow passengers Bill, Jim and John (with whom I'd had a Manhattan on Wednesday) and donated. The cioppino was served with butter rice, sourdough bread and pie bars made with blueberries and blackberries.

Karyn and I boarded a skiff skippered by deckhand and guide Charly Schmitt. Charly has a laugh that stays with you. I refer to it as "a hundred-yard laugh," or a laugh that I could hear from a hundred yards and think, "That's Charly."

Charly has plans to own his own boat one day. He is already a licensed captain and is saving his money and preparing himself.

We hiked into the East Brothers Islands and marveled at the Sphagnum Moss that seemed to cover nearly the entire island. It was so thick that in many places you could fall back on it like a mattress, and it gave the island an enchanted look. We spotted the remains of a dead bald eagle on the shoreline and we were cautioned that being caught with even a single feather could result in a $10,000 fine!

Once we had all returned, the *Liseron* weighed anchor and headed for Wood Spit, anchoring at the entrance of Endicott Arm for another beautiful evening on the water.

We settled in the Salon for a drink or two, read, listened, and talked, then went to our cabin at about 9:00 p.m. It was still light outside, and we were still wide-awake. We snuggled and listened to our book. The *Lusitania* was getting ever closer to its fateful rendezvous with the U-20.

Friday morning was mostly clear, with a soft light and no breeze. The *Liseron* pulled anchor and made its way up the Endicott Arm toward Dawes Glacier as we enjoyed another great breakfast consisting of candied cashew cranberry French toast with bacon, cheddar jack scramble, fruit, and oatmeal. Karyn loved the oatmeal and ate a hearty portion.

After breakfast Karyn and I stood in the fantail enjoying the view of Tongass National Forest as we motored along, we spotted three kayaks in the distance paddling toward us. And the *Liseron* slowed to a halt. A skiff was lowered, and we soon watched one of the crew members motoring out to the kayaks. The skiff and kayaks all headed back toward the *Liseron*, and soon, three National Forest Rangers came on board.

The rangers, two males and a female, were headed for the face of the Dawes Glacier. They were the very picture of handsome youthful vitality and endurance. They were patrolling a large swath of the waterways in the forest by kayak. Their patrol included spending time in several villages and educating youth about the National Forest they live in.

We met with them in the Salon and they told us a little about themselves and what they were doing. The senior ranger briefed us on their mission and then the other two spoke. The younger male is an educator, and was currently in training with the senior ranger to better prepare for his educational assignment. Slim, handsome, and positive, he projected the spirit of a professional.

The female ranger-in-training is also an educator. A tall, lithe brunette, she wore no makeup, and didn't need any. She provided an articulate overview of their latest training program, during which they took a group of kids into the National Forest for an amazing outdoor experience. They departed the *Liseron* and continued their patrol.

The *Liseron* anchored at North Dawes. We rode a skiff skippered by Jon to Dawes Glacier for an up-close look. When we turned left out of the bay and up toward the glacier, the water turned from green to blue.

As we approached the glacier, we threaded our way through a large field of small to medium-sized icebergs, most garage-sized and many studded with rocks and boulders both large and small. When we were about ½ mile away, we observed the glacier calving (breaking chunks off its edge).

The face of the glacier was bright blue at its base, appeared to be several hundred-feet-tall, and extended beyond sight into the mountains behind it. Keep in mind that generally only 10% of an iceberg appears above water! These were massive!

After we plied our way back through the ice field, Jon accelerated, and we sped back toward the bay and the *Liseron*—crossing back from blue to green water in the process.

Karyn and I had fun kayaking to a couple of small icebergs ranging from car-sized to train car-sized, always keeping the *Liseron* in sight as we paddled right where the water was in its transformation from green to blue.

After we were all back on board, it was anchor up and we headed for Taku Harbor for the night. This was our last night together and the vibe among us was interesting. We had become friends and the Salon was abuzz with conversation. We all exchanged contact information.

Dinner was grand. Fellow passenger Chip offered a toast to a fine voyage followed by a hearty assent by all. The minestrone soup was as good as I've ever tasted. The main course included seared filet mignon with a red wine reduction and compound butter, saffron risotto, roasted cinnamon chipotle, tri-color carrots, pumpernickel bread, and an awesome Chocolate Decadence with almond brittle. The conversation around the table was a near cacophony, accented with peals of laughter.

After dinner we were invited to a complete tour of the galley, engine room, support systems, and crew compartments, and to have any questions answered. We received a very complete briefing on the engines and other support systems including water filtration by our engineer, Johannes Bellow from Bremerton, Washington. It was a great briefing. He sounded like a smart, well prepared senior NCO briefing his new commanding officer on his area of responsibility.

We returned to the Salon and enjoyed a surprisingly entertaining—and well put together—slideshow of our cruise, photographed in large part, assembled, and presented by Katelyn Rennicke. Little did we know that in addition to her very able performance as our Naturalist and deckhand, Katelyn was also preparing this keepsake presentation. I've always enjoyed being around smart, strong women, and Katelyn is no exception.

As part of Katelyn's presentation, she talked about the 16 different types of birds we had observed ranging from Bald Eagles to Red-bellied Sapsuckers. She also talked about the six different types of marine mammals we'd encountered: Harbor seals, Stellar sea lions, Humpback whales, Dall's porpoises, orcas, and sea otters.

They were all magnificent to see, but the Dall's porpoises were by far my favorite. They are very strong swimmers and kept up with us easily as they frolicked in the water off our bow. They swam with us for a good ten minutes before disappearing, seemingly on command.

Katelyn's briefing included the scant land dwellers we had encountered to include coastal brown bears, North American black bears, Sitka black-tailed deer, red squirrels, minks, and about 100 banana slugs.

Fish included halibut, rock fish, King salmon, Dolly varden, and the incredibly ugly and undesirable sculpin.

We saw a good number of Moon and Lion's Mane jelly fish. We also observed sea stars, Nettles jelly fish, leather back chiton, and Dungeness crab.

Katelyn also talked about the great number of plants we had encountered and in addition to the Sitka spruce and Western hemlock we'd been surrounded by all week, she enumerated and identified fifteen other plant types we had encountered ranging from Skunk cabbage to heart-shaped twayblades.

We had a brief laugh about the Bald Eagles we observed mating, and when Katelyn mentioned the double-rainbow, there were hushed comments that swept the room like a wave. The double rainbow was symbolic of our week-long cruise from Sitka to Juneau.

Neither Karyn nor I ever heard a discouraging word, disagreement, or even a minor irritation. The crew performed impeccably and with great efficiency from start to finish, and Karyn and I could not have been surrounded by a more desirable mix of fellow passengers.

On our last day out, we had a good number of Humpback whales spouting and breaching about 500 meters in front of us. One became bolder and his distance from the boat at one point was about 100 meters, where he made a spectacular breach with a great splash of his tail. He continued spouting and breaching for a good ten minutes and then disappeared.

We all met in the Salon and shared stories and feelings. We were exhausted. What a week!

Anna Boone, our Guest Coordinator, gave us a briefing on services that would be provided in the morning, and set up a laptop for us so everyone could add or correct their contact information. A line formed.

Karyn and I slipped away at about 10:00 p.m.; exhausted, we showered, crawled into bed, and fell into a deep sleep.

I woke to the rattling of the anchor being hoisted before sunrise on Saturday morning. There was a kind of misty overcast as we sped past the forest that was soon pocked with a house or structure here, a dock there, and soon many structures, homes, and docks as we moved toward Juneau.

Soon, Juneau came into view. Boat traffic increased, and then we were passing or being passed by very large and small ships and watercraft.

The approach and docking were impressively smooth. We greatly enjoyed standing in the forward observation compartment, directly behind the observation deck, and watching as the crew maneuvered the boat to the dock and tied down the grand madam.

All our bags had been shipped to the Westmark in Juneau, and we were led to the hotel and bid adieu.

We checked into the Westmark, went to our nice room, and stripped. I took a quick shower and made room for Karyn's long-coveted bath while I got caught up with the *Wall Street Journal*. I hadn't received any news in a week and had almost no cell coverage while on the cruise.

We confirmed our reservations to fly to Taku Lodge for dinner in a float plane and made plans for the afternoon. We decided to see Juneau as best we could in the limited amount of time we had and went for it.

We walked over to the Mount Roberts Tram Ride. Karyn was fully in the tourist mode, and I was fully into the "Happy wife, happy life" mode, and enjoyed watching Karyn relish each new experience. It is hard to imagine someone who loves life more than Karyn.

We almost immediately encountered a small stand offering photographs with a grizzly. Karyn was excited and before I knew it, I was posing next to Karyn with a small club in my hand that appeared balanced on the chin of a grizzly bear, and Karyn shrinking behind me in great fear. The look on my face says it all.

We walked a good portion of Juneau and returned to the hotel in time to get cleaned up and head for Wings Airways down near the harbor.

After checking in, we were assigned a boarding group for the five aircraft. We were the "Moose" group and we were informed that our plane would be an orange-on-white Otter. We lined up and waited for the planes to fly into the harbor and taxi over to our docks. The pilots very skillfully taxied to their assigned dock, pivoted, and killed the engine.

We boarded a de Havilland Otter and headed for the Taku Lodge. I was seated in the co-pilot seat and had a good view off the nose of any other planes headed for the lodge. I observed them flying a couple different approaches. We swung wide out over some glacier fields then turned a short final.

After skimming over the glaciers, we made a sharp right turn into the water-way in front of the lodge. This was my first landing on pontoons, and I thought it was smooth.

Each plane disembarked, and we were soon mingling at the lodge. We were too early for dinner, so we took a hike out behind the lodge, which was okay but not great. I strongly recommend that you douse yourself well with mosquito repellant first.

Dinner was good. The salmon was perfectly cooked, and the beans were okay. The coleslaw was awesome.

We flew back to Juneau and walked back to our hotel. What a lovely little city.

We entered our room, hugged, kissed, and stripped. I drank a couple of glasses of a good port and we snuggled. We started listening to our book and fell asleep.

In the morning Karyn told me that the room was still rocking. She felt like she was still onboard ship. We headed down to check out early. Friendly hotel staff quickly located our box of fish and we walked down to the basement to retrieve it.

As part of the amazing service provided by The Boat Company, any fish we caught that we wanted to take home was fileted, vacuum packaged, and boxed for us to transport. We were carting about 25 pounds of halibut and rock fish back home to Prescott!

We arrived at the airport, checked our box and duffle-bag, and received boarding passes. Karyn asked the counter agent about how our bags would continue with us on to Phoenix. The agent explained that we would need to re-check our bags when we arrived in Sitka.

As we flew from Juneau to Sitka, an announcement was made that anyone continuing to Seattle should remain on the plane after we arrived in Sitka. For the first time, Karyn and I realized that we wouldn't be changing planes in Sitka!

We called for a flight attendant. When she came to us, we explained our dilemma to her. If we didn't have time to get off and re-label our box and bag for Phoenix, our fish would be left behind in Sitka, and after about 12 hours our hard-earned catch would begin to warm up and eventually become odiferous.

She assured us that would not happen. She told us that upon arriving in Sitka, she would make sure our box and bag were properly tagged. We gave her our baggage labels for the remainder of our flight to Phoenix.

Before taking off for our Boeing 737-800 ride to Seattle, the attendant came by and told us that she had personally gone into baggage, found our box and duffle bag, and re-labeled both. Our travel to Phoenix with Alaska Airlines went smoothly—and happily, our bags were on the baggage carousel waiting for us after we disembarked.

We walked to the parking garage across from Terminal 2, found our car and headed for home, cargo intact.

Our post office box was crammed-full. Karyn's cousin Linda had routinely checked our mail at the house and there was a small pile on the table. Our daughter Tori had spent the weekend and left us a box of chocolates and a nice card that said,

"Oh HAPPY me! Inside the words "THANK YOU so much" were printed with a nice hand-written note from Tori.

That night we crawled into bed, still bubbling with excitement, snuggled, and listened to our audio book. We turned it off just as the U-20 was lining up her shot on the *Lusitania* and we fell asleep.

"One more step and you're really going to get it!"

30

FAMILY

My paternal great-grandfather, John Osterman, was born and raised in Sweden. He immigrated to the United States, betrothed to Elsa Fagerstrom, a slender, light brown-haired young woman with delicate features who was six years younger than him, and also from Sweden. They planned to start a new life in America.

He was a handsome, light brown-haired, muscular young Swede of medium height, and after arriving in America worked and saved as much as possible, with plans to stake a claim on Kansas prairie land. He and Elsa would later become known as "Pioneers of 1869."

After John had established the homestead, the plan was for Elsa to join him. When the appointed date of Elsa's arrival neared, John packed for a long walk, and headed back north toward Salina to meet his bride.

As planned, they travelled on foot back to the homestead. Elsa had been busy preparing for the homestead, and brought a considerable collection of pots, pans, utensils, and other cooking items, linens, clothes, and household goods, as well as her personal belongings.

It was more than they could carry in one load, and they had to haul it in relays. John had already practiced this when he first walked out to stake his claim, carting about one hundred pounds of gear across the plains from Salina to the homestead in fifty-yard hops, fifty pounds at a time.

According to my father, after leaving Salina with Elsa, John noticed they had company. He had seen some movement behind them and grew concerned. He was armed.

He decided that he and Elsa had better shorten the distance between loads as they continued to hop-scotch across the prairie. Their company turned out to be Indians.

John never had to use his weapon. He correctly assessed that they were not "hostiles," and he was confident they were just following to see how this white man and woman, hauling all this stuff, would fare. This was common at the time.

It was not unusual for cross-country trekkers to drop or discard items as they grew weary, just realized they were hauling too much unnecessary gear, or expired. John and Elsa reached the homestead in good health with all their cargo intact.

According to family lore, although the native tribe wasn't pleased with the arrival of the white pioneers, John lived peacefully among them, and when they learned that Elsa was about to deliver her first child, they offered to provide a mid-wife.

John had already built a decent sod hut, began farming alfalfa, and built a frame home. Over the years he, Elsa, and his kids added on to it to accommodate their growing family as they started multiplying.

Among their surviving children were my grandfather, Samuel, who was born on September 10, 1882, followed by his brother Carl in 1885, and Godfrey in March 1888.

Great Grandfather John built his home in what became Assaria, Kansas, and was listed as a "farmer" in the 1880 census. He became well-known for introducing alfalfa to the local area.

My Grandfather Samuel enlisted in the U.S. Army in 1903. He was part of a force deployed to the Philippine Islands and assigned as an Army scout.

He later separated from the Army, reenlisted in 1908 and was assigned to the Ludlow Barracks, Philippine Islands, Headquarters Company, 21st Infantry as a scout in June 1910.

Samuel's older brother Frank served in the Army during the Spanish-American War, and his younger brother Godfrey enlisted as a military musician, playing in one of John Phillip Sousa's marching bands.

Godfrey was subsequently appointed to the Georgia Military College, serving as a major, with the title of Band Director.

He served as the Band Director for over 35 years. A college publication described him as, "A respected leader and incredibly talented musician, Maj. Osterman made a name for himself by taking inexperienced musicians and turning them into a well-rounded group."

His wife Maxa bequeathed a legacy gift of $100,000 to the Georgia Military College upon her passing in June, 2003.

Samuel married Francis Jankowski who had immigrated from Poland through Germany, and he became a building contractor. They purchased a house in Buffalo, New York, and raised a family. My Dad was born in 1920 when Samuel was thirty-eight.

Great Grandfather John died in 1920, at the age of 83, less than a month before my father was born. Elsa lived for another five years, until 1925, when she died at the age of 82.

My maternal great grandfather, John Frances Gaughan, Sr. immigrated to America from Ireland, with his wife, Mary, and records show that he applied for naturalization in the United States on April 26, 1901, at the age of 42.

According to Mom, Great Granddad John drank no alcohol. Just prior to sailing for America, Mary's brother convinced her that she should bring at least one bottle of spirits for "medicinal purposes."

She departed the ship briefly to go into town and purchase a bottle—and the ship left port without her!

She needed to be rowed out to the ship in the harbor with a bottle and a baby in her arms (my Great Aunt Mary), and according to Mom, Great Grandmother said, "Mr. Gaughan was so angry I didn't know what he was going to throw overboard first, the baby, the bottle or me."

Fortunately, it was the bottle. Interestingly, she always referred to her husband as "Mr. Gaughan" when she spoke of him.

They raised six children: John (my grandfather who later changed his name to Brian), James, Mary (possibly christened as "Mariah"), Rose, Bernice (also referred to as "Bridget"), and Nell (sometimes referred to as "Ellen").

My Grandfather John Frances Gaughan, Jr. was born on January 19, 1897, and was raised in Pittsburg, Pennsylvania. He enlisted in the U.S. Navy, just in time for World War I to come to an end. Talk about good timing!

Grandad Gaughan had been swept up in the Vaudeville craze and changed his name to Brian McDonald after he became an entertainer. He made the name change official on April 27, 1942. By that time, he had become a well-known singer and master of ceremonies.

He married an attractive model named Claire Weisser, who at the time was modelling for Coco Chanel. They had one child, my mother.

They divorced when Mom was about four years old. Mom remembered sitting on the judge's knee in his chambers, and him asking her who she wanted to live with. She also remembered singing him a song.

Grandma Claire later married a wealthy Jewish jeweler.

Granddad joined an extremely popular radio show, "Wilkens Amateur Hour," as the producer and master of ceremonies in 1936. The show originally began broadcasting on WJAS AM in 1935, and later aired on WCAE and KQV.

This program became one of the earliest television programs, broadcast on WDTV in 1950, and aired on radio and television for twenty-three years.

Over time, hundreds of Pittsburghers and other contestants competed for a chance to win the grand prize, and maybe be discovered.

Acts ranged from a sixty-eight-year old coal miner playing the "Cuckoo Waltz" on a concertina, to a popular performer named Margie Jean Dollman, the "Baby Cry Express," who was on for several weeks imitating crying babies to great peals of laughter by the audience.

Guest celebrity appearances included Gene Autry, Rudy Valley, band leader Baron Elliot, fighter Fritz Zivic, Roddey McDowel, Francis Langford, Jackie Heller, Broderick Crawford, Tyronne Power, and Jerry Colona.

In 1943, a young singer named Dino Crocetti from itty-bitty Mingo Junction, Ohio won second place. He changed his name to Dean Martin and went on to super-stardom after partnering with another up-and-coming talent named Jerry Lewis.

Mom's cousin, Gloria Okon, also had a successful career in radio and television. She made several television commercials, including as spokesperson for Arnold Bread. She was a gorgeous red head. Her son (my cousin), Tommy, starred in a Coke commercial with "Mean Joe" Green in 1979, where he handed Mean Joe a bottle of coke just as he came off the field from a tough game. It is one of the top-rated commercials in television history.

Grandad McDonald operated a speak-easy, promoted several wrestlers and boxers, and was head of a local entertainment fraternity, The Variety Club.

The Variety Club was originally started in Pittsburg by a group of entertainers to help a baby left on the steps of the Sheridan Square Film Theater and went on to assist children in other states.

The club was organized somewhat like a circus, and Granddad's title was "Ringmaster" (president).

He also served as master of ceremonies and general manager for the Ice Capades beginning in 1944, returning to MC the Wilkens Talent Hour from 1955 to 1957.

When he returned to the Ice Capades, he served as master of ceremonies and general manager for Ice Capades International.

While working for the Ice Capades, Grandad McDonald married one of his entertainers, Patricia Filippi. Everyone called her "Patty." She was an attractive brunette who had done well in skating competitions. She was a world champion baton twirler and a great entertainer.

They were married until she died of cancer. Grandad and Patty had a daughter, Kathleen (my aunt) who is one year older than me. She co-hosted a program on the radio in Williamsport, Pennsylvania for a period and I had the opportunity to hear her while staying in Williamsport. She sounded good and I was impressed with her ability as an announcer.

My older sister, Wendy, a pretty red head, was the original reason for Mom and Dad starting a Teen Club in Fairmount. That is how much they loved and cared about her.

And she didn't disappoint. A mother-of-four, she single-handedly raised her three sons and one daughter and helped each of them get a college education after her husband John, a truly wonderful man, died of a massive heart attack while shoveling snow on the first day of Spring 1998 in Baldwinsville, New York.

A cancer survivor, she lives life to the fullest, and is an amazing person. She started a vanilla business, producing and selling custom vanillas until the price of vanilla beans became exorbitant. My favorites were brandy, bourbon, and rum vanilla (unbelievably good in carrot cake, a variety of custards, and cornpone). When Wendy told me that she was folding the business, I stocked up on my favorites. The brand name was "Wendy's Vanilla," and was absolutely the best.

My brother Bruce is a successful wallpaper hanger. He has had about every business experience you can imagine before settling into his long-term profession.

Originally, he and a friend started a painting business at the behest of my father. Dad had just experienced a fire at his Carrier Circle Howard Johnson's Motor Lodge and hired my brother and his friend Bob to re-paint many doors that had been damaged in the fire.

A career was launched.

He and his then-partner tried operating a restaurant in a building they owned, unsuccessfully.

Bruce is one of the most talented wallpaper craftsmen in Upstate New York, and although he continues to manage his business and occasionally do some work, he is pretty much retired now.

Bruce and his wife Mary Jo own a nice little farm in Marcellus. The foundation of their house dates to 1792, and their property is beautiful.

During a difficult time in my life, I found sanctuary there, and will always love them for providing the necessary space and loving support I needed. If it were not for them, I might not be writing this memoir now.

My brother once planted Christmas trees in one of his fields, with the plan to cut and sell them—and then fell in love with them. He now has a pine forest. He also built a twenty-foot teepee on the same lot, perfectly surrounded by majestic pine trees.

He and Mary Jo have thrown one of the best 4th of July parties in the U.S., and his property has been the scene of some of the most outstanding, fun outdoor events you can imagine, including his son Bruce and daughter Jessica's weddings.

Brother Bruce came out and visited me in Arizona a couple of times. The first motorcycle he ever rode was my Triumph Tiger 650 in 1971 while I was living with Annie at 49th Avenue and Thunderbird. At the time, there was a large, open field to our west, and a big, stinky dairy just to the west of 51st Avenue. Bruce took my Triumph out in the field and roared around the mounds and gullies, dumping the bike once. It was great fun watching him.

He went on to be a Harley man. The first and only Harley I've ever driven was his Sportster. Bruce is solid and trustworthy. He plays a mean guitar, has a great voice, and has been in several bands over the years.

Bruce and Mary Jo raised two boys and two girls.

Much to his disappointment at the time, Bruce didn't get drafted for the Vietnam War, and was unable to enlist.

My brother Brian has always had the entrepreneur spirit. Through trial and error, he and his wife Lynn established one of the best residential cleaning services in Upstate, New York, "American Maid."

They raised a daughter, Heidi, and are currently helping raise a granddaughter, Lexi (Alexis). Lexi is now a tall, beautiful blonde teenager and has learned to play the piano and sing quite well. She is also very athletic.

Brian has been out to Arizona a couple of times and had a fun adventure with me in the desert, back when I was still with Annie. We all decided to camp in the desert while Brian and his friend Alex were visiting.

They went out for a beer and ice run, and after it grew dark and late, it occurred to me that they might be in distress. I grabbed my flashlight and revolver and went for a stroll down the dirt road from our encampment, looking for them. I had recently been released from the Maricopa County Hospital after getting in a wreck on my 650, so I was a bit hobbled. They were stuck in the dirt about ¼ mile away. I helped push the car out, and back we went to our campsite.

I had dug a hole and lit some charcoal in the bottom of it. When they were burning brightly, I lowered a big Dutch oven of ham-hocks, beans and seasonings into it and covered it. It had been cooking for many hours and we feasted in the dark much later as we all crouched around a big campfire and talked.

Brian and Lynn own a nice house in Eastwood. He is an honest, reliable man, and served as my best man when Karyn and I married. He is also a talented poet and song writer. Bruce completed a DVD featuring a couple of songs Brian wrote.

Back in the '70s, while Brian was driving through Kansas, he stopped to locate the family homestead, picked up a piece of sandstone from the original foundation, and gave it to Dad. Dad hired a local handy-man to incorporate it into the brick front-steps of his house on Shotwell Park.

My little sister Kerry is the first person I can ever remember loving. Dad jokingly referred to her as his fourth son, "Harry," and they were close. Kerry was a tomboy with dazzle.

She worked in the Syracuse public school system with severely developmentally disabled children and enjoyed her work tremendously. She retired in June 2017 and continues to do part time work with the school district and volunteer work at a local hospital. She is sweet, caring, and can take care of herself. She raised three sons, all solid men.

When she contacted me many years back and informed me that her husband of thirty years was leaving her for a high school sweetheart he'd hooked up with on Facebook, Karyn and I purchased her an airline ticket to Phoenix, and she stayed with us for a couple of weeks at the Treehouse. It was during rodeo week in Prescott, and I took her down to Whiskey Row on a Friday night.

I was the wing man that every girl deserves when she is feeling blue. We drank and danced from one end of the Row to the other, and she met several handsome rodeo cowboys.

When she returned to Syracuse, she was ready to get on with life.

All five of us siblings get along well, and care deeply about each other. All of us have been loving and supportive toward each other during difficult times, and we celebrate the good times.

My son Daniel currently works for Albertsons Companies, Inc. at their main distribution center. He has worked his way up in the organization from warehouse worker to supervisor of the IT Department.

He is married to Angela, who I first met when she was a cute, perky little Junior ROTC cadet at Trevor Brown High School in Phoenix, and I was an Air Force Major seated in the review stand watching her team perform drill.

They married and held their reception in the Mountain Club clubhouse here in the pines, just outside Prescott.

Daniel and I have enjoyed numerous excursions together, including drives across the U.S. and Canada, deer and quail hunting, and most recently, a trip to New Zealand with our wives.

Over the years, our gift-giving has evolved exponentially from a gift card to one year giving a Gold Nugget Bucket to Daniel and Angela, and an Instant Pot for us. This year Daniel and Angela gave us a full tenderloin, which he butchered into twelve filet mignons before my very eyes up here in the Treehouse. From my perspective, it was an amazing feat of butchering simply because I had never seen anything like that before and didn't know he had that skill. He also sent me the YouTube video link that he learned from. They also gave us a nice Weber grill. Daniel is a master griller and smoker and provided me with some great pointers on grilling when we sampled four steaks at dinner over a good bottle of red wine. I could cut my steak with a fork.

In return, we filled their home freezer with a wide variety of meats.

For the uninformed, The Instant Pot is a recent all-in-one gizmo. You can use it to sauté, steam, pressure cook, and slow cook. You can also use it to steam rice, sterilize, and make yogurt.

Karyn took right to it. She has excitedly cooked innumerable meals from a small stack of Instant Pot cookbooks ordered from Amazon. I, on the other hand, seem to be Instant Pot challenged. My garlicy green beans were a total flop.

There are Instant Pot support groups across the country, and I understand why. Although I did not seek any support, I am seeing some improvement, and I believe that one day the Instant Pot and I will bond.

Just as it appeared that I might not be able to adapt to new cooking technology, Daniel and Angela gave Karyn and me a joint birthday present that has renewed my hopes for redemption: the ANOVA Sous Vide Precision Cooker. Wow! I can cook sous vide. I can't imagine a smarter way to cook but it's time intensive.

Daniel and Angela are raising two daughters, Jasmine and Katherine. Jasmine is musically inclined; her favorite instrument at the time of her graduation from high school was the baritone sax, and she is currently living somewhere in Texas and not in communication with her family.

Katherine is a budding writer and scholar. She graduated from Barrett, The Honors College at Arizona State University, and continues working on her master's and travelling when able.

She is holding down her pet-sitting business and a part time job on campus working for the campus Public Broadcasting Station (Channel 8). She also provided me with some assistance in publishing this book.

Karyn and I "adopted" my co-worker, Tori (Victoria) in 2009. Tori and I met while she and I worked on the same student team for the University of Phoenix. After spending a great deal of time together (and sharing Honey, her golden retriever who hunted with me for several seasons), Tori became a permanent part of our lives. Karyn and I think of her as our daughter, and she has reciprocated.

Tori is a beautiful, articulate, well-educated woman making a career in the financial services industry. Recently, Tori was promoted to a regional manager position with Merrill Lynch, and I couldn't be prouder.

And can she ever snowboard! She's currently teaching her nephew Andy snowboarding. I saw a video of Andy, age 4, riding a snow board much better than I ever could. He is a smart, sharp, young fellow with a great mentor.

We have acquired a mutual taste for scotch, good wines, and mead. I've enjoyed many pleasurable evenings with Tori and her many friends, to include Kate and Sara, at the Superstition Meadery in downtown Prescott sampling their many offerings. My favorite is Desert Monsoon, made with Prickly Pear cactus fruit and local honey. If I were only allowed one alcoholic beverage ever again, this would be my choice.

She is an intrepid world traveler, serving honorably in the United States Air Force, and then with the Air Force Reserve.

As I heard more about genetic testing, just out of curiosity, I submitted a saliva sample to ancestry.com, and received an ethnicity estimate. The report shows me as 100% European, with the following approximate amounts of ethnicity: Europe West

22%, Europe East 19%, Ireland 15%, Scandinavia 14%, Great Britain 13%, Iberian Peninsula 9%, Finland/Northwest Russia 7%, Italy/Greece 1%.

After marrying Karyn, I acquired a new family.

Karyn's father Tod, who passed in 2015, was a wonderful man. He was a bit of a jokester with an infectious smile and laugh. Karyn adored him—he raised her well. He taught her to ride her bike, built her first skateboard for her, and helped her feel protected. He loved her and she knew it. She loved mussing his hair just to make him laugh.

Tod enlisted in the Navy in 1945 after graduating from high school in Prescott, Arizona in 1944. While still in basic training at Great Lakes, the Japanese surrendered. Tod explained that when the Japanese learned that he had joined the war effort, they decided that surrender would be their best option. What a guy!

He became one of the few optometrists in Flagstaff, Arizona during the 1950s, 60s, and 70s. He was well-known and well-liked. He had a gentle demeanor and I liked and admired everything about him.

He was a flying enthusiast. He had owned several airplanes and had built his own, a Kit Fox with a 100 hp Rotax engine. I had the wonderful opportunity to fly it once, just before he and I shook hands on a deal to purchase it from him. It was a great-flying little 2-seater.

He later managed to survive a jolting wreck in his Kit Fox. He totaled it after stalling at an altitude of about 50 feet on takeoff and plunging right wing first into the ground.

About a month prior to the wreck, he and I had agreed that Karyn and I would purchase his plane and a cool custom trailer that it could be transported in for $25,000. The plane was well-built with customized seat covers (done by Beverley) and a cool paint design. It was a nice airplane. I was overjoyed that it would also come with a special-built trailer, and envisioned fun road/flying trips in the future.

I felt really bad for Tod, but also grieved for the plane.

Much later, when his health had deteriorated significantly and the end was near, still at home and under the care of Beverley (his second wife), Karyn and Ryndi, he provided instructions to not resuscitate and passed peacefully. I considered it to be a very brave and dignified death.

His farewell was well attended. Many who knew and loved him came to talk about him and laugh about his many antics.

He had built a clever remote-control glider with a talking female pilot (his wife Bev) who responded to his radio calls with funny quips. He had also built many model planes over the years, a few I am fortunate to own now. I often look at them and feel deeply appreciative that I had the opportunity to know Tod.

Karyn's mom, Helen Lawrence, was also a pilot. A retired schoolteacher, she was strong-willed, fiercely independent, and an aviation pioneer. She was the first female pilot to land a T34 at Luke Air Force Base while serving as an officer in the Civil Air Patrol.

She is also responsible for electric fuel pumps being installed on Piper Cherokees. While preparing for her check-ride for her Instrument ticket, she rented a Cherokee for some instruction at Pulliam Airport, Flagstaff, Arizona.

As she rose off the runway, arching off to the left, her engine quit. Below her was a floor of trees, with a road not too far away, and not a lot of altitude. She crashed hard, just barely making the I-17 and narrowly missing a semi. They pancaked on the asphalt, demolishing the airplane. Both she and her instructor survived. She broke her back and filed suit.

Part of the settlement resulted in the recognition that they needed to install fuel pumps on like models. The next time you are out flying in your Piper, after you lift off and start your turn, glance quickly at your fuel pump switch, look up for a moment, and say, "Thanks Helen!"

Over the years, I've grown to know Karyn's Uncle Bill and Aunt Bobby and have developed a strong love for both of them. It seems impossible to know two more wonderful people.

Bill grew up in Prescott. His father, Elmer Lawrence owned the Eagle Drugstore in downtown Prescott at the intersection of Gurley and Cortez and owned and operated a travel agency. His mother Mable became a talented, well-known local artist, specializing in oils, pastels, and watercolors. We have several of her paintings hanging in the Treehouse, and there are numerous more hanging in private residences and owned by the Sharlot Hall Museum in downtown Prescott.

In his late teens, Bill was inducted into the Smoki tribe, braving the rituals, including being dropped bare-foot and naked in the middle of the desert at night, and finding his way back home.

He learned to perform the snake dance and other rituals and received the snake-bite tattoo as part of his initiation into the Smoki.

Bill enlisted in the Army Air Corps in World War II and managed to get into pilot training. Eventually, he began flying the B-25. Instead of going to war, he was assigned to train pilots.

As an instructor, he primarily trained twin-engine bound students in the AT-10 Wichita, a wood and fabric twin-engine trainer nicknamed "The Bamboo Coffin." He told me that every one of them had different flight and stall characteristics; instructors routinely flew them first to determine how the plane would behave with a student at the controls. According to Bill, in slow flight, you could stick your hand out of the window and induce a stall in that wing.

It would not take off with frost on its wings. He and the student would sit in the run-up area, tail facing to the west so the plane's flight surfaces would get the full benefit of the rising sun. When the wings were sufficiently defrosted, they would go fly.

After his discharge from the Air Corps, although still attracted to aviation, he had no interest in flying a plane full of passengers and opted to work other positions with Bonanza Airlines instead. He once told me that he wasn't sure he could have stayed awake doing something that boring day in and day out.

Bill and Bobbie met while both worked for Bonanza in the late 1940s. Bill worked a variety of ground positions, and Bobbie was a very pretty, petite former John Robert Powers model and had worked in the Scripts Department for CBS Radio in New York City. She had an intelligence and quick wit that clearly set her apart from the other ladies. After a stint working at the newly reopened Nellis Air Force Base just outside of Las Vegas, Bobbie was hired as a stewardess and flew the route to Reno.

When Bonanza Airlines was certified as a scheduled airline in 1949, Bobbie was selected to fly one leg of the inaugural flight on December 15th, 1949 and flew many of the routes after that. Some of the passengers she got to know included celebrities such as Randolph Scott, Donald O'Conner, Tommy Dorsey, and, best of all, Santa Claus!

It was Santa Claus who got Bill and Bobby together. At the time, Bill was station manager for the Prescott terminal. Bobbie routinely would see him about twice every week, three minutes at a time, for approximately two years, when he would hand her the manifest for the First Officer.

Bonanza flew Santa into towns along the "southern route," much to the delight of many children, and while in Prescott, Bill showed the entire entourage the town, including many introductions to local Prescottonians. He invited Bobbie to spend the night with his family in Prescott, and they hit it off and were married in April.

Bill rented planes after the war, was instructor qualified, and continued to fly for some time before developing a love for boating and sailing. For many years they owned a beautiful 45-foot yacht and served terms as Commodores for the local yacht club.

While still instructor qualified, he taught his dad to fly. When his dad, Elmer, flew his cross-country ending at Phoenix Sky Harbor airport, Bill went to the tower and informed the controllers that his dad was in route to Sky Harbor and he wanted to observe him. As Elmer approached Sky Harbor, he announced, "Sky Harbor Airport, this is Elmer Lawrence, and I'm coming in for a landing!" much to the amusement of the forewarned controllers.

Elmer purchased an Aerocoupe, supposedly a nearly un-crashable airplane with very stable flight characteristics. One day, Elmer took a friend out to fly on a very warm day and attempted to take off on the uphill runway. He didn't gain any altitude and crashed just on the other side of SR89.

Rescuers ran over to the crash and found both pilot and passenger bruised and confused, but otherwise fine. The Aerocoupe was demolished.

Karyn and I flew up to Seattle in January 2020 to celebrate Bill's 95th birthday in Tacoma. As always, he was upright and sharp. While there I had the wonderful opportunity to converse with Bobbie at great length. One year older than Bill, she is beautiful and has remarkable poise and grace.

Over some drinks, Bill and I talked about some fistfights we'd been in. I told him about the only time I had duked it out with three guys at the same time.

Bill told me about one day in high school, while walking to class, he spotted a chubby, pale, bespectacled boy being shoved around by the school bully. He stopped and watched as the bully knocked the kid's glasses off, breaking them.

Bill, who lettered in football for three years, knew the kid and his family. He also knew that when his acquaintance went home from school, he would catch hell from his dad when it was revealed that his glasses had been broken in a fight. The thought of that really pissed Bill off.

Bill jumped into the fray, grabbing the bully, and hitting him with a hard right, and a good left, which knocked him down. He then jumped on him and gave him several good face-plants into the concrete sidewalk. Soon, he was ordered to the office to explain himself, which he did.

The principal told Bill that he expected he would never hear of such an incident again and returned him to class.

After class that day, Bill walked over to the bully's house to speak with his parents. The bully's dad came out of the front door with a hatchet in hand and demanded that Bill get off his property immediately, and the bully avoided Bill for the rest of his senior year.

Bill then went over to the bespectacled kid's house and explained to his parents what had happened, sparing the kid from any further punishment.

Karyn spent a summer with Bill and Bobbie in Springfield, Oregon while her parents worked on resolving their differences, ultimately agreeing to divorce. Bill and Bobby became second parents, and her cousins Allyn, Elizabeth, and Jennifer were more like sisters. All three cousins grew up to be attractive, strong, successful women.

Allyn, Elizabeth, and Jennifer moved to Alaska and lived there for many years. Elizabeth moved back to Tacoma, Washington a good number of years ago and went to work for the school district, and Jennifer died in her home in Anchorage in 2018.

Allyn found a new love for southern Arizona near Patagonia, sold her property in Homer, and purchased acreage with plans to build her new home and own another horse one day.

Elizabeth recently retired from the Tacoma school district.

Bobbie and Bill celebrated their 69th anniversary.

Beverley Lawrence is Karyn's stepmother. Tod and Bev had a wonderful marriage. Both flying enthusiasts, they bought, flew, and sold several airplanes over the years, and they loved each other deeply. Tod fully accepted Bev's children, Ricky and Ryndi, as his own.

Beverley is a master quilter, owns a long-arm quilting machine, and over the years has produced several beautiful quilts for Karyn and me, including a really nice silhouette quilt of Karyn and me that Bev made as a wedding gift.

Ryndi was the wild child. With willowy, natural good looks, a fearless lack of inhibition and a precocious style, she kept Tod and Bev on their toes throughout her teen years.

Lo and behold, Ryndi is now known as the "Ryndinator" professionally, helping arrange a variety of significant agreements for the establishment of largescale solar arrays, and taking little bullshit. She's a blast to spend time with and I've grown to admire her and her husband, John, greatly. She is currently in the process of building a consulting business in the solar industry, working closely with previous work associates.

Beverley's son Ricky was born with Marfan's Syndrome, a genetic disorder that affects the body's connective tissue. He was tall, very lanky, and had heart and liver issues throughout his life. He was a hard worker, could really tell a joke and was a good guy. He worked in the construction industry and travelled all around the country on different projects over the years.

Ricky's former girlfriend "Kat" is a professional chili and wine taster, and a lot of fun! They took cruises together and lived life to the fullest right to the very end, when Ricky took control of his end-of-life and bravely dictated his hospice instructions, passing quietly while staying with his mom, Beverley.

Karyn's brother, Rick, is a "Big Five" Arizona hunter. He and his wife Annette have a great little oasis on the edge of Camp Verde, Arizona. Rick is retired from the tire and brake industry, and Annette retired from Northern Arizona University.

Karyn's cousin on her mother's side is Linda. Linda is remarkable. She has a placid ranch-woman look that disguises a keen intellect.

A long-time employee for Fann Construction in Prescott, she rose with the company since its early days and now looks forward to retirement with her husband, Dan.

Over the years, Karyn and I have spent a fair amount of time with Karyn's niece, Jamie, and Jamie's long-time beau, Lance. Their long-term romance culminated in a beautiful cruise in the Puget Sound where Jamie and Lance married onboard ship, joined by their friends and family. They also had a professional videographer onboard who videotaped the ceremony using a cool drone.

Jamie is a licensed captain in the Puget Sound, so it seemed most appropriate. She is currently an executive with Starbucks in Seattle, but dreams of the day she will own a ship to captain in the Sound. She recently completed her MBA.

Lance, tall, handsome, and clear-eyed, grew up ranching. His family owns a 600-acre ranch in Texas, nestled near Mount Pleasant and Mount Vernon, and that's where the rest of his family lives and works. Lance took an interest in physics and graduated with a Bachelor of Science in Physics. He is also a talented surveyor.

2019 was "The Year of Babies," for my family. My niece Courtney gave birth to Daisy Mae, and my nephew James (aka: Jimmy) fathered a son, Jack. Karyn's niece Jamie gave birth to a son named Mason William Hollingsworth. My nephew Tom and his lovely wife Michelle added a daughter this year, now with four members of their little tribe.

Over the years I have noted several quotes about not being able to choose your family. I disagree. Over an unmeasurable expanse of time, my family has chosen me, and I them. Like a universe forming, various planets materializing around their suns, my family has grown around me, and I within them, constantly expanding, developing, and evolving in proportion and quality. My family.

Atherton

SALINA, KANS.

John Osterman, "Pioneer of 1869"

Granddad Sam in the Philippines

Granddad Sam (center in uniform) with Elsa Osterman standing to his left

The Commandant, 1921

Published by The Senior Class of the Georgia Military College
Milledgeville, GA.
contributed to Georgia Genealogy Trails, by Dena W.

To Capt. Robert Grant Cousley, U.S.A. One whose untiring efforts, loyal endeavor and zealous care has been for the interest and the betterment of every student activity, whether scholastic, military, athletic or social; disciplinaian of the first class, a culutred gentleman, an inspiring leader, and a steadfast friend, we affectionately dedicate this volume of The Commandant.

Carlos H. Horne - Editor in Chief
J. Berner Tingle - Business Manager

Faculty

Col. K. T. Alfriend

Capt. R. G. Cousley,
Military Instructor

Maj. L. M. Moore

Maj. T. H. Bonner,
Athletic Director

Maj. R. M. Cabell,
Commandant & Instructor in
Chemistry

Maj. C. E. Edwards, Instructor
in Latin

Maj. W. D. Morrison,
Instructor in History

Maj. H. W. Martin,
Instructor in Physics

Maj. Godfrey Osterman,
Band Director

Maj. H. Rolston,
Insturctor in Mathematics

Maj. R. W. Russell, Instructor
in Modern Languages

Mrs. T. A. Reese,
Instructor in English

1st Sgt. Fred Ayres,
Assistant Military Instructor

Sgt. W. M. Reese, Assistant
Military Instructor

Frank Osterman

Grandad MvDonald with wise-cracking, cigar-smoking Charlie McCarthy on his lap

31

SEVENTY AND ALIVE!

I have a strong hunch that after I finish this book and it has gone to press, I will have so much more I want to write about. Every time I turn around, life takes an interesting new turn. How quickly circumstances can change in a blink.

We are currently immersed in the COVID-19 pandemic. Gratefully, Karyn and I have been spared so far, as have all our family members and close friends to the best of our knowledge. Two of our friends have contracted it while living in London, and experienced rather mild symptoms, including a fever, a brief, painful dry cough, and a loss of taste and smell. The toll nationwide and worldwide has been horrible, with so many people dying one of the very worst ways, gasping for breath until they are too exhausted to try anymore and asphyxiate.

For whatever the reason, we seemed to have been caught by surprise, even though ninety-eight years ago we had almost the same thing happen with the Spanish flu. A handful of countries reacted quickly and seem to have dodged the bullet. We did not. In spite of ample intelligence and multiple resources available, and early warnings within the Administration, we blew it. Please note that back in 1918, although many tragic mistakes were made, we didn't waste any time or effort blaming Spain. This further reminds me of the "three envelopes" joke. If things go appropriately, our current commander-in-chief will be preparing his own three envelopes soon.

At the time that I am writing this, I have no known health issues, and everything seems to still work quite well. Nor does Karyn have any issues. She is a beautiful, fit, trim and healthy sixty-eight-year-old—always the love of my life, and always ready for our next adventure.

We have been rather happily cooped up in our Treehouse, enjoying our new bedroom addition, and eating quite well; thanks to Instacart we've both gained a few pounds. After experiencing home delivery for this long, I'm hooked!

The only thing I really miss is swimming. The YMCA pool has been closed for a couple of months now, and I cannot wait to be back in the water swimming laps again! This is the longest I have gone without swimming since I was in my early twenties. I even swam in Vietnam every chance I got. When we were guarding Namo Bridge. We had a little spot just down from the bridge where we could wade and swim, and there was a brief span of sandy river shoreline where we sometimes stripped to the waist and wrestled, on occasion for bets in MPC.

While serving as an Air Force Radar Operator, Air Weapons Controller Technician, Air Weapons Controller, and Air Weapons Director, I was subject to numerous inspections. Depending on the type of inspection, I could also be subject to positional evaluations and testing. All test questions and correct answers referred to as the Master Questions File, or "MQF", were kept locked in the Stan/Eval office "top-secret" safe, and periodically, I was permitted to review them. One of the "classified" questions asked was, "What is the key to airpower?" The correct answer was "flexibility." I strive to remain flexible.

Thus, I have replaced swimming with walking and a newly purchased NordicTrack elliptical for now. I couldn't ask for a more beautiful and interesting neighborhood to walk in than Mountain Club. When the Hassayampa Mountain Club was first established in 1926 it spanned roughly 800 acres. When incorporated in 1936, the Club, then known as the Hassayampa Mountain Club, measured more than a full section of land, or a square mile, plus. Through a series of deals and land swaps, not all beneficial to Mountain Club, we now cover a span of about 450 acres. Not much else has or will change all that much. We only have about ten buildable lots left in all of Mountain Club. We own two parks within our boundaries both protected by covenants, and have a seven acre preserve on our eastern boundary maintained by the City of Prescott. We own the water distribution system and clubhouse, and all are maintained or supported by a robust cadre of volunteers—and the annual assessments paid by our loyal Mountain Club members.

Our road next to the house was dirt until about three years ago when the county paved it. They did a beautiful job. On average, the road has a typical weekday traffic count of well-below 25 vehicles, and even less on the weekend. It is both quiet and serene. I look forward to getting back in the pool, but I'm not suffering.

The walking is great. I don't recall a stroll taken anywhere else in the world that I enjoyed it as much as my routine daily walks through Mountain Club.

During our forced staycation, Karyn has had more time to focus on her spiritual path. She is an ardent follower of Eckankar, a spiritual path based on personal experience with the inner light and sound. I teased her once, asking her, "So does that mean that someone like Helen Keller wouldn't be able to participate?" Her answer was, "No (with a bit of a scowl)." Oops. She later explained that, "Light and sound are manifestations of the inner light and sound, and light and sound is how we can experience God."

As Karyn's mom, Helen, neared end of life, she and Karyn talked about Karyn's spiritual path. Karyn had a neat little plastic case with a small stack of HU cards. According to the teachings of Eckankar, HU (pronounced like "Hugh") is an ancient name for God, and as Karyn has explained, when sung with love in your heart, you can both send and receive love. Karyn feels that it can bring peace and greater clarity. You would think if your name were Hugh, you might kind of enjoy participating in a HU chant, or song.

Helen expressed an interest in singing "HU." Karyn showed her how to do this and gave her a card that contained instructions on singing the HU, and the benefits. The next week when Karyn visited with her mom again, Helen asked her for another card. When Karyn pulled out the case and offered a card to her mom, Helen's eyes lit up. She pointed at the case and said, "Can I have that?"

Karyn gave her the case and cards, and apparently Helen passed them all out. She also began singing HU regularly and told Karyn that it "really worked." I am still not singing HU. Maybe on my deathbed. (I might be feeling a little anxious.)

My sense is that Eckankar is overall reasonably unimposing on one's beliefs, and probably one of the least offensive set of religious tenets I have encountered on my stroll through life. One time when Karyn was at a conference in Minneapolis, she mentioned to one of her associates that I believed all religions were pretty much made up. He agreed. Karyn loves Eckankar and I love Karyn.

I feel somewhat amazed that I am still alive and kicking. Fifty years ago, I was stunned that I was still alive after my little adventure in the Marine Corps, and just nine days before I was going to turn twenty. As it turned out, my Marine Corps time wasn't the end of my close calls, but hopefully there will be no more, and here I am!

I am currently wrapping up my third and probably final year as President of Mountain Club for now. I'd like to give someone else the opportunity to provide good order and discipline for the Board. Where has the time gone? I let the other Board Members know early on that I was a "Three-year kind of guy," and I meant it. I will be open to serving another officer position on the Board if nominated. If not, fine.

I found that I generally started getting tired of what I was doing employment-wise after about three years and don't like that feeling. I will not be vacating this office because I'm tired of it; I want to step down before I feel that burnout, as I have in the past and detested.

The only exception jobwise was when I worked as a mediator and supervisor for the EEOC. I loved it. I was almost 67 and just wanted to take some time off, stop working all the time—and I was at a place when I could. Otherwise, I would probably still be mediating for the EEOC. I feel a deep loyalty to some of the folks I enjoyed working with there. Some remain in contact and I greatly enjoy hearing of their many accomplishments in the intervening years since retirement. I continue to provide any assistance I can in support of their future career moves.

Along the way I have learned the importance of loyalty, and its closest relative: respect. You can demand neither. You must earn both. Over the years I have noted many folks in leadership positions who did not fully comprehend that concept as they continued climbing the organizational ladder. As they climbed higher, if they were a bully, then no doubt a coward, they felt less support from those around them and they got uglier.

Instilling fear will only get you so far. Cowards can be hard to spot until the pressure is on, such as a firefight or diplomatic brinksmanship, when much is at stake. If you have clearly identified a bully, you have clearly identified a coward early enough to prepare for their inevitable collapse or total lack of effectiveness under enough pressure.

I deeply admire people and organizations who keep their word, and act in an honorable manner.

Karyn and I were set to fly to Lihue on Kaua'i, August 24th, 2018; planning to check into the Makai Club Resort near the North Shore, which we had booked through Diamond Resorts. Karyn, ever the happy planner, had made our resort reservations (after considerable research) and booked and paid our airfare, roundtrip with Hawaiian Airlines. We had flown Hawaiian to New Zealand and liked them quite well.

She had also paid in advance for our parking at Sky Harbor Airport, a rental car with Alamo, a helicopter "ECO Adventure" over Kaua'i with Blue Hawaiian Helicopters, and a tour of Lydgate Farms Hawaiian Chocolate plantation, complete with a full tour of the production area and wrapping up with a rather sophisticated chocolate tasting. We also practiced snorkeling.

Mother Nature had made other plans. On August 21st, 2018 Hurricane Lane made landfall and began dumping 52 inches of rain during Lane's brief stay.

When we first learned of the hurricane barreling toward the islands, we decided to cancel. We contacted everyone, and they were all very understanding. We received a complete refund from everyone, including the airline.

We booked our next attempt to visit Kaua'i departing May 9th, 2020, flying with American Airlines this time and getting a great fare deal. We planned and paid in advance for everything we had wanted to do on our first attempt, including the Lydgate Farms chocolate tour again, and added the Luau Kaiamaku, excluding only the helicopter flight. We decided we would book that after we got there if we could comfortably fit it in. We had reservations at the Westin Princeville Ocean Resort.

Apparently, it is true. You can't fool Mother Nature. As we started hearing more about COVID-19, we realized that our plans had been foiled again. When we arrived, we would immediately go into quarantine for the duration of our stay. Once again, without exception, everyone refunded any money they had received from us in advance, and American Airlines unflinchingly refunded our airfare.

I told Karyn that I could be "fairly dense" sometimes but thought that maybe somebody was trying to tell us something—and it might have something to do with Hawaii.

We ordered some chocolate from Lydgate Farms and Karyn loved it. We took a chocolate tasting tour with them online using Zoom, complete with a good explanation of the chocolate making process and samples they shipped to us. What a blast! Facilitated by Megan Gitler and hosted by Will Lydgate, we sampled two 70% dark chocolates, one of them called Palm Blossom Honey. OMG! We also sampled "chocolate nibs," made with 50% milk, coffee, and cacao nibs. That was my first time and they are delicious!

Will is very humorous and extremely likable. A fifth generation Hawaiian, he grew up totally immersed in the local culture and speaks Hawaiian. Probably a great guy to sit and drink a beer or two with. If we ever actually make it to Hawaii, we plan to visit the Lydgate Farm. I would recommend the online Zoom tour to anyone who loves chocolate. FYI: it is a fun "couples thing" with a favorite drink.

Last year Karyn and I purchased the ½ acre immediately to our west. At the time of purchase, this property had been neglected for many years, and when we explored it, we discovered several shabby little structures that had been constructed in the years past, probably by kids, and a lot of junk. We cleaned it thoroughly and had it professionally "fire-wised." What a diamond in the rough it turned out to be! We placed a picnic table and umbrella on the high spot and love our little secluded place behind the house.

A couple of years ago when Dave was helping us make the basement a decent spot for work and storage, he hired his masseuse to assist him in wrestling some bulky construction materials into the renovation.

His assistant and masseuse, Sandy, a lean, tough-looking little woman with long, grey hair pulled back provided me with her contact information on request and soon became my masseuse too. What a gal! For the first time in my life I'm getting a massage every other week and enjoying it immensely! She is a self-proclaimed 59-year-old "hippie-capitalist" and has been a licensed masseuse for over 25 years. She spent many years living like a beautiful gypsy, working at Renaissance Fairs around the country, and participating in many gatherings of like-minded folks from coast to coast. Quite the fearless adventurer. She now owns her own house for the first time, and her closest companion is her second Great Pyrenees named, of all things, Deja Vu. I've known Deja Vu since she was a puppy. One hundred pounds plus of herding white fur, muscle, and a head the size of a basketball, who greets me with great cheer every time I show for my scheduled massage, and who with a gentle nudging nose, guides me into the house.

Several years back, I was talking with my sister-in-law, Mary Jo. She reminded me that I had once told her that my favorite place in the world was her backyard—all seven acres of it—which I truly meant at the time. I found great refuge just hanging around their farm during a rough period of time in my life. I have never been treated with greater kindness. Thank you, Bruce and Mary Jo.

I told her that I had a new favorite place, and she was visibly crestfallen.

My new favorite place is here in the Mountain Club, on our property. I know all my neighbors and I'm comfortable with all. Our neighbors directly across from us, Doug and Jill, are wonderful. Doug is rated as a "Super Host" by Airbnb. They have assisted in giving the neighborhood a much-needed facelift and unity. Sitting on our deck is like resting on a small slice of Heaven. Facing to the east, my view consists of treed hillsides far into the distance until they turn to a blue-gray and disappear below a far distant ridgeline. Immediately to our east is my neighbor's large stone house and small cottage on the other side of the road. Both structures are handsome and sturdy in appearance, built by grandfather, father and son back in the mid-1940s and 1950s—all the rocks collected locally back in a time when you could collect truck-loads of rocks with impunity. They have proven to be excellent neighbors.

Directly in front and on both sides are large, healthy mature Ponderosa pines, and many oak trees that are alive with a multitude of birds, squirrels, lizards, numerous other insects and little critters, and in season, cicadas. It appears that we have a healthy population of plateau fence lizards running around too. They are fantastic insect eaters and absolutely of no threat to anything much larger than a cicada. One of our most common birds is the raven. They can be a little messy sometimes, but they are a trip. They have many odd and interesting vocalizations and behaviors, seeming to communicate back and forth frequently.

There have been times when I have had as many as two dozen ravens descend into the trees around the house, cawing like crows sometimes, or many emitting their very distinct "gkronk, gkronk, gkronk," with other grumbling, mewing or whatever sounds mixed in. A couple of times while sitting on the deck, I've had a raven fly down out of a nearby tree, land on the rail of the deck, and study me briefly before flying off. They are big, wary, and intelligent, sometimes referred to as "wolf birds." I've called back and forth with them on numerous occasions.

We spotted a three-foot king snake one time just as it was slipping under our shed, and before that, a garter snake in our flower box. I hope they are everywhere. They are both prodigious rodent and insect hunters, taking an occasional small bird if able, and fully encouraged to stay for as long as they like.

We've spotted coyotes, feral cats, racoons, stray dogs, javelina, skunks, bobcats, lots of mule deer, squirrels, chipmunks, assorted birds, and on a couple of occasions a person peeking at our property (one of whom I recognized) out back, all caught on camera.

Although we didn't see it on camera, Karyn and I spotted a good-sized desert tortoise across the street from us and ran over and picked it up to keep it out of the road. Many desert tortoises have been adopted, and many are notorious escape artists. I suspected that we had captured an escapee based on his appearance and calm behavior, and it turned out that I was right. Doug and Jill knew someone who owned a desert tortoise, called them, and indeed it was their little feller. It was quite content being fed butter lettuce by Karyn until his mom and dad came and picked him up.

We constructed a new master bedroom which stretches partially into our newly acquired property to our west. Besides giving us considerably more room, which spurred the purchase of a new Tuft & Needle bed, it provided us with more room to hang some wonderful pen, pencil, charcoal, and ink drawings. Back in about 1992, Karyn attended a Health Fair at the Phoenix Convention Center. While there, she noted a local Native American Artist named Dennis Mehan, also known as Brother Soaring Eagle. She purchased one of his intricate drawings on the spot, entitled: *Indian Power Symbols ALL MY RELATIONS Mi TaKuye Oyasin.*

When she brought it home and we got a look at it, we both agreed that it was one of the most interesting things we had ever owned. His relations included very carefully depicted creatures ranging from butterflies, tortoises, ravens, elk, bears, hawks, eagles and more.

Little did I know, Karyn had also ordered two additional drawings based on our birth dates. Mine: *New Life Moon Red Tail Hawk April 12 Red Thunder.* As with his first drawing, the creatures and the face of a strong, beautiful native woman are intricately detailed and associated with my "relations." Karyn's is equally intricate and interesting: the strong, detailed face of a native man and a wondrous collage of equally detailed and intricate creatures including birds, an otter, mountain lions, a wolf, various reptiles, and more adorn hers. I received mine for my birthday and Karyn's for hers. What fantastic birthday presents! I look at them daily with a smile.

Frequently, the silence is nearly complete for many minutes at a time. Just my own thoughts. An occasional hiker might spot one or both of us sitting up on the deck and wave and call to us as they go by. This is a greater peace than I felt at 7,500 feet MSL, air clear and calm, plane fully trimmed out, power setting just right, and the radio turned down; left hand resting on the yoke, right hand holding Karyn's.

Now my left-hand rests lightly on the arm rest of the rocker-bench we built and stained, and my right hand still holds Karyn's.

EPILOGUE

NOT THE END

Memories become misty over the years, and only the strongest impressions remain crystal-clear. I still remember the unforgettable beauty and sense of freedom on the Oswego River.

Some sights, sounds, and smells of combat are deeply etched in my memory: the feeling of mortar rounds impacting near my fighting position as the ground jumped, throwing debris on me; the snapping sound of a near miss, the feeling in my ears and nostrils when something exploded very near-by and the scent wafted over me, or when I witnessed some of the most gruesome sights imaginable—so many years ago; still like it was yesterday.

I also deeply remember tender moments—a look, a touch, a caress, a kiss, or an intimate exchange—throughout my being, and I hope forever.

I truly desire that the experiences I had while serving with the EEOC will be among the lasting memories that I hold and treasure for the rest of my life.

Each of us takes our journey down an uncertain path. The decisions we make are what define us, what we become.

On that clear bright Spring day, as I sat at the conference room table on the 22nd floor and looked across into the pretty sleep-deprived face of the Respondent's attorney, I thought about the spectacular view just outside our perch: the Papago Buttes, Camelback Mountain, Piestewa Peak, and the Sky Harbor control tower.

My mind went back to 1976 and losing my job as a cabbie. What seemed like the end was only the beginning—the beginning of my journey to nowhere and everywhere.

Now I am the freedom of the river and the fallen soldier. I am the curious lover and dreamer of dreams. The man I am is all the men I have been. I have become the experiences and they are me.

The petals of the lotus are many, but the flower is only one. Let us live together life among life, taking one battle at a time and going on with grace and dignity as we strive ever more to be and share the best of ourselves. Life is not about existing, it's about living. And I've come to live out loud, to make each moment something to remember—for me or for someone else—for in giving we also receive. And I have received many blessings in my lifetime, not the least of which is my wife and soul mate, Karyn. I'm in her and she's in me.

If my story is beneficial to your world view, if it helps you see life differently, if by sharing it I've opened your eyes to something new, then I am happy.

My journey has taken me from warrior to peacemaker, from trouble maker to problem solver, from pawn to sovereign of my own kingdom.

And I continue to tread my path.

"The goodness of a man runs much deeper than a moment in time." (Jack Bartlett in Heartland)

Vietnam War Memorial Speech

This is the speech I gave in Payson, Arizona, May 5, 2000 when providing the dedication to the Vietnam War Memorial Moving Wall.

Thank you to the numerous citizens of Payson and the surrounding areas for making this wonderful, unifying event possible.

This dedication highlights the strength and vitality of Payson, as well as the patriotism of my fellow Arizonans.

I viewed this wall for the first time in 1985 with my son Daniel. We visited Washington, D.C. as part of a father-son summer sabbatical.

At the time, I remember standing before the wall and feeling absolutely dumbfounded.

I found the name of my closest friend etched in the dark granite and traced my finger lightly across his name.

I felt a sense of amazement at how quickly the time had passed; I also felt grief for the many years of life my friend Dale Thompson hadn't been able to enjoy; and gratitude that this monument ensured his sacrifice wouldn't be forgotten.

As long as I live I will never forget that moment, nor will I ever forget the moment when I pulled Dale from his fighting position and looked at the handsome features of his noble young face in the glare of illumination as a fire-fight raged around me. I knew he was dead, but no tears came to me in the early morning darkness.

I was a battalion scout assigned to Charlie Company, 1st Battalion, 26th Marine Regiment, First Marine Division, and the multiple explosions, whining shrapnel, constant pop and whiz of rifle fire, and rising casualties around me in the early morning fight stunned me and demanded my immediate attention.

I returned later and silently assisted his squad leader in wrapping Dale in a poncho. I still shed no tears, and that was the last time I saw him.

My tears came 16 years later. My son saw me cry as I stood at that wall, looking at the seemingly endless black ribbon of granite.

About one year ago I met a very interesting fellow named Adrian Cronaur. As many of you will recall, Adrian was the Air Force disk jockey portrayed by Robin Williams in the movie *Good Morning, Vietnam*. Adrian and I spoke at length about the war—and about our feelings.

We talked about the many men and women we had known over the years, whose lives had been permanently altered by the war.

This war took its toll on both of us, and many others—in *many* ways. Most importantly, it took away our innocence, as so many wars have taken the innocence of young men and women, and in many ways that other American conflicts have not.

We ended our conversation by agreeing that the one thing that Vietnam Veterans needed to hear most when they returned from their duty overseas, and in many instances still needed to hear, was "Welcome Home."

So, on behalf of the State of Arizona, and the Arizona National Guard, to all the Vietnam Veterans here today, "Welcome home."

The ultimate price of freedom is the price that service members pay with their lives. The ultimate price of freedom is: the denial to these young men and women to ever laugh with their families again; to watch their children and grandchildren grow, to play at the lake, to kiss someone, or simply to smell the fragrance of a beautiful flower. The ultimate price is that none of these 58,219 service members will ever hear the words, "Welcome home." The ultimate cost of freedom is written on this wall.

And, lest we forget, many MIA and un-returned POWs from Vietnam and other conflicts haven't, and may never hear those important words. Our thoughts need to be with them today…

I want to believe that none of the 58,211 men and 8 women whose names are etched on that wall have been forgotten. I want to believe that when someone reads a name from that wall and speaks that name ever so quietly to him or herself, that somewhere in the cosmos, the spirit of that person smiles invisibly, and says, "That's me!"

I ask as a personal favor to me that you please visit my friend Dale Thompson at Panel 23W, Line 107 and say my friend's name, at least once. Dale Thompson.

I want to believe that the price of freedom, etched so starkly on this wall, will never be forgotten by those who benefit from this ultimate sacrifice; and that they will continue to instill an appreciation for these brave spirits, in the hearts of the generations to come.

In 1969 Kris Kristofferson and Ned Forster wrote a song they entitled *Me and Bobby McGhee*, which was made popular by Janis Joplin. The song said in part, "Freedom's just another word for nothin' left to lose, and nothin' ain't worth nothin' but it's free."

For the men and women who were serving in Vietnam at the time, these lyrics were just part of the constant drum-beat that equated the value of their service as being worth "nothin'."

But we know now that the cost of freedom is indeed very great. Please, make no mistake about this; the price of freedom is written on this (pointing) wall. God bless America.

Thank you.